The Europeans

Studies on the European Polity

BRENT NELSEN, SERIES EDITOR

Europe and the Middle East:
In the Shadow of September 11
Richard Youngs

Sustaining European Monetary Union:
Confronting the Cost of Diversity
Tal Sadeh

The Europeans:
Political Identity in an Emerging Polity
David Michael Green

The Europeans

Political Identity in an Emerging Polity

David Michael Green

LYNNE
RIENNER
PUBLISHERS

BOULDER
LONDON

Published in the United States of America in 2007 by
Lynne Rienner Publishers, Inc.
1800 30th Street, Boulder, Colorado 80301
www.rienner.com

and in the United Kingdom by
Lynne Rienner Publishers, Inc.
3 Henrietta Street, Covent Garden, London WC2E 8LU

Library of Congress Cataloging-in-Publication Data
Green, David Michael, 1958–
    The Europeans : political identity in an emerging polity / David Michael Green.
        p.   cm.
    Includes bibliographical references and index.
    ISBN-13: 978-1-58826-355-1 (hbk. : alk. paper)
    1. National characteristics, European.   2. Europe—Civilization—1945–
3. Europe—Politics and government—1945–   I. Title.
    D1055.G73 2007
    940.55—dc22
                                                            2006033581

British Cataloguing in Publication Data
A Cataloguing in Publication record for this book
is available from the British Library.

Printed and bound in the United States of America

The paper used in this publication meets the requirements
of the American National Standard for Permanence of
Paper for Printed Library Materials Z39.48-1992.

5   4   3   2   1

For Liz, Bud, and Janet

For until the great majority of Europeans, the great mass of the middle and lower classes, are ready to imbibe these European messages in a similar manner and to feel inspired by them to common action and community, the edifice of "Europe" at the political level will remain shaky. . . . Hence the importance of basing any European project on firm and deep cultural and social foundations that are to some extent independent of economic and political fluctuations, even of the much vaunted trends of mass democracy and popular capitalism.

—Anthony Smith (1992: 73, 75)

Contents

List of Tables and Figures   xi

Acknowledgments   xiii

1   Introduction: The Study of European Political Identity   1

2   The Idea of European Identity   33

3   Are There Any "Europeans" in Europe?   51

4   Who Are the "Europeans"? Explaining Variance
in Levels of European Identity   71

5   What Does It Mean to Be "European"?
The Nature and Content of European Identity   109

6   How "European" Are the Europeans?
The Depth of European Identification   131

7   Conclusion: European Identity and Its Context   147

Appendixes
    1   Summary of Elite Informants Interviewed   167
    2   Summary of Targeted European Identifiers Interviewed   171
    3   Summary of Respondents to the Survey of European
       Identifiers   173

4 Summary of Survey Datasets Analyzed   175
5 Basic Script for Interviews of Elite Informants   177
6 Basic Script for Interviews of Targeted
     European Identifiers   179
7 Survey of European Identifier Instruments   181
8 Summary of Ancillary Events Attended During
     1998 Fieldwork   187

References   189
Index   197
About the Book   203

Tables and Figures

Tables

3.1   Identification with Europe   53
3.2   Identification Levels for Various Geopolities   56
3.3   Identification with Europe, by Country, Format One
         Identity Questions   58
3.4   Identification with Europe, by Country, Format Two
         Identity Questions   59
3.5   Identification with Europe, by Country, Format Three
         Identity Questions   60
3.6   Identification with Europe, by Country, Format Four
         Identity Questions   61
3.7   Identification Levels for Various Geopolities, by Continent   63
4.1A Effects on European Identification, Using Member-State
         Variables, Format One and Format Two Identity Questions   74
4.1B Effects on European Identification, Using Member-State
         Variables, Format Four Identity Questions   79
4.2   Effects on European Identification, Using Member-State and
         Political-Cultural Variables, Format Three Identity Questions   82
4.3   Effects of Independent Variables on European Identification,
         Using Member-State and Political-Cultural Variables,
         Format Three Identity Questions   84
4.4   Comparative Levels of Attachment to Europe   97
4.5A Effects on European Identification, Using Political-Cultural
         Variables, Format One and Format Two Identity Questions   101
4.5B Effects on European Identification, Using Political-Cultural
         Variables, Format Four Identity Questions   102

5.1	Is There a Shared European Cultural Identity?	111
5.2	Content of European Identity, by Nationality	113
5.3	Content of European Identity, by European Identity Level	115
5.4	Factors Linking EC Countries Together, by Nationality	117
5.5	Factors Linking EC Countries Together, by European Identity Level	118
5.6	Aspects of Europe Most Attached To, by Nationality	120
5.7	Aspects of Europe Most Attached To, by European Identity Level	121
5.8	Ways of Life, Standards, and Values That Are Specifically European	122
5.9	Meaning of Being European—Open Response Question	123
5.10	Meaning of Being Part of Nation—Open Response Question	124
5.11	Meaning of Being Part of Region—Open Response Question	124
6.1	Causes Worth Risks and Sacrifices, by Nationality	133
6.2	Causes Worth Risks and Sacrifices, by European Identity Level	134
6.3	Should EC Countries Assist Another in Trouble?	136
6.4	Various Questions Regarding Personal Sacrifice, by Nationality	138
6.5	Willingness to Sacrifice for European Unification, by Nationality	140
6.6	Willingness to Sacrifice for European Unification, by European Identity Level	141
6.7	Willingness to Sacrifice for Regional, National, and European Polities, by Type of Sacrifice	142

Figures

| 3.1 | European Identification over Time | 67 |

Acknowledgments

THIS PROJECT HAS HAD a long incubation period leading to its present form. It was originally conceived of in the early years of my graduate study, when it occurred to me that European integration studies could well benefit from some of the analytical approaches employed by the subfield of comparative politics, and that the matter of a continental identity could be as crucial to shaping historical trajectories—even in its absence—as nationalism had been in previous centuries.

In addition to my substantive advocacy for attention to the question of European identity, I would also be pleased—at the risk of being perceived (incorrectly, I hope) as immodest—if the form of this study added a small rivulet to the great stream of contemporary political inquiry, steering that river slightly more in the direction of solid empiricism and slightly away from improbable grasps at theory, slightly more toward real-world relevance and slightly away from what one political scientist has rightly described as the discipline's current "instinct for the capillary." Whether those are worthy goals, and whether this book makes a positive contribution toward achieving them, must ultimately be the judgment of each reader. Here, I can only indicate my own prescriptions and aspirations.

This book has been a fairly massive undertaking for a single scholar, and in fact would have been impossible without the contributions of many good and generous people. I have benefited along the way from countless helping hands, some of whom I am now pleased to also call my friends, all of whom I wish to know the deep extent of my gratitude.

In graduate school, I was well served indeed by some excellent training on the road to becoming a political scientist by profession. I am particularly grateful to Paul Diehl, Jim Kuklinski, Paul Schroeder, and Dina Zinnes for the wonderful vistas of methodology, epistemology, philosophy, and substantive content they opened for me, and for their support of my work. I only hope this book will make them proud of their contributions to my development as a scholar. I am also very grateful to Mark Pollack, Graham Wilson, and Crawford Young, who gave extensively of their time and insights in helping to shape an earlier version of this study.

Others, as well, made smaller but still crucially helpful contributions. My hat is off to Cedric Jourde for translation assistance with my survey instrument, and to Michael Schatzberg, Bob Turner, Charles Franklin, and especially Paul Martin for many hours of generous assistance on methodological issues and strategies. I am grateful for the survey data made available by the Inter-University Consortium for Political and Social Research (ICPSR) in Ann Arbor, and for the prompt and repeated assistance of Robin Rice, Kim Tully, and others at the University of Wisconsin's Data and Program Library Service in accessing those data.

My various ventures into the field for purposes of this study were really more fun than anyone should be allowed to have while at work. This was in no small part because of the generosity of the Europeans who volunteered their time and thoughtful responses to my questions and made my data collection easy, interesting, and truly pleasurable. I thank them profoundly, one and all, and especially two who helped facilitate my contact with multiple interviewees and thus greatly improved the scope of the project: many thanks to Jörg Mathias and Aidan Gilligan. I would also very much like to thank the staff of the College of Europe, the Congress of Europe, the People's Europe Conference, and the European Parliament (especially Member of the European Parliament David Martin and his staff) for throwing open their doors to this Yankee interloper with notepad, pen, and endless questions. I am especially indebted to Colin Bartie, who started off as an interviewee and quickly became a friend, and who, along with his wonderful family, has been an endless source of gracious hospitality and professional assistance with this project over the years.

Recently, I have had the good fortune to work with Lynne Rienner and her excellent staff in the preparation of this book. I very much appreciate all of them for their interest, support, and nurturing of the project, but none so much as series editor Brent Nelsen, my comrade-in-arms in the trenches of European public opinion studies. Brent has been great, as has the Rienner team, and I thank them for their help in bringing this work to fruition.

I also owe a debt of gratitude to my family, friends, and colleagues, who have supported my efforts over the years, sometimes simply with their interest in my work, sometimes more directly. I wish to thank Debby and Pat, and Bill and Shirley, in particular, for their steadfast moral support, and my dear friends Jackie and Bill Slee, for the constancy of their efforts to help me realize my goals. The others are too many in number to mention here, though I hope they will all know how much I appreciate their many contributions.

Finally, I dedicate this book to Liz, Bud, and Janet, who were unyieldingly generous in their support, and unsparingly gracious in understanding the commitment required to wrestle a project of this scale to the ground. This book is their book, too, and they have earned my deepest loving gratitude in helping to bring it to life.

—David Michael Green

1

Introduction: The Study of European Political Identity

The Prince must have the people well disposed toward him. Otherwise, in times of adversity, there is no hope.

—*Machiavelli*

IMAGINE THE FRENCH REVOLUTION had not occurred. Imagine that Napoleon had not assembled a people's Grand Armée and swept it across the face of Europe. Imagine that this army had not produced a reciprocal effect wherever it marched, that it had not fostered the construction of nation-states all over the continent. What if there had been no unification of Italy, no powerful new Germany? For that matter, imagine that the United States had not united much at all, but had remained a set of loosely affiliated (or perhaps even antagonistic) separate countries.

Now suppose that World War I had never transpired. Nor Japanese imperialism, national socialism in Germany, the Holocaust, nor all of World War II. Imagine that North America, Latin America, Africa, and much of Asia remained, to this day, European colonial possessions, and that the United Nations was an exclusive club for a small handful of member-states, if it had come into existence at all.

Consider a world this fantastically different from the one we inhabit, and then ask a simple question: What historical change—what single factor—could account for unraveling so many of the most salient developments of the past two centuries? There is only one answer: political identity. Or, more specifically for purposes of this exercise in counterfactual history, one particular form of political identity: nationalism.

With the possible exception of the explosion in scientific and technological prowess experienced in recent centuries, it is difficult to imagine a single phenomenon that alone can fully or partially account for more of the most consequential developments of this period than does nationalism. In addition to playing a prominent role in all the great conflicts of the past two centuries, and to restructuring the world through colonialism and then again through decolonization, nationalism has filled the hearts of countless millions of men and

1

women across the planet, often giving a sense of meaning to their lives that is otherwise unavailable to them as individuals.

But what if nationalism had never happened? Or what if political identity in the historical period we call modernity had possessed radically different characteristics? Suppose it had not stirred the hearts of men and women and moved them to make the greatest sacrifices as well as to commit the most unspeakable crimes in its name. What if there had existed, instead of the emotionally charged primordialisms at the core of most nationalisms, more of a reciprocal, cerebral, and benign sort of relationship between nations and nationals, such that the *pays* could only expect as much as it was willing to tangibly provide in return—a sort of rational business transaction, a quid pro quo, in place of a passionate and unidirectional adoration as strong as any?

If that had been the case, none of the crucially defining events and developments of modernity would have turned out the way they did, and many of them would be completely unimaginable at all. Of course, this hypothetical scenario is not what happened. Instead, an extremely powerful emotional force—political identity, in the form of nationalism—has gripped the world for at least two centuries, and has written many of the major chapters of its modern history. Yet the counterfactual questions above show not only the power of political identity, but also the consequences of its particular character and form. Those questions remain as significant as ever, and the current political environment is as determined by their answers as was the past.

This book examines a relatively new sort of mass identity, found in Europe and very much the product of the peculiarities of both recent and extended European history. This European identity has characteristics significantly different from those of nineteenth- and twentieth-century nationalisms, a fact that, beyond the many implications for Europe itself, raises a host of possibilities about the very nature of political identification as a general social and political phenomenon in the new millennium.

There are multiple possible interpretations of this anomalous European identity, and several of these are discussed in the concluding chapter to this volume. One, however, is most intriguing. It posits that European identity is a vanguard, articulating the emerging nature of political identification in the epoch the world is now entering, the period following modernity. It suggests that other identities may come to take the same form that European identification now does today—just as Europe previously pioneered nationalism and many other sociopolitical phenomena, including the very structure of international politics prevalent in the world today (the Westphalian system), before exporting them far beyond the boundaries of that small bit of real estate at the western end of the Eurasian land mass.

In short—and at the risk of employing a term both constituted of multiple meanings and simultaneously fraught with all manner of social, political, theoretical, epistemological, and moral baggage[1]—what today's Europe suggests is nothing less than the possibility of a *postmodern identity,* with all the deeply significant changes likely attendant to such a major development.

The historical counterfactuals presented above show how consequential such a development might be to the unfolding of global history. Just as the history of the past two centuries would have been dramatically different had nationalism been either nonexistent or of a different character, so too will the unfolding of the coming era be significantly altered should political identification take a different shape from the one we've known to date.

One way to grasp this is to again engage in some retrospective historical analysis, but this time from the vantage point of the future. In the introductory chapter to her edited volume *National Histories and European History* (1993), Mary Fulbrook tells an imaginative story of European integration, looking back from the other side of the twenty-first century. A multicultural, multiethnic, and multilingual "United States of Europe" has been forged, complete with a European identity and historians to write (invent?) its history as the triumph of progressive forces over those of backward provincial opponents.[2] While certainly not everyone's vision of Europe's ideal future, Fulbrook's clever extrapolation from the experience of European nation-states is notable for the prominence it gives to the role of identity in the creation and maintenance of viable polities. Any number of other scholars have also pointed to the same crucial nexus,[3] some illustrating the relationship from a negative perspective, substituting a discussion of the risks of ignoring identity for Fulbrook's portrayal of its positive capacities.

What is certainly clear, in the end, is that identity matters. It has mattered in Europe and the world in the past, it matters in the present, and it is highly likely that it will matter in the future. And, arguably, it matters especially in Europe, home over the previous half century to the world's most creative experimentation in the design of political institutions and of polities themselves. Europe at the millennium is a social scientist's laboratory, and—among others—it begs the question of political identity.

But this question has received insufficient scholarly attention to date. In 1969, Leon Lindberg and Stuart Scheingold wrote of a "permissive consensus" on the part of the European body politic[4] that was sufficient to sustain the integrative efforts of elites. That same year, however, former European Commission president Walter Hallstein was already warning of the dangers inherent in building an economic and institutional edifice on the weak foundation of indifferent public support. Hallstein ominously noted that "the construction of Europe is unfinished," and that the continued failure to involve citizens in the process meant that "even those parts, which are already set up, could be jeopardized" (Papcke 1992: 67). More recently, but still a decade before monetary union, Karlheinz Reif noted that so many competences have been transferred to

Brussels that, combined with the lack of mechanisms available for citizens to influence policy outcomes there, the legitimacy of the European Union (EU)—and therefore the Union itself—was at risk (1993: 134).

For these reasons, and because the complexity of contemporary Europe provides for students of political identity a fascinating academic case study, independent of any consequences on the ground, this book seeks to examine the question of European identity in its multiple dimensions, both theoretical and empirical. It finds that a European identity does indeed exist, though it is a minority sentiment, and one that is particularly prominent among elites and sympathizers of the integration project. Moreover—and perhaps more significantly—this identity is of a different quality than political identities typical of the past. Where nationalisms tend to be highly emotionally charged identities, often built on some primordially defined and exclusivist content, European identity emerges as more of a dispassionate, cognitively oriented persuasion for those who possess it, rooted in normative values such as peace, democracy, human rights, and—ironically—diversity and tolerance. As noted above, multiple interpretations of the identity are possible based on these conclusions, but the most compelling of these (theoretically and normatively) is that the continent's complex, contingent, multilevel, instrumental, and emotionally desiccated form of identification may be a harbinger for the future of political identities more broadly, beyond Europe's borders, under the cultural conditions of a world transitioning beyond modernity. This and other interpretations of the book's findings are discussed in the concluding chapter, but before examining these ideas and the observations on which they're based, it is worth detailing more fully why a study of European identity matters.

The Significance of Identity

The accomplishments of the European Coal and Steel Community (ECSC) and its successor institutions—up through and including the European Union—are surely remarkable developments in modern history. This is true for a number of reasons. First, nowhere else in the world has a supranational (or, more accurately, a suprastate) governmental structure developed such breadth of competence, such institutional elaboration, and such genuine, autonomous power. Second, this development has occurred in *Europe,* of all places, site of history's most intense and destructive national rivalries over religion, commerce, colonialism, territory, power, and prestige—rivalries that culminated in centuries of increasingly fierce fratricidal conflict. Indeed, beyond the noteworthiness of its very existence, all the more remarkable is the fact that European integration occurred directly on the heels of the worst of these conflagrations.[5]

The explanation for this astonishing development, and the integration project's real purpose—to prevent the reoccurrence of such catastrophes—is itself a third reason European integration deserves scholarly attention; it represents perhaps the most promising experiment to date in efforts to transcend the millennia-old curse of war between states. Though the capacity of current institutional structures to guarantee against militarized conflict is dangerously overestimated by some, the boldness and successes of the project are nevertheless noteworthy (in addition to being underestimated by others). Finally, European integration has been remarkable for the rapidity of its development, however rocky that process has been. Even theorists of international politics, who might be expected to take a longer view on the matter, too often neglect the extended temporal scale of historical state- and nation-building processes—the closest analogues to European integration—when wringing their hands at the "slow" or stalled development of the project (e.g., Haas 1975). But a broader perspective on these events instead suggests that tremendous change has occurred in a relatively short time. Desmond Dinan cogently summarized the scale of the achievement over a decade ago, well before the occurrence of monetary union and enlargement across the old Iron Curtain, perhaps the greatest integrative leaps to date:

> The EC's [European Community's] pervasiveness tends to obscure its uniqueness and relative newness. The voluntary sharing of sovereignty by nation-states—the ever closer union envisioned in the treaties of Rome and Maastricht and implicit in the term "European integration"—is unprecedented in modern history. Before World War II, the kind of European Community with which we are so familiar today was a pipe dream. Nations jealously guarded their sovereignty (national authority) and cooperated only on the basis of intergovernmental agreement. Less than fifty years ago, France and Germany were implacable enemies. (1994: 2)

In short, the postwar achievement of Western Europe is unprecedented and remarkable, and should not be underestimated. Yet—without diminishing in any way what has been accomplished—neither should it be overestimated or misconstrued. While the institutional superstructure of European integration has developed with great rapidity, it rests precariously on a foundation of mass public indifference and, all too often, even antipathy. Moreover, whatever popular *opinion* holds of the European Union and its various projects, a European *identity* clearly has not developed to capture the hearts and minds of most Europeans. I argue that such an identity is not only interesting and significant, but also in fact crucial—and therefore worthy of attention—for four reasons, ranging from the purely academic and semantic to the very pragmatic.

First, recent events in Europe (particularly public reactions to the demands and sacrifices associated with the run-up to monetary union, then later the rejection of constitutional referenda) only reinforce the argument that the success of European integration may be jeopardized by any approach that assumes too much of institutional development without sufficient regard for the significance of popular identities. To date, while the former has received enor-

mous attention and has prospered accordingly, the latter has been left generally unattended and thus largely underdeveloped. Even if the preservation of
existing institutions is all that is at issue, the affective ties of the European
body politic are likely to be critical to Europe's future, as indicated in the Anthony Smith quotation that prefaces this book. And, to the extent that even further integration is desired or pursued in Europe, the issue of identity will become increasingly critical.

Second, the character of popular identities in Europe has other profound
material implications, as well. Not least of these concerns the desire to make
war "unthinkable" and "materially impossible," as the EU's founders intended, an outcome that cannot be guaranteed without concomitant shifts in
identity. Only when there is no "we" and no "they," but only "us," can war become entirely unthinkable—by definition—for at that point there are no possible adversaries left to engage one another.

Third, European identity matters for social scientists, who have heretofore
largely defined the concept of "integration"[6] according to the trajectory of developments in postwar Western Europe. This usage allows a single, recent, and
erratically evolving case to define what should be an autonomous social science
concept. It also unhelpfully restricts wider application of the concept and more
generalized theorizing across geopolitical levels (e.g., to localities, nations, regions), and across cases. As well, the extant definition diminishes clarity of
usage and the distinction between integration and other concepts, such as interdependence, alliances, treaties, international regimes, international organizations, globalization (albeit on a regional level), and state-building.

Finally, as described previously and discussed in further detail in the
book's concluding chapter, European identity is worth our attention because it
represents something substantially different from that which has heretofore
been observed in the world. This alone makes it interesting, significant, and
worthy of investigation. However, if this form of identification also points the
way toward the future shape of political identity beyond the shores of Europe,
it is therefore all the more important. Each of these reasons for addressing European identity is discussed in greater detail in the pages that follow.

The Welfare and Viability of Polities

It has so far been suggested that the attention of both scholars and actors to
questions of political identity is important, for the multiple and specific reasons detailed above. Nevertheless, students of European integration might be
tempted to dismiss the general argument on the basis of what could be considered substantial prima facie evidence to the contrary: namely, the European
Union exists, and has grown considerably and rapidly, despite little engage-
ment of its body politic in the process. Yet, while this observation is true, it
should not be taken as a guarantee of the EU's longevity. As David Easton and

Jack Dennis noted, polities are dependent on a level of "diffuse support [that] forms a reservoir upon which a system typically draws in times of crises, such as depressions, wars, and internecine conflicts, when perceived benefits may recede to their lowest ebb" (1969: 63). Machiavelli made the same point, as indicated in the quotation introducing this chapter.

It seems likely that this logic would apply to the European Union as well, and therefore the degree to which the EU now remains aloof from popular identification bodes ill for its continued development and even existence, especially should events and conditions strain the patience of Europeans (even if such conditions are, in fact, actually unrelated to European institutions or their policies and behaviors). In this regard, it must be noted that the project of European integration has thus far largely taken place in highly munificent times, economically and politically; Europeans at all socioeconomic levels have experienced levels of wealth and peace unprecedented in the continent's history. This has been an ideal climate in which to launch the EU experiment, but the institutional products of such favorable conditions are not necessarily indicative of solidified European integration. What happens if times get tougher? European states and, to a lesser extent, their constitutional regimes, largely withstood the corrosive effects of the Great Depression and World War II (though governments were generally more expendable) because of the reservoirs of identification and loyalty upon which they could draw. What would happen to the EU and its existing institutional achievements in the face of meaner times? A lack of diffuse support could very possibly result in rapid breakdown, especially should those institutions be popularly perceived as either a cause of such woes or a barrier to their remedy, with such perceptions perhaps being driven by either genuinely or opportunistically Euroskeptic politicians and media outlets.

The first argument for the significance of popular identities in Europe, thus, is that the European Union—notwithstanding its achievements to date—remains a "shaky edifice" that may not necessarily withstand substantial pressures should Europe's future winds blow ill. Indeed, it lacks the very foundation of deep public attachment on which to make such a stand. This argument, moreover, is more than just speculative—muted manifestations of such effects have arguably already been observed to date. Louise van Tartwijk-Novey suggests, for example, that such pressures and their resultant disagreeable effects characterized the public reaction to the Maastricht Treaty at a time of general discontent and anger:

> Dissatisfied with the recession and rising unemployment, resentful of the influx of immigrants, fearful of the future for France's agricultural sector and apprehensive of the reappearance of their historical rival, a single Germany, the French voters directed their anger at the treaty. Unfortunately, Kohl could offer Mitterrand only little solace as sections of the normally pro-European German population had also begun to show signs of souring on the merits of further integration. While the Maastricht Treaty was not given a public referendum in

Germany, the treaty still had to be approved by the German parliament, and the domestic political debate over the treaty was coinciding uncomfortably with the realities of the costs of German reunification. Attached as they were to the D-mark, as a symbol of their country's postwar success, Germans began to have second thoughts about relinquishing it to a single European currency, and with the mounting costs of reunification many felt that their country could ill afford the further burden of [the Economic and Monetary Union]. In fact all across the Union no government leaders were in any position to rally to the treaty's defence as the political establishment and their prize treaty took a severe public beating. (1995: 12–13)

Indeed, as the run-up to monetary union required sacrifices in several member countries, hostility to the EU grew, feeding the power of extremist politicians on the right. This was certainly an ironic outcome for an organization contrived chiefly for the purpose of transcending nationalist sentiments and their pernicious effects.

And while the above passage demonstrates public hostility to a particular EU initiative seeking sectoral enlargement, it might just as well have referred to existing EU institutions or the integration project itself. It is not hard to imagine how this absence of public affect might be mobilized against EU institutions in the future, particularly should they be regarded as costly by citizens experiencing lean times. A cursory examination of the treatment of Europe by some national media and politicians reveals an already long-standing tradition of beating up on the EU, even in good times. Moreover, that the effects described above evidently took European leaders by surprise only underscores the argument that policymakers and scholars alike have devoted insufficient attention to the question of popular sentiments, loyalties, and identities, and that the European polity therefore remains at risk. Martin Slater summarizes well:

A second reason for looking more closely at elite-mass relationships concerns the broader question of the viability of any political community. One of the central issues in integration theory is that of the popular legitimacy of political institutions. Almost by definition, the building of a political community means the creation of a sense of community or solidarity among the people of a given region. It is this sense of solidarity which gives legitimacy to the Community's institutions. A viable political community needs the allegiance of its mass public as well as that of elites. In the case of the European Community, a lack of public commitment to Europe tends to be seen as a major threat to the existence of the Community. (1982: 155)

If, as argued above, Europe is now a grown-up polity, then it must face the challenges incumbent upon all adults. In particular, if it is to expect the progress made over the past half century to be able to weather difficult storms—let alone if there is to be further development—then the foundations of the European project must be built on firmer grounds than the shifting sands of public indifference and occasional hostility that presently (fail to) buttress the Union. The best bulwark for ensuring the success of European institutional integration, then, is an equally developed positive affect among Europeans. In short, like any polity, a successful Europe requires a robust European identity.

Prevention of War

Without question, the prevention of war has been at the heart of centuries' worth of dreams of European integration. In fact, it has been the motivating force behind most of those dreams (Nicoll and Salmon 1990: 2; Squires 1994: 9). But whatever the dreams of the Dantes or Kants of distant days, even more apparent is that the issue of peace between European states was the guiding principle for the architects of the current European project. As Dinan notes, "To a great extent, the EC was a security system for Western Europe" (1994: 2). Miles Hewstone relates this history in memorable terms: "Fear, says Barzini (1983), was *the* prime motivation. Fear of Russia's military might, fear of America's economic might, and the Europeans' fear of themselves. As Barzini says of these Europeans: 'They know anything might happen in Europe because everything has happened'" (1986: 3, emphasis in original).

Fresh on the heels of three Franco-German wars in almost as many generations, this concern weighed heavily on the French in particular. In 1950, France was once again brought face-to-face with its recurrent national security nightmare as the British and Americans became indifferent toward, if not encouraging of, German remilitarization in the context of the increasingly all-determining exigencies of the Cold War. For Germany, meanwhile, the primary foreign policy goal of the day was the rehabilitation of its moral reputation and readmittance to the international community of civilized states, following the disaster of national socialism and World War II.

It was both in, and because of, this context that Jean Monnet struck upon his plan for a lasting solution to ongoing French security fears (Monnet 1978). Likewise, when French foreign minister Robert Schuman issued his famous declaration of May 9, 1950, leading to the development of the European Coal and Steel Community, his clear and famously articulated intent was to make war between Germany and France "not merely unthinkable, but materially impossible" (Schuman 1994: 12; Nicoll and Salmon 1990: 8). What is more, this goal of preventing war remains even today at the core of both elite and nonelite perceptions of the European Union's raison d'être. Survey and interview research by Josephine Squires demonstrates that political and business elites are apt to choose "putting past rivalries behind us and living in peace with the people of neighboring countries" more often than any other factor in describing their sense of what European identity constitutes (1994: 156–158). Similarly, former German chancellor Helmut Kohl, one of the strongest advocates of further integration, highlighted the nexus between integration and peace in comments responding to domestic opposition to the Economic and Monetary Union

(EMU) program: "'In spite of recent criticism of the European Union, the federal government and myself personally are determined to do everything to make the integration process irreversible,' the chancellor said. Integration was and remained 'the effective insurance' against nationalism and war" (Atkins and Barber 1996: 2).

So why should this pursuit of peace in Europe somehow be seen as problematic? In and of itself, of course, it is laudable. The danger, rather, is in the potential for disaster that accompanies assumptions that Europe's institutional achievements to date somehow provide adequate bulwarks against future war. An example of this fairly common sentiment is Asbjørn Sonne Nørgaard's assertion that "war between any two member-states is unthinkable because of the extremely high costs and the close political ties among governments" (1994: 274). But to the extent that it is EU "integration" that is relied on to deter such war, the risk of unexpected future conflagrations would seem enhanced, ironically, however remote such conflicts certainly are today. It is not that European institutions and integrative efforts themselves in some way promote the prospects of war (though their potential to actually *divide* Europeans rather than to integrate them is discussed below). But it could be the case, rather, that a failure to swiftly mitigate rising potential conflicts might be the product of a hubristic assumption that EU institutions alone make war "unthinkable."

As earlier comments in this chapter make clear, the accomplishments of the European Union are by no means insubstantial. However, they are but one element of a host of equally remarkable developments that, individually and especially collectively, provide much better explanations for Europe's "long peace" of the previous six decades. Among these factors are

- moral revulsion following two world wars and the Holocaust,
- the unifying pressure on Western Europe emanating from the Cold War complex of US dominance in the West and the perception of a Soviet threat from the East,
- French and British nuclear capability,
- German popular pacifism,
- the unprecedented affluence of the postwar period,
- the loss, due to decolonization, of a major potential source of international conflict (Britain's willingness as late as the 1980s to fight the Falklands War is instructive here),
- the loss of desire for territorial acquisition—another traditional source of international conflict—due to the ascendance of economic power relative to military, and due to changes in international norms, and
- the tendency, as Bruce Russett (1993) and many others have noted, of democracies not to fight one another.

European institutions, in short, should not be assumed to have rendered war on the continent "unthinkable," though they have likely played an important role in helping to diminish its probability. Ultimately, however, the fundamental (and indeed definitional) preventive for war is common identity, or the making of potential cleavage lines politically irrelevant in the popular mind. The very phenomenon of war is dependent at its core on a division between one people and an "Other," and is not possible to the extent that identity is shared and such a distinction cannot be made. In other words, if an enemy cannot be specified—cannot be *identified*—it cannot be demonized or engaged in combat. But today's Europe is not that integrated, and scholars and policymakers must therefore avoid being seduced by the belief that the current form of European "integration" satisfies the historical purpose that has driven visions of a unified continent down nine or more centuries—namely, the pursuit of peace. It is the integration of popular identity that will be required to accomplish this goal, if it is to be accomplished, and not the construction of remote, let alone sometimes-loathed, institutional structures in Brussels.

Indeed, it is even conceivable that institutional development alone could actually *exacerbate* tensions between Europeans, rather than ameliorate them.[7] If, for example, a particular EU project was seen to have costs for one or more member-states because of provisions demanded by others, resentment from within the former might well be directed toward the latter, toward "Europe" itself, or toward both. As described above, this is exactly what appeared to be transpiring as the EU sought to implement monetary union. Thus the French and Italian publics, forced to sacrifice slivers of welfare-state benefits in order to qualify for what many already viewed as the dubious privilege of losing their national currencies, were bound to resent Germans and their strict criteria for EMU membership qualification. More recently, others in the monetary union have been angered by the rather cavalier manner in which France and Germany have busted their post-EMU deficit-spending limitations. While such resentments are, of course, far short of war,[8] they can nevertheless provide a climate ripe for escalation toward war by xenophobic political actors seeking to capitalize on the social and economic costs of integration. Dominique Moïsi illustrates the effect:

> Instead of being perceived as a goal or even—less ambitiously—as a solution, the European Union is seen as either the problem or an irrelevant answer to the daily preoccupations of the French: unemployment and insecurity. In a contradictory manner, the EU is seen as being both too intrusive in a bureaucratic sense and too impotent on the international stage. From the diktats of Brussels to the failure of Europe in Bosnia, the European project is losing its allure and purpose for France. The growing discontent is shrewdly exploited by Jean-Marie Le Pen's extreme right. (1996: 20)

Moreover, there is some evidence that the popular alienation of Europeans from Europe was not new to the period preceding monetary union. Van Tartwijk-Novey describes similar manifestations, with similar effects, in the "post-Maastricht tension" of the early 1990s:

In fact it was quite apparent that they [EU citizens] possessed no shared feeling of being "Europeans" at all. . . . This combination of lack of faith in the
leadership and uncertainty about the future was in turn giving rise to a re-
newed sense of nationalism. This divisive nationalism, together with a mistrust of European Union motives and methods nearly set the clock backwards
on Union progress. First, in the place of the Maastricht Treaty's professed
unity, a dangerously divisive rivalry between national politics and Union
agreements had arisen. . . . As governmental leaders exhibited their inability
to offer solutions to faltering home economies, halt growing unemployment,
ease the steady rise in the number of immigrants from Eastern Europe and
North Africa, and assuage worries that national identities were under threat
from Brussels, a reactionary xenophobic upswell gave new support to the far
right. (1995: 15–16)

Thus, the question must be asked, were monetary union or any other institutional unification project to go forward while in the process alienating
substantial numbers of European citizens from Europe or from one another, by
what definition would this constitute integration? The answer, of course,
points to the fallacy of substituting either institution-building or economic
convergence and interdependence for an apprehension of integration rooted in
notions of popular identity. Again, there should be no mistake but that Western European countries are now far from war with one another—no doubt as
far as they have ever been since the advent of the modern system of states. But
that said, believing that war is today "unthinkable"—or at least that it is unthinkable due to the development of existing supranational institutions—recklessly courts disaster. Today's reactionary xenophobes may lack both the
power and the maleficent designs of their predecessors of the 1930s, but it is
worth remembering that there would be no European integration to speak of
today were it not for the intent of the EU's founders to avoid the rise of just
such actors and the sentiments they represent, sentiments for which the
Union's founders had developed a healthy and well-justified fear (Squires
1994: 9). Ultimately, real assurance of preventing war in Europe requires nothing short of the advent of a widespread common identity, thus eliminating—
by definition—an enemy against which to fight.

Conceptual Implications

To date, the question of political integration in Europe has been treated as a
phenomenon of international politics. For most of the period in question, this
has been appropriate, because integration has been perhaps more a *process* involving multiple states than a resulting *condition*. Increasingly, however, it is
both. As an emerging polity in its own right, as opposed to either a process
alone, or a collection of units with common purpose (e.g., the North Atlantic
Treaty Organization [NATO]), the European Union must now be treated accordingly by scholars, thereby entering the domain of comparative politics,

and subjecting itself to the sorts of questions appropriate to the study of existing polities. What are the salient institutions of this polity, and how do they relate to one another? How deeply does the polity penetrate its respective civil society? How does it relate to the political units that constitute it and to external sovereigns? What sort of actors and politics characterize its decisionmaking processes? What is the relationship of the polity to its body politic? And, in particular, what is the degree and character of political identity associated with the polity?

But such analysis is made difficult by a certain imprecision of terminology, particularly with respect to the definition of the word *integration*. Indeed, employing this term—at least in its general, unmodified sense—in the absence of considerations of identity, is rather conceptually problematic. That is, to what extent may a polity be said to be integrated when little or no sense of unity or communal consciousness exists? Thus a third reason that identity matters, I argue, is that it is crucial to, though now largely absent from, a conceptually meaningful definition of political integration.

What *is* integration? As Michael Hodges (1978: 247) has suggested, there is little concurrence on the very meaning of this term, a lacuna that has had serious implications for the ability of the field to successfully describe, explain, and predict within its domain of interest. Nor is Hodges the only scholar of integration to note the field's embarrassment of definitional riches. As early as 1971, for example, Fred Hayward (1971: 314–315) identified five conceptually distinct definitions of regional integration, as well as a disturbing general lack of clarity in defining integration at the national level. More recently, James Dougherty and Robert Pfaltzgraff (1990: 432–434) presented twelve definitions, including those from two scholars for whom entries appear *twice*—once with original and once with revised versions. Finally, Carol Glen (1995: 9–10) described a spectrum of definitions, associated with each of integration theory's four major analytical schools, ranging from transactionalism's shared sense of community to neofunctionalism's incremental institution-building. She also noted that within the field, disagreement remains as to whether integration constitutes a process (per Ernst Haas [1958] and Leon Lindberg and Stuart Scheingold [1970]), or a condition (per Amitai Etzioni [1965]).

Despite this lack of consensus regarding the meaning of "integration," scholars have by and large been satisfied with employing the term to describe the sort of institutional development that has occurred in Western Europe since 1952. Effectively, that is, integration is what Europe does. There are several problems, actual and potential, associated with such an apprehension. In the first instance, the focus on Europe's activities on the ground has produced a working definition of integration that stresses those domains—and only those domains—in which Europe has been successful. Thus, for most scholars and policymakers, the term *integration* refers to the economic and institution-building processes that have characterized the European postwar experience.

Even from a perspective solely concerned with the needs of social science, this is a problematic development. Cases should not define concepts, especially single cases, cases of relatively recent origin, or cases characterized by erratic development—all of which are attributes of European "integration."

The danger presented by such a scenario is at least twofold. First, if cases define concepts, what happens should the case mutate into another form? What if the European experience had been generally characterized by political (i.e., defense and foreign policy) cooperation and consolidation rather than economic—as might well have happened, had not the French National Assembly rejected the European Defense Community (EDC) and European Political Cooperation (EPC) in 1954? Would the concept of "integration" therefore shift in meaning accordingly, and if so, can it really be said that it has any autonomous meaning of consequence? Of even greater importance, the second danger of a sui generis definition of this or any other concept is that it diminishes the possibilities of both comparison with and cross-fertilization from other areas of inquiry. There may be much to be learned about European integration, for example, by its comparison to state-building experiences and by the borrowing of theoretical ideas from studies in that field. But to the extent that a concept is defined by a single case, such comparisons and exchanges of ideas are structurally impeded.

A more useful definition of integration would allow for its wider application, both across polity levels (e.g., continents, countries, regions), and across cases within each of those levels. Andrew Gamble and Anthony Payne (1996: 257, 262), in their comparison of regional projects throughout the world, demonstrate the manner in which a revised and identity-based conception of integration would permit more universal geographical applicability. Thus they find that East Asia currently manifests the least degree of regional integration, because multiple identities impede consolidation around a single regional one. Europe, meanwhile, shows the most potential for integration, despite some internal differences over the nature and definition of a European identity. Whatever the particular findings of their study, however, the salient point for purposes of this discussion is that a social science concept such as integration should possess a meaning that is generalizable, and is autonomous of the vicissitudes of any given case.

A second problem with the current conception of integration is that it doesn't even meet standards of fidelity to its own historical meaning. The idea of European integration is, of course, hardly a new one. Political philosophers have proposed and considered various integration schemes for at least nine centuries, with the long-lost Roman Empire clearly a lingering inspiration for many of them. Though the nature of these plans has varied in terms of the degree and type of integration proposed, a central component to most has been the notion of eliminating war on the continent (Squires 1994: 9), which, as argued above, would require shifts in popular identity to guarantee, short of imposing "peace" from on high as Napoleon and others have attempted.

Such pacifying aspirations were clearly on the minds of those who launched the modern European project a half century ago. And, just as clearly, their vision of integration transcended mere institutional development or economic consolidation. As Desmond Dinan notes, the European Union's founding father had more in mind than simply "suprastate-building" when he initiated the contemporary process in 1950: "For Jean Monnet, a senior French official who pioneered the idea of sectoral economic integration, the ECSC was not an end in itself but part of a process that would culminate in a European federation transcending the nation-state. Such a goal was inherent in the word 'community,' which distinguished the new arrangement from traditional forms of intergovernmental collaboration and international organization" (1994: 2).

Sophie Duchesne and André-Paul Frognier concur that "the dream of the Community's founding fathers was, ultimately, to see the emergence of a European identity" (1995: 193). They note that while the intention of the founders was never to replace national identities entirely, the development of a genuine polity at the European level required a strong foundation in mass European identity. In contemporary usage, then, employing the term *integration* to refer to that which, as Dinan and Duchesne and Frognier have noted, was explicitly excluded from the original definition held by the founders, distorts the traditional meaning of the term.

Indeed, conceiving of integration in the absence of identity risks producing absurd outcomes. The EMU convergence criteria, for example, put onerous burdens on certain European states in order to qualify for joining the monetary union, burdens that were not always welcomed by their respective publics.[9] If the euro were to have been created at the cost of wholesale French or Italian resentment and antipathy toward either Brussels or Germany (which was behind the stringency requirements), could this outcome then legitimately be called "integration"? Put a bit more lyrically, one might ask: What is integration profited if it shall gain the euro and lose the Europeans? Such a scenario should remind us that economic and institutional consolidation in the absence of—or, potentially, even diminishing—a shared sense of identity cannot plausibly be described as integration.

A third problem with current usage of the term is that integration so construed is difficult to distinguish from other concepts of international relations and comparative politics, including such notions as interdependence, treaties and alliances, international regimes and organizations, globalization (on a regional level), and state-building (again, in regional garb). Institutional integration (and its preeminent manifestation, the European Union) shares extensive definitional overlap with each of these ideas. This is especially problematic because, at their core, several of these other notions refer to a voluntary and self-revocable intergovernmental relationship of autonomous constituent units, surely *not* what the concept of integration is meant to convey.

On the other hand, none of these notions can be construed to refer to the sort of shared sense of identity or "we-ness" for which the term integration is perhaps solely useful. Reconceptualizing integration in this regard would address each of the concerns articulated above, providing scholars with a conceptual definition that is autonomous of any single case, fully distinct from other political science concepts, and faithful to the historical and philosophical meanings long associated with its lineage. Finally, it would also have the probable additional effect of redirecting scholarly attention toward a property that is critical to the welfare of any polity, the question of identity.

Such a conceptualization is not without precedent in the theoretical literature on European integration, particularly its earlier variants. Karl Deutsch, for example, alternatively defined integration as a "sense of community" in which individuals share a commitment to resolving common social problems by means of "peaceful change" (1953: 5), and a community as a common culture of "stable, habitual preferences and priorities in men's attention, and behavior, as well as in their thoughts and feelings," where "many of these preferences may involve communication" (1957: 88). Similarly, Ernst Haas incorporated identity concepts into his definition of political integration, but not exclusively, only with respect to regional integration, and without much concern for the attitudes of nonelites: "Political integration is the process whereby political actors in several distinct national settings are persuaded to shift their loyalties, expectations and political activities toward a new centre, whose institutions possess or demand jurisdiction over the pre-existing national states" (1958: 16).

Moreover, the emphasis on elites in Haas's theoretical work bore more than a passing relationship to the reality of early European integration. Kevin Featherstone (1994) has shown, for example, the degree to which Monnet's original vision in building the European Coal and Steel Community (the EU's original predecessor institution), and especially its executive, the High Authority, was an elitist project. Indeed, by demonstrating the degree to which that strategic "error" would cost the EU and its predecessors and limit their aspirations, Featherstone underscores the importance of public support and identity to the concept of integration. Articulating this critique, Monnet's fellow federalist Altiero Spinelli put it best: "Monnet has the great merit of having built Europe and the great responsibility to have built it badly" (quoted in Featherstone 1994: 150).

In short, some of the original and seminal theoretical work on European integration did indeed take care to emphasize the identity question. But not enough. And subsequent studies have focused far more on institutional developments and related themes in considering and (often implicitly) defining integration. But, in fact—I argue—identity is actually *the* crucial element in defining true political integration, and social scientists should treat it accordingly.

Identity After Modernity

A complete catalog of the reasons for studying European identity must include mention of the fact that the identity is unique. And, more important, that it may represent the leading edge of a wholesale new form of political identification, which has the potential to be to postmodernity what nationalism was to modernity.

Given that nationalism has arguably been the most consequential political force of the past two centuries, no exaggerated argument is necessary to make the case for the potential significance of European identity to international and domestic politics. If this identity—which appears to represent a sea change from the nationalisms of the past—only obtains in Europe, that alone is a highly consequential development. If, on the other hand, it also represents a new form of political identification that will characterize postmodern societies generally, its ramifications and significance are enormous in scope. This question, and alternative interpretations of the trajectory of political identities in Europe, are addressed in the concluding chapter. The point here is simply to underscore the degree to which such possibilities make European identity highly worthy of attention.

* * *

As I have argued, European identity matters for at least four reasons, ranging from relatively narrow conceptual academic interests to implications that affect the highest of high politics. Identity in Europe matters, first, because Europe is no different from any other polity with respect to the requirement of broad positive affect necessary to sustain it, especially through more challenging chapters in its future. It matters because it is, at the end of the day, the only true preventive for war; those who cannot differentiate themselves from others cannot fight those others. It matters because defining integration in the absence of common identity, as has heretofore been the case, makes little conceptual sense. And it matters because it may point the way to a wider form of political identification that will come to characterize postmodern societies everywhere.

With these philosophical justifications in hand, we may now turn to the more prosaic but equally daunting questions of just how to measure European identity.

Methodology and Sources

Identity questions are among the most difficult in the social sciences with which to grapple, for reasons that are further elaborated in the next section of this chapter. Suffice it here to say that identities are amorphous, contextually influenced, and sometimes fluid. They operate at a subconscious level for most individuals, and can be highly controversial when conscious. None of these characteristics facilitate the work of scholars seeking to understand and explain identity—indeed, all of them hinder such investigations.

Nor is an understanding of such a nuanced and recondite phenomenon profited by reliance on a single methodological approach to the topic, a characteristic that unfortunately describes most extant work on European identity. As John Brewer and Albert Hunter (1989: 11) note, most methods bring certain strengths *and* certain weaknesses to the topics to which they are applied. The cogency of this argument is easy to see in considering methodological approaches to the question of European identity. Survey methodology, the principal research vehicle of prior work on the topic, provides an excellent, and virtually indispensable, resource for generating broad, reliable conclusions about a population and for making comparative statements about various subpopulations within it. But the burdens of collecting—not to mention analyzing—10,000 or more responses to a bank of questions require standardization of prompts and responses to an extent that can seem almost comical, especially where identity is concerned. Forcing respondents to characterize their affective sentiments toward a community by selecting one of four predetermined responses to a uniform question prompt strips the resulting answers of all of the nuance, contingency, and depth of sentiment surrounding identity issues that were alluded to above. Anthony Smith underscores this point in the context of a general critique of empirical work on the question of European identity:

> Though there have been many studies of the economic organizations and political institutions of the European Community, relatively little attention has been devoted to the cultural and psychological issues associated with European unification—to questions of meaning, value and symbolism. What research there has been in this area has suffered from a lack of theoretical sophistication and tends to be somewhat impressionistic and superficial. This is especially true of attitude studies, in which generalizations over time are derived from surveys of particular groups or strata at particular moments. In few areas is the attitude questionnaire of such doubtful utility as in the domain of cultural values and meanings. (1992: 57)

Smith is perhaps overly pessimistic, but he is clearly on solid ground in pointing to the liabilities of overreliance on survey methodology in understanding identity questions. Yet, on the other hand, scholars opting to capture the detail of European identity through the alternative means of conducting extended interviews on the ground (and few have so opted to date) risk either drawing inferences that are highly suspect given the necessarily limited size of the informant pool, or refraining from reaching such conclusions at all, for the same reason. In their book of the same name, Brewer and Hunter (1989) propose "multimethod research" as a solution to this quandary, and this is precisely the strategy that has been employed in this study.

Both quantitative and qualitative methodological tools were applied to four distinct data sources (in addition to a review of existing scholarly literature, and participation/observation at events listed in Appendix 8). The main methodological techniques employed included interviewing of elites and nonelites, and various forms of statistical analysis. The latter are composed of the following:

- Univariate measures of the dependent variable (e.g., means, percentages); these measures are employed chiefly in Chapter 3, which explores the extent of European identification in Europe.
- Bivariate measures of the dependent variable juxtaposed against a single independent variable (e.g., cross-tabulations, comparison of subpopulation means, Cramer's-V measures of the general relationship between two variables); these are utilized throughout most of the chapters that explore the empirical themes detailed below, especially Chapters 5 and 6.
- Multivariate measures of the relationship between the dependent variable and multiple independent variables (e.g., ordinary least squares and ordered probit regression analyses), in order to determine the impact of each of the latter on the former, while controlling for the simultaneous effects of the others; these measures are utilized primarily in Chapter 4.

These statistical techniques, as well as the interpretation of interview responses, have been applied to data gathered from four key sources: interviews of targeted European identifiers, interviews of elites, original survey data, and extant survey data.

Interviews of Targeted European Identifiers

Locating and interviewing European identifiers in every European Union member-state would have been impossible, given the limitations imposed by cost and the eleven or more languages spoken in EU countries at the time of fieldwork. In order to circumvent these limitations, I attempted to locate venues where (1) the broadest and most diverse possible sample of individuals—especially with regard to nationality—would be present; and (2) a large number of this same group would be likely to possess relatively high levels of European identity. Three such venues met these criteria perfectly, and interviews were conducted at each. The first of these was the fiftieth-anniversary Congress of Europe, held in May 1998 at The Hague, site of the original Congress, chaired by Winston Churchill, which had launched the modern European integration movement from the debris of World War II. Some 2,500 participants from across Europe attended the conference, and interviews with as many as time permitted (about a dozen) were conducted over the course of the weekend.

The original Congress of Europe, in 1948, had created three significant institutions: the Council of Europe, the European Court of Human Rights, and the College of Europe. The latter, situated in the Belgian city of Bruges, provided a second ideal site for locating a concentration of European identifiers from across Europe. Students there participate in intense, one-year postgraduate training programs in law, politics, economics, or human resources. These students are diverse in background, if not in age (the average is twenty-five, with the range probably between twenty and thirty), and many will become Europe's future leaders and staff its managerial corps. There are about 260 students at Bruges, from thirty-five countries, who speak an average of four languages each. The campus was visited in May 1998, and a series of often lengthy interviews was conducted with these students, in addition to one focus-group discussion. At least one informant from each of the then-fifteen EU member-states was interviewed, as well as several from non-EU countries.

A third venue, similar to the Hague Congress, was provided by a June 1998 gathering in London called the People's Europe Conference. It was sponsored by the British government as part of a public outreach program that was a centerpiece of its then-concluding rotating presidency of the European Union. Roughly 1,000 people attended the conference, held on the London School of Economics campus. These participants were also drawn from across Europe—but with rather a large portion from the United Kingdom—and interviews were conducted over the brief period of the conference.

Finally, interviews were also conducted at various field locations in Britain and Ireland. These informants—mostly European sympathizers but also some ardent Europhobes—were identified via their association with advocacy groups, from College of Europe alumni lists, and via the "snowballing" referral technique. In sum, nearly eighty such targeted informants were interviewed in May, June, and July 1998. The average length of these interviews was about one hour, though many lasted two hours or longer. Appendix 2 summarizes these various interview sources by location and informant nationality. Appendix 6 presents the script that provided the basic structure for these interviews (though departures to ask additional questions were frequent, with the interviewer following important leads as they arose in conversation).

Interviews of Elites

In addition to interviews of key European Union figures who were well-acquainted with matters related to European identity, two of the questions examined in this study required more extensive fieldwork, and interview data were therefore collected from various actors well-positioned to feel the pulse of their respective communities. In order to examine the play of a European identity in the context of complex, multilayered, and sometimes antagonistic competing identities, four regions in the United Kingdom were visited: Scotland, Wales, Northern England, and Greater London. These visits took place at a remarkable time for Britain, as the implications of devolution were being felt and splashed across the front pages of newspapers, and as questions of identity were generally quite high in people's consciousness.

Ireland, on the other hand, provided excellent grounds for testing the instrumentalist hypothesis of European identity. This country has experienced phenomenal development in the previous decades, catapulting it from the ranks of the EU's poor to the ranks of its wealthy, and from an agricultural country to a high-technology and service economy, without much bothering to stop at industrialism in between. What is more, it is a commonly held belief (and one that is constantly sustained by the many signs denoting EU sponsorship of various infrastructural and other projects) that Ireland's development has had everything to do with its EU membership, by virtue of multiple factors, including Irish access to the common market, the massive investment of Structural and Social Funds that poured into the country, the foreign direct investment that flowed in because of European access, and the autonomy from Britain that EU membership has facilitated. Clearly, it was widely perceived that Ireland has gained tremendously from joining Europe. Would this mean, as the instrumentalism hypothesis would predict, that the Irish would be more "European"?

To answer these questions, interviews of elites were conducted in the UK and Ireland (and these interview data were used in conjunction with other data sources). Altogether, more than sixty individuals from various domains—including government, politics, business, labor, media, nongovernmental organizations, private research agencies, and academia—sat for interviews regarding European identity in May, June, and July 1998. They ranged from local reporters, to key administrators, to several members of parliament (MPs) and members of the European Parliament (MEPs), and included both a current member of the European Commission and a former Irish taoiseach (prime minister). These interviews were generally held at the workplace of busy informants, and tended therefore to be briefer than those with the targeted identifiers. The average duration was perhaps forty minutes, but they too could sometimes be quite lengthy—one informant spent four and a half hours in (quite high-quality) conversation on the topic of European identity. The names of these elites are presented, along with their respective titles and organizations, in Appendix 1. Appendix 5 details the basic script for these conversations, though again, departures were followed wherever they appeared promising. Follow-up interviews with MEPs and staff were also conducted at the European Parliament during the summers of 2002 and 2004.

Original Survey Data

In addition to the targeted interviews described above, the gathering of large numbers of probable European identifiers at conferences in The Hague and London presented an excellent opportunity to collect further data from respondents at a volume well beyond what is generally available to qualitative researchers.

Of particular interest was the chance to explore hypotheses and questions either not at all or poorly addressed by existing survey data (see below)—for example, on parental attitudes, which could be used to test the socialization hypothesis. Toward this end, a two-page, thirty-eight-question written survey instrument was created, with the aim of including questions probing every theme and hypothesis of the study that was amenable to written response. English and French versions of the survey (see Appendix 7) were distributed to participants at the respective final mass meetings of the conferences. Additionally, notice of the survey was posted on the electronic mailing list of Britain's Young European Movement, a group of pro-Europe activists of mostly college age. Twelve members of the group requested copies of the survey by e-mail and responded to it electronically. It is estimated that the survey required approximately twenty minutes to complete. Altogether, 271 surveys were completed by respondents from thirty-one countries, resulting in the Survey of European Identifiers (SEI), a new dataset specifically tailored to respond to the questions and hypotheses contemplated in this study.[10] Appendix 3 details respondents by number, locale, and nationality.

Extant Survey Data

Finally, a host of existing mass survey data is available for purposes of interrogating the topic of European identity. More than a hundred survey codebooks from the extensive library of datasets at the Inter-University Consortium for Political and Social Research (ICPSR) were downloaded and reviewed. All datasets that possessed a valid measure of European identity were employed in this study, as were some others that are otherwise relevant even though they do not include such a dependent-variable question. Appendix 4 lists these surveys, and the respective dates they were fielded. The most extensive and carefully administered of these are the series of Eurobarometer surveys, which were initially deployed in the early 1970s, subsequently became adopted by the EU as an in-house project, and are now fielded at least every six months. Eurobarometer datasets always include all member-states of the EU in their sample, and sometimes a handful of other countries as well. Surveyed countries vary somewhat across the other datasets, as does the apparent quality of the administration.[11] The surveys analyzed herein all polled widely, however, with almost every sample at or above 10,000 cases. In total, 260,143 respondents from twenty existing survey datasets were examined (of whom 12,213 are duplicates from one survey, Eurobarometer 36-0, which has two dependent-variable questions); Chapter 4 takes up this analysis.

Supplied national weights were applied wherever possible, so that samples from each country would be proportionate to their respective populations.[12] Where necessary, and as documented in the chapters that follow, new variables were constructed from permutations or combinations of existing data, or from external data, in order to operationalize various concepts in question. In addition to standard demographic and attitudinal data, all employed surveys capture a number of respondent attitudes and attributes that provide insight into political identification at various levels of community in Europe (i.e., local, regional, national, and European).

Three basic dependent-variable question formats were employed across these various surveys, with a permutation of one of them representing a fourth format:

• *Format One:* The first format asks respondents, "Which of these geographical groups would you say you belong to first of all?" Respondents could choose among their town, their region, their country, Europe, and the world as a whole. A follow-up question asked them to specify their second choice from the same list. This format is found in Eurobarometers 6, 10A, and 12, the three European Communities Studies, and the three World (and European) Values Surveys. For most of the analyses undertaken in this book, the two-question responses have been recoded into a single constructed ordinal variable, in which the omission of Europe as a mentioned choice is coded "0," the selection of Europe as the second choice is coded "1," and the selection of Europe as the first choice is coded "2." In the case of the 1999–2001 World and European Values Survey only, a fourth category is added, in which European identity can also be actively rejected (as opposed to just omitted) by respondents.

• *Format Two:* The second identity-question format asks respondents, "Does the thought ever occur to you that you are not only [nationality] but also a European? Does this happen often, sometimes, or never?" This format is employed in Eurobarometers 27, 30, 31, 33, and 37-0.

• *Format Three:* For the third format, Eurobarometer 41-1 poses to respondents the same question described in Format Two, but asks them to locate their response on a 10-point scale—with "1" representing "Not at all also European" and "10" representing "Very much also European"—rather than choosing among the three ordinal responses.

• *Format Four:* Finally, in the fourth format, inquiries are made in separate questions about the respondents' feelings toward the same polities/ geographic levels listed under Format One (town, region, country, etc.). For purposes of this study, the key question posed is the fourth in this series, asking, "How close [attached] do you feel to . . . Europe [or] the European Union?" Respondents could choose from "Not close [attached] at all," "Not very close [attached]," "Close [attached]," and "Very close [attached]." This format appears in the International Social Survey Program (ISSP) 1995 survey on national identity, and in Eurobarometers 36-0, 51-0, 54-1, 56-3, and 58-1.[13]

*   *   *

This study thus draws from a variety of sources, and types of sources, in order to examine a series of questions related to European identity. This multimethodological, multisource approach benefits the research in at least three ways. First, the sheer volume of sources improves the credibility of the conclusions reached, in the same way that increasing the number of respondents to a survey boosts statistical significance. Second, drawing on multiple types of sources is critical for the examination of a phenomenon as complex as is political identity. The combination of qualitative and quantitative approaches within a single study is especially felicitous to understanding the subtleties of the topic, permitting an analytical triangulation upon the targeted question. And finally, the use of a broad number of datasets is also helpful, because it permits examination of trends and changes in patterns of European identification over time.

Obstacles to the Study of Identity

Questions of identity are at once among the most recondite and recalcitrant in the social sciences. There are not often votes to count, nor commercial transactions to tally, nor even much visible manifestation whatsoever, short of sporting matches and militarized disputes, though scholars have used all of these in attempts to operationalize the concept. Even the meaning of identity itself—and the boundaries and content of its various incarnations—can be controversial, let alone theories purporting to explain it. Moreover, simply referring to identity as an "it" arguably constitutes a grave conceptual error, for a great deal of evidence suggests that identities are multiple and simultaneous, and not even restricted to the political/geographical kind at that. Identities can also be moving targets, changing as does the individual's current context or life experience, and thus increasing the difficulty the researcher faces in characterizing them.

Additionally, while scholars and others may give a good deal of thought to identity questions, for many people—almost certainly the vast majority— such questions rarely migrate to the level of consciousness. Though their identities may even be quite strongly held, these sentiments tend to reside in the subconscious, or in a thousand subtle manifestations of everyday life. And finally, apart from all these issues, there is the very difficult pragmatic problem facing the social scientist as to how something as complex, nuanced, and sometimes controversial as identity can be operationalized and measured in any meaningful way.

Though these obstacles, discussed in further detail below, are daunting, especially in their collective impact, they do not preclude researchers from investigating this topic and generating interesting and reliable conclusions. They do, however, constitute serious caveats that any consumer of identity scholarship would be wise to consider.

Perhaps the most significant of these caveats is that identities are not singular and exclusive, as the empirical work based on Eurobarometer data and other analyses clearly demonstrates. Not only might individuals maintain affective ties to several levels of political organization (e.g., municipalities, regions, nations, states, supranational regions, the world) simultaneously, but they may also do the same with respect to associations from other social domains as well (e.g., family, religion, ethnicity, race), with some of the latter at times even conflicting with or eclipsing political affinities.[14] Nor, for many individuals, are identity constellations necessarily static over the course of a lifetime. Charles Tilly makes the point eloquently:

> Any actor deploys multiple identities, at least one per tie, role, network, and group to which the actor is attached. That others often typify and respond to an actor by singling out one of those multiple identities—race, gender, class, job, religious affiliation, national origin, or something else—by no means establishes the unity, or even the tight connectedness, of those identities. That sickness or zealotry occasionally elevates one identity to overwhelming dominance of an actor's consciousness and behavior, furthermore, does not gainsay the prevalence of multiple identities among people who are neither sick nor zealots. It actually takes sustained effort to endow actors with unitary identities. (1998: 4; see also Smith 1992: 59)

Fortunately, the fact that people maintain complex identity structures does not preclude measurement of levels and changes with respect to any one or more of these identities; but it does suggest caution, especially in trying to affix onto individuals a single identity label.

As indicated above, there are also very good reasons to believe that identities are far less constant than, say, a nationalist demagogue or a primordialist-oriented scholar would care to admit. Indeed, a good deal of evidence—including much collected in the field for this study—suggests that political identities are fluid and contextual rather than static and fixed. One who is considered a Glaswegian in Edinburgh, for example, may well be a Lowlander in Inverness, a Scot in London, British (or, perish the thought, English) in Spain, and a European in Africa. Nor are these purely ascribed identities either; many informants interviewed for this study reported alterations in their own feelings of who they were, depending on their location at the time. Dormant identity-related feelings may also be stimulated by perceptions or events, not least of which include sporting matches pitting local or national teams against one other.[15] Indeed, fieldwork for this project twice took place during the height of the quadrennial World Cup football competition, the emotive power of which should not be underestimated, deeply affecting as it does more than just the "hooligans" who rioted across France during the 1998 tournament.

In part, recognition of this question invokes the debate between "primordialists" (e.g., Geertz 1973; Smith 1992) and "constructivists" (e.g., Anderson

1991; Judt 1996; Gamble and Payne 1996b; Hoover 1975)[16] on the very nature of identity itself, and particularly on the extent to which it is malleable (see Chapter 2 for further discussion of the dispute between these approaches). Yet the issue of context extends beyond the scope of this debate, for even if the primordialists are correct in asserting the relative fixity of identity, as long as one is still willing to admit to the existence of multiple simultaneous identities— something seemingly rather difficult to deny—the probability of their relative flux remains high. Moreover, these multiple identities and their modulation as a result of contextual changes are precisely what informants frequently describe in discussions about their own identities, as demonstrated above. It would seem clear, in short, that identities respond to changes in stimuli and environment, offering an additional challenge to scholars who would seek to understand and explain them.

There are other special challenges, as well, that are attendant to the study of identity in general, and to a focus on European identity in particular. One of the most vexing of these concerns the difficulties involved in attempting to extract thoughtful responses from informants on subjects to which they may have given little conscious thought. While identities matter to scholars, the individuals who possess them may traverse entire lifetimes without much consideration of their own identity, or of the idea that there is even anything to consider at all—that identities, in other words, might be anything other than simply immutable patrimony. Identities may be enormously salient for a given individual, and yet rarely enter that person's consciousness, perhaps, in part, precisely because of their ubiquity. To the extent that they are the products of affective, and not cognitive, psychological processes, obtaining data useful for purposes of generating meaningful insights into identity may be extremely difficult, and perhaps impossible. Doing so under the constraints imposed by a mass survey methodology only exacerbates this difficulty. As Oskar Niedermayer and Richard Sinnott note:

> We can only agree that measuring such things as diffuse and specific orientations towards internationalized governance, sense of community and European identity, democratic values, and policy orientations is problematic. Some of these problems are inherent in research on mass culture and public opinion; for example, problems arising from the artificiality of the interview situation. In cases where the issues concerned are of low salience, there is always the danger that the interaction involved in the interview situation generates an attitude which would not otherwise have existed. Over and above this, there is the general problem of validity: do the data tell us what we want to know? Are the answers to particular questions valid indicators of the particular attitude we want to measure? (1995: 3)

Another obstacle to the study of political identity concerns the distinction— one that is often lost in the popular and sometimes even scholarly press—

between nation and state, or more generally, between a community and its associated institutions. It is certainly clear from the historical record that these two are intertwined, and it is also clear that institutions often play pivotal roles in the fostering and strengthening of identities.[17] Nevertheless, it is important for scholars, at least, to maintain a distinction between the two concepts. It is far less clear, however, that individuals on the ground do so, and this is especially the case where Europe is concerned. Indeed, the very term *Europe* is probably far more likely to evoke in the minds of Europeans the idea of the European Union (i.e., Europe's "state") than it is to conjure up images of a single people with a shared set of interests, attributes, and destiny (a European "nation"). To a certain degree, conflation of these concepts is inevitable, but nevertheless needs to be recognized and guarded against. The two concepts are quite different, precisely to the extent that (once again employing the national analogue) a scholar of French identity, for example, would not wish to equate that concept with the French state and its many vicissitudes and multiplicity of regimes.

Finally, apart from the conceptual, theoretical, and epistemological problems alluded to above, there are some very pragmatic concerns that researchers must face when grappling with identity questions. Chief among these is the problem of constructing the most appropriate dependent-variable measure. As previously indicated, four survey-question formats have already been applied in the European case, and arguments could be advanced as to why one is superior or not with respect to the others, or even that an entirely different measure is required to accurately represent the concept in question. Is a format that requires respondents to compare their degree of European identity to that of other identities preferable to a nonrelative one in which the former is simply evaluated in its own right? Is it preferable that respondents should be able to describe their feelings along a continuous scale, as opposed to having to conform their response to fit within one of several fixed categorical options?

The answers to these and related questions are unclear, and perhaps impossible ever to discern. Moreover, it is arguably preferable to have multiple measures of any phenomenon of interest, rather than relying on a single construction, despite the risk of having to interpret potential variances in responses to the multiple formats (as is precisely the situation with European identity—see, especially, Chapter 3). This interpretation problem becomes especially daunting when, as is again the case with European identity, question formats tend to be aggregated in time, such that one format appears in a certain decade, only to be replaced by other formats in subsequent decades. This makes it difficult for the analyst to determine whether changes in identity measures reflect actual changes in identity over time, or simply the change in question format, or some of both. One likely effective solution to this quandary would be to place each of the question formats on a single survey, thus allowing comparison of responses taken from the same individuals at the same moment in time. With the exception of two questions posed on Euro-barometer 36-0, however, this has not been done in a mass survey to date, but all three main question formats were included on the SEI original field instrument that was distributed in support of this study, for precisely this reason. Thus, at least some highly circumscribed evidence may be analyzed to determine how these various dependent-variable measures relate.

The foregoing discussion suggests that the obstacles to studying identity—and especially European identity—are many and formidable. It is not meant to suggest that the task is impossible, but rather that it requires considerable care to be executed meaningfully and reliably. This care must not only be applied in interpreting findings from empirical analyses of the data, but long before that as well, during the stages at which such empirical work is designed. Above all, the caveats discussed above should underscore the risk inherent in relying on a single data source or a single methodological approach to this most complex of phenomena.

Structure of the Book

This first chapter has introduced the themes of the project, the rationale for examining the topic, the scope of the study, and its methodologies and limitations. In Chapter 2, the stage is further set for making an original contribution to what is known about the topic by reviewing the idea of European identity *as* an idea, looking at its history, asking whether a shared identity across a continent of diverse nations and languages is even possible, and if so, what substantive elements might be employed in constituting it. The chapter also examines some efforts that have been made to foster identification with Europe, both private and EU-sponsored.

The book next turns to its core task, addressing five key empirical questions concerning the phenomenon of European identity. Of initial and obvious importance is the extent of European identification; Chapter 3 establishes that there are in fact a considerable number of Europeans who possess some or even a great deal of European identity. The second question concerns whether, to what extent, and how identity changes over time, which Chapter 3 also addresses. The third question—perhaps the most central of the six empirical topics—asks, "Who Are the 'Europeans'?"—or more precisely, what factors cause levels of identification with Europe to vary from individual to individual? A wide range of hypothesized answers to this question are tested in Chapter 4. These hypotheses have been organized into four general categories, according to the type of factor invoked by the posited relationship:

- those hypotheses that resort to *attributional* factors (e.g., socioeconomic status, age) to explain varying levels of European identification;

- those that consider the relationship of other *attitudinal* factors (e.g., ideology, postmaterialism) to the dependent variable;
- those that refer to certain *social-psychological* processes and characteristics (e.g., socialization, political efficacy) to address the question;
- and those that are derived from *political-cultural* aspects (e.g., nationality, religion).

The fourth empirical question of this book probes the meaning of a European identity for those who possess it. This discussion, in Chapter 5, seeks to determine the nature and content attendant to this rather unique creature of the political animal kingdom, the supranational identity. Finally, a related fifth question asks how deep this identity runs, and explores whether European identity is fleeting and peripheral even among those who possess it, whether it is capable of producing the sort of emotions and behaviors for which other forms of identity (e.g., especially, nationalism) are notorious, or whether it is something in-between or of a different character altogether. These questions are addressed in Chapter 6.

Concluding the book, Chapter 7 summarizes the findings of this analysis and considers their wider implications. In particular, the discussion seeks to grapple with the character of political identity, broadly construed, and to consider its place in a world that is quite likely experiencing wholesale structural change at the political, economic, and cultural levels, perhaps including the replacement of the Westphalian order of autonomous (nation-)states with some new system. This discussion considers whether the entire notion of political identification—a phenomenon of extreme consequence and widely recognized as a major defining characteristic of modernity—will change beyond recognition in a postmodern world.

Much has been written about the deterioration of the sovereign state. Can the nation long remain unchanged in such a context? What are the implications of globalization and other contemporary developments for how and whether people identify themselves today? The final chapter of the book explores themes such as these, and presents the argument that political identity may be so reconfigured and so diluted in our postmodern world as to no longer be recognizable in the form we've grown familiar with over the past two centuries or more. This seems true in Europe, at least, which may be the harbinger for crucial changes coming on a far broader scale.

Notes

1. Postmodernity must be clearly distinguished from postmodernism for purposes of this study. I do not employ, and remain only partially convinced of the utility of, a postmodernist epistemology, agenda, or style of analysis. In any case, I seek here only

to distinguish between two historical phases or, more properly, two sociocultural modes. For Western societies, modernity can be dated from the Enlightenment, if not the Renaissance, until late in the twentieth century when, among other developments, industrialism gives way to information-based economies, nuclear families to more complex relationship webs, and nationalism to new forms of political identification, including that which is the subject of this book. More broadly, even assuming that the process of cultural development is monolithically sequential and unidirectional (which it may very well not be), other (non-Western) cultures may experience transitions from one mode to the next at various different chronological moments (some are still transitioning *to* modernity), which is why these are better understood as modes than periods. In any case, I employ the term *postmodern* herein in a very literal sense—referring to a societal condition following the condition of modernity—rather than as a set of epistemological assumptions or political commitments that collectively inform a particular style of inquiry, analysis, or discussion.

2. Paul Howe (1995: 32) argues that such a reinterpretation of history has already begun.

3. See, for example, Halecki 1963: 372; Delanty 1998: 39; Llobera 1993: 78; Papcke 1992: 66; Reif 1993: 131; Laffan 1996: 82; Slater 1982.

4. Actually, it is premature, even today, to speak of a real European body politic. The fact that elections for the European Parliament tend to be contested over national issues is only the most telling political indicator of this status. In terms of mass political consciousness, Europe is probably better described as twenty-seven national polities vaguely and tenuously joined together in a far-off place called Brussels. This could change somewhat, however, now that the euro has become entrenched and even powerful, or, to choose another example, should Europeans be driven together by a growing transatlantic breach.

5. Of course, this was no coincidental accident of history. Experiments in international organization tend to follow disastrous meltdowns of the existing form. The Concert of Europe, the League of Nations, the United Nations, the Bretton Woods system, and the European integration project can all be understood as fitting this pattern. Nevertheless, the rapidity of this swing from full-blown militarized conflict to nearly unprecedented institutional embrace and shared sovereignty is breathtaking, and clearly left some participants behind the transitional curve. Chapter 4 describes one particular, and poignant, manifestation of this effect at the College of Europe during its first years of operation.

6. Use of the term *integration* is immediately problematic, especially in light of the arguments advanced in this book. Integration has heretofore been widely—and, I suggest, somewhat inappropriately—used to refer both to the processes and events that have taken place in Western Europe since 1952, and to the study of those processes. The concept of integration as defined in this book, on the other hand, concerns the question of popular identities. Integrated political associations are those in which there exists "a we-feeling among a group of people—they are a political entity that works together and will likely share a common political fate and destiny" (Easton 1965: 332), irrespective of levels of institutional development. In the European context, this means creating a political space "where men and women of every country will think as much of being European as of belonging to their native land and wherever they go in this wide domain they will truly feel 'here I am at home!'" (Winston Churchill, quoted in Hewstone 1986: 202). While the avoidance of standard usages of the term *integration* is certainly in the interest of semantic clarity, doing so would nevertheless require some rather inelegant (and frequently reiterated) syntax. Therefore, without prejudice to the arguments presented herein, the term is used in both its "correct" and "incorrect" mean-

ings, with the hope that the intent in each case emerges apparent. While the former concerns the development of a common identity, the latter (and common) usage refers chiefly to institutional development and elaboration, as well as to the economic unification and harmonization that continue apace in Europe.

7. This is true, moreover, in at least two senses. Apart from the conditions described here, it has also been argued by some scholars (e.g., Bueno de Mesquita 1981) that alliance partners are actually *more* likely to fight one another than they are to fight others.

8. Though not short enough of war to prevent Calvin Trillin (1997: 6) from raising the issue in his poem "European Unification: The Short Version":

> Those nations will unite as one—
> The Europe that's supposed to be.
> The euro is the final touch
> Unless it causes World War III.

The poem, fortunately, is meant as humor. But, like all such humor, it is of course only funny to the extent that it bears some resemblance to reality. (*European Unification, The Short Version*—Copyright © 1997 by Calvin Trillin. Originally appeared in *The Nation*. This usage granted by permission of Lescher & Lescher, Ltd. All rights reserved.)

9. Truly a picture that spoke a thousand words, *The Economist*'s cover photo of rioting French opponents to monetary union under the headline "France Prepares for EMU" (1995a) well illustrates this point.

10. In order to maintain comparability to Eurobarometer and other existing surveys, however, and to avoid the prickly question of who should be considered a European (respondents from Russia? Macedonia? Turkey?), only those 227 respondents from EU-15 countries are included in the analyses herein.

11. Many multinational surveys are fielded separately in each country by local firms, and thus coding and quality of reporting can vary.

12. In some cases, these weights had to be modified or created. In all cases, only data from EC/EU member-state respondents (at the time of the survey) have been included. In the analyses presented in Chapter 4, mean values were substituted for all missing independent variable data in order to maximize the number of included cases in regression models. For Eurobarometer 41-1, this strategy was also employed for the interval-level dependent variable; for all other datasets (with ordinal-level dependent variables, and analyzed using the ordered probit procedure), missing dependent-variable cases were dropped, thus maintaining the appropriate number of cut-points in the model.

13. In the latter two surveys only, the question prompt asked respondents how attached they were to "the European Union," as opposed to "Europe." Conceptually, of course, these are very different animals, and it is quite conceivable that an individual could, for instance, possess very strong attachments to Europe while loathing the European Union. Whether respondents make this distinction to the extent that these two surveys should be excluded on the basis of not being true measures of European identity is a judgment call to be made by the researcher and his or her audience. For purposes of the analyses in this book, they have been considered sufficiently similar approximations of the concept to warrant inclusion. It should be noted, however, that the resulting data (see Table 3.1) suggest some possible degree of distinction between the two ideas in the minds of respondents.

14. In Britain, one survey asked respondents, "What is important to your sense of self-identity?" Britishness and English, Scottish, or Welsh nationalism ranked below

six other factors, such as "My principles and values," "My interests," "Being a parent," and "My circle of friends" (Leonard 1997: 23).

15. One informant described how he felt German when in London, European when in the United States, and Western when visiting Latin America, while a second informant inverted the effect, saying "At home [in Ireland], I feel proud to be European, while away from home, I feel proud to be Irish." And, illustrating the contingent effect that events (as opposed to location) may have on identities, another said that he also felt very European in America, but also felt German when the French were fighting for the presidency of the European Central Bank.

16. Crawford Young (1993: 21–25) helpfully reviews the nature and lineage of these two political identity approaches, plus a third: instrumentalism.

17. Indeed, rather than the idealized model in which the nation gives birth to the state, there may be as many instances in history of the state creating the nation. For Arjun Appadurai, the nation is "the ideological alibi of the territorial state" (1996: 159). A more tangible application of this notion may be found in the comment attributed to nationalist activist Massimo D'Azeglio, following the creation of his country: "Now that we have made Italy, we need to make Italians."

2

The Idea of European Identity

For a thousand years or more, men have dreamed of uniting Europe. What stave and scimitar, chariot and battering rams, horse and Heinkel, Caesar, Charlemagne, Henry, Louis, Napoleon, Briand and Hitler failed each in his own way to achieve, what Yalta failed to prevent, may yet be voted into being by the peoples of the Continent. Where the sword failed the ploughshare, the microchip and the ballot box may, indeed must succeed. An empire without an emperor, this continental union will be the first to come into being without the use of force.
—David Lewis (1993: 12)

THE PROJECT OF EUROPEAN integration is a relatively new phenomenon, as polities go, but the idea behind it is not. Political philosophers have been contemplating the perceived need or desirability of unifying Europe for centuries, as the following pages document. This chapter seeks to place the idea of European integration and the related notion of shared European identity into their historical and theoretical contexts. The chapter treats four main themes related to these core subjects: the history of the idea of European unification, the theoretical possibility of a European identity, the potential constituent elements of such an identity, and efforts that have been made to foster European identification. Together with Chapter 1, these discussions set the stage for the empirical investigations that follow.

The Idea of Europe

The earliest viable appearance of either the polity or the idea of a unified Europe emerged, most historians agree, with the efforts of the Franks in the seventh and eighth centuries, culminating with the crowning of Charlemagne as emperor of Rome in 800 C.E.[1] (Rome was more of a global than a strictly European power, and no one living on the continent during the empire's rule would have considered him- or herself European.) The Franks were consciously attempting to unify the continent, in the face of its increasing fragmentation, and in fact were able to do so within limitations.[2] Coincidentally (or perhaps not?), the borders of what was the Frankish state are nearly an identical match to the region occupied by "The Six" (France, Germany, Italy, the Netherlands, Belgium, and Luxembourg), those countries that launched contemporary integration efforts with the European Coal and Steel Community of 1952.

Rivals to the emperor and to the newly emerging states, the popes of the Middle Ages also advanced the idea of European unity as an ideological weapon in their battle for supreme secular political power to complement their religious authority. Rallying around the notion of common Eastern and Islamic enemies, the Crusades marked the first instance of Europe presenting a united front, under papal leadership. Later, the idea of European identity flagged, as economic decline, the Plague, and division within the church took their toll, but it would once again be revived by all sides in power disputes among the church, the emperor, and national monarchs. Pierre Dubois, for instance, issued a pamphlet in 1306 calling for European unity for the purposes of launching another crusade, though in fact it was little more than a plan to unite Europe under the king of France. Yet it contained elements of supranationalism, especially related to dispute resolution, which are still visible in today's institutions. In the end, though, the Europe of the medieval period was more a cultural fact than a political one. Increasingly, Europeans were coming to share institutions and cultural attributes, such as universities, feudalism, and chivalry, but not common governance.

The fall of Constantinople in 1453 revitalized plans for European unity, and a nascent identity was formed from distinction against the Turkish "Other." Heikki Mikkeli notes, "there appears to be no doubt that the term 'Europe' began to acquire more and more emotional charge in the period following the fall of Constantinople. In literary circles at least, Europe was conceived of as a unit with positive connotation, and one worth defending against outside enemies" (1998: 34). In particular, a series of proposals for peace within Christendom were advanced in order to facilitate a unified response to the Turkish challenge.

But little came of these, and Europe would shortly thereafter be more divided than ever by its internal religious wars of the sixteenth and seventeenth centuries. A notable solution to these was advanced by France's Duke of Sully in 1638, who envisaged a supranational parliament to resolve disputes between states. William Penn and other Quakers also began advancing similar European peace plans in the period shortly thereafter. Another, by the French Abbé de Saint-Pierre, stimulated widespread debate beginning in the early eighteenth century, including a midcentury "realist" critique by Jean-Jacques Rousseau, who found the plan for supranational governance naive. Still later, Immanuel Kant and other German philosophers would join the quest for a workable European peace plan. They failed to achieve their goal, of course, and shortly after the publication of Rousseau's response to the Abbé, the continent was deeply convulsed again by the French Revolutionary and Napoleonic Wars.

But Europe's cultural unity remained, and philosophers such as Edmund Burke could argue that the shared patrimony of Christianity, monarchy, Roman law, and other customs meant that "no citizen of Europe could be altogether an exile in any part of it. . . . When a man travelled or resided for health, pleasure, business or necessity, away from his country, he never felt himself quite abroad" (Mikkeli 1998: 59).

After 1815, Napoleon would claim that his intention had all along been merely to add a political unity to the cultural unification that Burke and others found to be already powerfully developed. But the former's vision of Europe was to appear a bit too French in character for his adversaries, who banded together to ensure its demise. Instead, Napoleon did succeed in stimulating more conferences and peace plans, including a notable one by the Duc de Saint-Simon (which called for both a parliament and a king of Europe), as well as the more substantial Concert of Europe. The Concert, a series of nineteenth-century summit meetings of European great powers, was a moderately successful attempt to transcend raw balance-of-power politics with a management system for international crises. It did not last long, but it did contribute to making the nineteenth Europe's most peaceful modern century. It also helped reify the notion of Europe. As Inis Claude noted, "A conception of European solidarity, of a community of nations, took root in the nineteenth century and found its expression in the operative agency of the Concert of Europe" (1971: 26). Unfortunately, this period was also the beginning of the heyday of nationalism on the continent, and political philosophers such as Johann Herder and Georg Hegel privileged the state above any idea of European supranationalism (though other thinkers and actors, such as Johann Fichte, Philippe Buchez, and Giuseppe Mazzini, would hold European unity as their ultimate goal, to be reached through nationalism). Other Romantics were explicitly pro-European, including Victor Hugo, who envisioned a "United States of Europe" leading the charge for humanism worldwide.

From 1830 to 1880, the idea of Europe received the most attention yet, with the influential work of Pierre-Joseph Proudhon articulating the specifics for a system of European federalism, and that of Johann Kaspar Bluntschli extrapolating principles to the continental level from the experience of his native Switzerland. But no such union was developed, of course, and following a period of pessimism about Europe's future, the continent not only destroyed any remaining semblance of the Concert system, but plunged itself into its worst-ever pair of conflagrations, nearly committing political suicide in the process. Between the wars, however, the spirit of European unification was again revived, and a number of philosophers and political figures, including José Ortega y Gasset, published pieces on the subject during the 1920s. Among the most prominent of these was Austrian count Richard Coudenhove-Kalergi's book *Pan-Europa,* and French premier Aristide Briand's plan (backed by Gustav Stresemann, his German counterpart) for European federalism. Briand's ideas never caught on with other European governments, and were in any case buried along with any other such notions in the disaster of World War II.

Coudenhove-Kalergi's ideas, on the other hand, flourished in the form of a movement named after his book, which was popular before and after World War II. From this Pan-Europa movement, and from the ideas and convictions of resistance fighters such as Altiero Spinelli, the ground was laid for European integration to actually be launched in the postwar period, centuries after philosophers and statesmen had begun articulating the idea. Politicians of all ideological stripes were involved in the early conferences and schemes, but Winston Churchill, Europe's most popular political figure, was especially prominent (though Churchill's vision of European unity was more limited than that of "federalists" such as Spinelli).[3] In 1946 he made a speech calling for a "United States of Europe," and in 1948 he chaired the Congress of Europe, from which came the Council of Europe, the European Court of Human Rights, and the College of Europe.

In the end, though, these would prove to be peripheral—though not insignificant—developments. The real engine of European integration would not take the form of large public conferences characterized by acrimonious debates in which delegates proposed and then rejected grand schemes. Instead, per the theories of Jean Monnet, the work would be done by political elites, acting in an incremental fashion. The "Monnet method"—or neofunctionalism, in academic parlance—was the basis of a proposal for the formation of a joint Franco-German coal and steel community that Monnet proposed to the French government in 1950. Taken up by sympathetic foreign minister Robert Schuman, and enthusiastically approved by German chancellor Konrad Adenauer and in the United States by the Harry Truman administration, the proposal was issued on May 9, 1950, as the Schuman Declaration. It called for the formation of the proposed coal and steel community under the direction of a supranational High Authority, for the express purpose of making war in Europe not only "unthinkable," but "materially impossible." Italy and the Benelux countries signed on, and the European Coal and Steel Community went online in 1952. After centuries of intellectual struggle for European integration, this was Europe's first real supranational political institution of any consequence.

The rest, as it is said, is history: in half a century this small and narrowly focused community has grown to include nearly full economic integration of a region encompassing twenty-seven countries, with several more now in the queue, along with some considerable amounts of social and political integration. Some observers estimate that half the laws that govern Europeans today originate in Brussels, as opposed to the respective national, provincial, or local capitals. Yet, significantly, none of this considerable achievement necessarily implies the existence of a European identity to complement such developments in economic and institutional integration.

Is a European Identity Possible?

Two questions must be of paramount concern in any theoretical consideration of European political identity. First, is such an identity conceivable? That is, could it realistically exist? And second, assuming an affirmative answer to the first question, what would be the constituent elements or defining characteristics of such identity? Whatever empirical answers to the first question might be ascertained (these are discussed in Chapter 3), scholarly opinion has been decidedly mixed.

Philip Schlesinger's assessment of the prospects for development of a European identity is doubtful. Schlesinger notes the lack of common culture across the European continent, which leaves the integrationist reaching for certain "core values" around which to unite disparate nations: "A typical shopping list could include democracy, private property, the market, Roman law, renaissance humanism, Christianity, individualism, and rationalism" (1993: 14). This stretch is required because, unlike in traditional nation-states, European integration "cannot be based upon the classic simplifying nationalist criteria of ethnicity, consanguinity, language, or religion. For Europe is simply too diverse. Any eventual Euro-state—at least if it were to be democratic— would have to be both civil and pluralistic in character and be premised upon a flexibly inclusive conception of European identity. Quite a tall order!" (1993: 9–10).

Anthony Smith concurs, applying his knowledge of nationalism and nation-building to articulate a cogent skepticism regarding the prospects for a European identity. Europe's lack of shared experience and symbols provides two primary reasons for Smith's doubts. He notes that Europe possesses no pan-European educational system, but only a series of national systems. Likewise, it has only national media, and these outlets tend to report their news (even weather reports) from a national perspective. Smith also finds that Europe lacks a shared set of myths and symbols, those elements that he finds crucial to the development and maintenance of national identities; there is no European Bastille Day or shrine to European kings or saints, and hence there is no shared sense of community (1992: 72–73). Moreover, Smith's "primordialist" approach to identity suggests to him that there never will be such symbols. With the continent lacking a premodern history capable of providing the necessary emotional content to sustain an identity (1992: 62), he asks, "who will feel European in the depths of their being, and who will willingly sacrifice themselves for so abstract an ideal? In short, who will die for Europe?" (1995: 139).

For others who are also skeptical about the possibility of a common European identity, the issue is less a lack of shared historical and cultural content as it is one of positive differences irreconcilably dividing peoples. Max Haller, for example, finds Europe's "crazy-quilt" linguistic diversity and its tripartite religious division (within Christianity alone) daunting obstacles to a shared European identity (1994: 243–245). John Keane makes much the same argument, adding national identity and custom to language (he counts fifty, without a common linguistic base) and religion as prominent cleavage lines within Europe. Keane also suggests a third major theme in the catalog of obstacles to European identity. Not only does Europe lack a shared culture while possessing salient differences, but it also lacks as fundamental an element of identity development as clear physical or intellectual lines of demarcation between Europeans and non-Europeans (1992: 57).[4] Is Europe synonymous with the European Union? If so, what about the Norwegians, who were twice offered membership but declined? Are they not Europeans? What about the Swiss? And if the Orthodox Greeks are Europeans, why not the Russians?[5]

There are other reasons, beyond those catalogued in the above discussion, to be pessimistic about the prospects for establishing a specifically European identity. Any such project would clearly face a number of obstacles, not the least of which being substantial disagreement on the core elements around which such an identity could be built. But the flip side of this problem also constitutes a second major obstacle, namely, the difficulty inherent in locating identity elements that are common to Europeans yet distinct enough from certain other non-Europeans, in particular those of the remaining countries of the West. The differences between Europe and the United States or Canada on any number of key defining elements—individual liberty values, industrialization, classical heritage, Christianity—are unlikely to be prominent enough to form the basis of a distinct identity, assuming they can be articulated at all. And this obstacle only grows in magnitude each day, as globalization sweeps Western culture and values across the globe.

Moreover, a third problem that faces would-be architects of a European identity is the fact that national and local competitors have hardly disappeared from the scene. Identities are not mutually exclusive, but the pool of affective sentiment that any given individual has to allocate to various recipients is probably zero-sum, if only in a relative sense, so the gain of one means a loss to others. What is more, today's Europe is at a distinct disadvantage compared to local and national governments with respect to the possession of both material and nonmaterial desiderata whose allocation may produce instrumental effects on identity. William Wallace makes this point well, comparing Europe's identity prospects to the nation-building experiences of the recent past:

> The nineteenth-century nation-state in Western Europe successfully resolved the political problem of reconciling political community with the framework of law-making and enforcing power, thus providing a secure sense of identity and status for the former and legitimacy for the latter. Identity was strengthened by emphasizing the characteristics which distinguished members of each national community from outsiders; indeed by exaggerating the differences between stereotypical members of each national community and

their neighbours. Visible symbols of national unity reinforced the sense of solidarity. Heads of state were surrounded with pomp and ceremony; national monuments were erected; national parliaments and the judicial system were dignified with splendid buildings to reinforce their authority. Reinforcing symbolism with self-interest, every West European government also thought it wise to cement the loyalty of its citizens through redistributive tax policies and the beginnings of social welfare, to provide every citizen with a tangible sense of having a stake in the state. The [European] Community system has no comparable symbolic or financial resources at its disposal, nor has it any prospect. Sources of legitimacy remain firmly at the national level, the visible involvement of national ministers in Community bargaining still providing much greater popular reassurance of accountability than the fledgling activities of the European parliament. (1990: 103–104)

Combining these obstacles with the aforementioned lack of well-defined borders makes the case against a European identity appear daunting. And yet, perhaps the biggest impediment may be a contemporary sea change among the publics of postindustrial societies, which suggests a lowered salience of politics and political associations than in the past, and a general rejection of dogmas and divisive ideologies. It is the attitudinal complex of postmodernity, in short, that may constitute the biggest obstacle to the formation of *any* new identity today (for further elaboration of these ideas, see Chapter 7). Where mass populations could once be rallied to capture their own state or someone else's in the name of religion, nation, or class, such behavior is less imaginable in today's postmodern societies. Skeptical of all-embracing (or perhaps any) ideologies, and seemingly ever-more committed to a pragmatic pursuit of prosperity, history may have indeed ended for contemporary Europeans (Fukuyama 1992), and with it, identity as we have known it for at least two, if not five or more, centuries.

On the other side of the ledger, however, there are reasons to suspect that European identity could be a going concern, and not everyone who has examined the question is pessimistic about its possibilities. Michael Wintle begins in the same place Smith does, with an analogy to nation-building processes, but then departs in a rather different direction. Wintle argues that the achievements of national elites in constructing "universal high culture" across previous centuries provide evidence of the capacity to do the same in the European context. Moreover, he finds indications of movement in that direction already afoot, in the form of converging education standards, educational exchanges, and the organization of a burgeoning European civil society. Finally, Wintle is encouraged by the findings of historian Robert Bartlett, who argues that a European identity was previously already created during the High Middle Ages (Wintle 1996: 19–22). Salvador Giner also finds reasons to be optimistic about the prospects for European identity, indeed arguing that a European society is already clearly in sight. Giner also points to characteristics and experiences that have been converging for all Europeans, ranging from changes in life expectancy to secularization of society, the development of welfare capitalism, and economic prosperity. He suggests that skeptics of European identity should reconsider the depth of various salient cleavages within national polities, not only for the lack of coherence they imply for the much touted nation-state, but also for the remarkable similarity in their configuration across the European continent, suggesting further shared experience in Europe (1994: 22–26).[6]

Beyond these observations, several others should be added. The oft-mentioned contemporary trend toward diminution of the power and capacity of the state (Strange 1996) can only be heartening to any polity competing with it for the capture of popular hearts and minds. Second, the migration of competences from Paris, Rome, and other state capitals to Brussels may well accelerate in the wake of the euro. If ever the neofunctionalist notion of spillover might be expected to prove accurate, the repercussions from the advent of a common currency should provide that occasion. Moreover, as this process advances, Europe may be perceived to be providing more and more of the desiderata—including, it may claim, peace and prosperity—which earn (or, more cynically, buy) public allegiance.

An attempt to create a European identity would also clearly benefit from the increasing cosmopolitanism that characterizes contemporary Europe, in the form of massive increases in travel, commerce, and media exposure, much of it of the EU's own doing. The continued repudiation of nationalism and its products of the first half of the twentieth century work in favor of a common identity, as well. And, Europe's attempts at generating meaningful symbols (flag, anthem, etc.), the object of much derision today, may in fact resonate given enough time and proper circumstances. Finally, the content of European identity may strike an appropriate chord for our time. Though seemingly paradoxical on its face, the "unity in diversity" theme and its implied notions of openness and tolerance may inspire devotees on a continent that is growing ever-smaller each year.

At its core, the debate between skeptics (e.g., Smith) and optimists (e.g., Wintle) is fundamentally a clash between primordialist and constructivist approaches to identity. Both are (correctly) wont to begin with the same premise, namely, that we can learn something valuable from the nation- and state-building analogues to the European enterprise. Primordialists take from this history the lesson that Europe can never develop a common identity, precisely because it lacks the substantive material that nations employed in crafting their identities. That is, Europe lacks the necessary history of shared experience, symbols, and destiny from which to derive an identity, items that cannot otherwise be created from whole cloth. Constructivists, on the other hand, draw just the opposite conclusions from the very same cases, focusing instead on the relative historical proximity of supposedly immemorial identities, and on the efforts and tools of their construction.

While this is not the place to attempt a resolution of this debate, it should be noted that advocates of the primordialist paradigm carry a heavy burden, and time, quite literally, is not on their side. Studies such as those by Linda Colley (1992) and Eugen Weber (1976) document the process by which the most established of states *created* national identities, and did so fairly recently (relative to primordialist time scales) at that. There is thus no a priori reason to believe that Europe could not achieve a similar effect, given time and the proper set of conditions. As Ariane Chebel d'Appollonia notes, "History reminds us that the idea of nation emerges slowly like its symbols. It took many wars and revolutions for it to take shape. European identity today is as symbolic as national identity was for centuries" (1998: 67). Thus, asks Wintle, "How can we dismiss European cultural identity in the 20th century when the EU has only been in existence since 1957?" (1996: 22).

A European identity therefore probably possesses the same potential to develop as national identities have enjoyed. (Nor can differences in language, religion, or ethnicity sustain an argument against this claim, for these very same obstacles faced nation-builders in what are today considered national success stories.) At the same time, given the postwar changes in the public's attitudes toward politics discussed above, it would probably be inappropriate for Europe to aspire toward the same goal that nation-states have sought, often with near-success: to be all things to all people. That sort of identity, with its attendant demand of a "die for it" intensity of loyalty, may have become an anachronism more associated with Europe's past than with any of its likely futures. But there would appear to be no theoretical reason why a mass European identity of a different, more circumscribed sort could not come to exist. As in nations before it, European identity would probably grow in tandem with the expansion of the geographical scope of communication and commerce, and the development of European governmental institutions at its core. And, even more so than for the nation-state, loyalties to Europe are likely to be heavily dependent on instrumental perceptions of benefits derived.

All of this will take time, if it happens at all. States may be born overnight, but identities grow more slowly.[7] Notwithstanding this general pace of development, the capacity of events to dramatically alter the situation should not be discounted. Conflict, and its required reification of an "Other," has shown itself to be an especially potent facilitator of identity formation (e.g., Colley 1992). Anthony Marx (2003) has also theorized that the (often violent) marginalization of some internal pariah group is another historically proven strategy in the forging of identities. Thus, if Europe were to successfully present a common (or perhaps better yet, almost common) front to an external problem or threat, this accretionary timetable might perhaps be dramatically accelerated. Moreover, for maximum effect in articulating identity borders, the demonized "Other" should probably be as close in shared characteristics as possible to those whose common identity is being built, since distinctions vis-à-vis other communities will be inherently clearer. Thus, the "best"-case scenario for a European Mazzini would probably be a major (though not necessarily militarized) rift in the Atlantic community, with, say, a Poland seen as an internal pariah aligned with the adversary.

A version of this scenario, in highly muted form, does in fact appear to be transpiring at the moment, though events are now fluid, and certainly capable of being overstated and misinterpreted (as does Robert Kagan [2002, 2003]). The years of the George W. Bush administration have been difficult ones for transatlantic relations, but the breach that has opened up between Europe and the United States is less deep and less permanent than some have suggested, and is not due to Europeans having lost their sensibilities in a fit of Venusian pacifism or other such delusions. The coming years will probably be critical in determining whether the present moment represents an aberration or a turning point in the longer historical sense. At the moment, in any case, it would appear that Europe is simultaneously too divided, too weak, and too timid to contemplate calving itself off from the Western alliance to form a fully independent entity, complete with its own popular identity as such. Such an outcome is not, however, impossible to contemplate, and is certainly more probable—even if the probabilities remain low—than it was just a short time ago. But should such an independent and integrated Europe appear in coming decades, the current antagonisms and resulting differentiation with the United States (again, perhaps also coupled with the marginalization of some internal pariah) may be seen to history as having provided a useful definitional core around which a European identity was further articulated and mobilized. Indeed, when asked what defines Europe, many informants interviewed for purposes of this study replied, "Not American."

The notion of a European identity, in sum, provokes controversy even at the level of theoretical plausibility, and it becomes even murkier when considering the mix of constituent elements that might constitute its substantive character (discussed below). That said, it would seem that those primordialists staking out the position that such an identity is an impossibility have saddled themselves with an untenable historical and theoretical burden. Rather, the potential for a European identity should be seen as the more-or-less direct analogue of the potential for national identities in their early formative years. As discussed above, the EU would face substantial normative barriers that France or Britain never did, should it attempt to forge an identity just as those and other states did. But these have more to do with changed political conditions and contemporary prohibitions against the use of certain identity-building tools than they do with the fundamental project of overlaying a wider identity onto a patchwork of local and regional rivals. Clearly, the potential for a European identity exists (though perhaps not in the exact form of the political identities to which modernity has made us accustomed). Moreover, existing surveys as well as the data collected specifically for this study allow us to address the question empirically, moving beyond the preceding discussion of its notional plausibility. These findings are presented in Chapter 3. Related themes are explored in Chapter 5, which examines the meaning of a European identity for those who possess it, and in Chapter 6, which measures the depth of those sentiments.

Elements of a European Identity

If the optimists are correct, and a European identity can in fact be crafted, what might be the stuff of its contents? Myriad scholars have weighed in on this question, many responding with laundry lists of core European commonalities. For Michael Wintle (1996: 13–16), such a list includes the Roman Empire, Christianity, the Enlightenment, industrialization, shared knowledge of language, and a common physical environment. Soledad García's list (1993: 7–9) points to Hellenism, Roman law and institutions, Christianity, the Renaissance, the Enlightenment, Romanticism, welfare society, and the cross-fertilization of diversity. And Václav Havel (1996) has argued that Europe's core values are its commitments to an undivided continent, to individual freedom, and to the universalism of humanity. Such approaches to defining the content of European identity[8] are helpful to an extent, though their ironic effect may be to highlight the lack of an agreed-upon definition, and the dependency of the various conclusions on the values of the observer. No doubt this is what caused the European Commission to punt when tackling the issue in 1992: "The term 'Europe' has not been officially defined. It combines geographical, historical, and cultural elements which all contribute to the European identity. The shared experience of proximity, ideas, values, and historical interaction cannot be condensed into a simple formula, and is subject to review by each succeeding generation" (quoted in Mikkeli 1998: 213–214).

Meanwhile, others have pointed to rather more odious elements that they claim define a European identity. Max Haller (1994: 248), for example, sees "Euronationalism" as a new identity being constructed to suit contemporary interests, and conveniently omitting from Europe's story religious intolerance, colonialism, slavery, and the subjugation of minorities and powerless social groups.[9] A more common theme, however, concerns the presence or necessity of the "Other" as the characteristic around which identities may be defined. Perhaps the most relevant, and certainly the most prominent, articulation of this notion is provided by Edward Said's 1979 theory of "Orientalism," which has been characterized as "a collective notion identifying 'us' Europeans against all 'those' non-Europeans" (Mikkeli 1998: 230–231), and facilitating the dominance of the former over the latter. Ariane Chebel d'Appollonia echoes this notion, arguing, "There is no identity without alterity" (1998: 68).[10]

Finally, stock must be taken of a new model of European identity that has grown prominent in the literature. Like so-called Western patterns of nationalism, this model emphasizes civic values and practices over essentialist definitions of community—*demos* over *ethnos*. And, in an ironic twist, it underscores the significance of diversity as a defining characteristic of European identity. Brigid Laffan (1996: 99) provides a good example of such thinking, arguing that European identity should be built around three principles: shared destiny, tolerance of diversity, and emphasis on the civic dimension of nationality in place of dubious historical myths.[11]

Joseph Weiler (2001) makes rather a similar argument in his essay on the nature of European federalism (assuming the term is applicable in this context, if only for purposes of discussion). Weiler employs the term *demos* slightly differently—as an integrated and singular public serving as ultimate sovereign to any given polity—and locates its role in European integration differently as well. However, he shares the concerns of Laffan and others regarding the significance of tolerance to the project, even amplifying that notion to a singular pride of place in the pantheon of European ideals. Since, according to Weiler, Europe lacks such a *demos* standing behind its constitutional federalism (as demonstrated by the very choice of language in the Treaty of Rome's preamble: "Determined to lay the foundations for an ever closer *union* of the *peoples* of Europe"—emphasis added), it must instead rely on a particularly healthy, mature, and virtuous form of voluntary tolerance and national subordination to Brussels as the animating force behind its constitutional order. By embracing others within the polity as they are, rather than (arrogantly) attempting to assimilate all into a singular *demos*, and by voluntarily subjecting themselves to the rule of those others acting collectively, Weiler argues that the many tribes of Europe in fact display both a more practical and a more laudable form of federal unity, based on constitutional tolerance.

In the end, the character of European identity resists any precise and exclusive definition, and anyone who attempts a definitive cataloging of its elements is no more likely to produce a widely accepted formula than was the European Commission. Europhiles and fans of the integration project need not necessarily be despondent at this prospect, however. It is not entirely clear that national identities would be any more amenable to precision of definition should one query citizens possessing them, even including those patriots who have in the past gladly risked life and limb defending their nations.

Efforts to Foster a European Identity

Even with their overwhelming emphasis on economic and institutional aspects of European integration, EU leaders have on occasion attempted to foster higher levels of identification with Europe, often in spasmodic episodes recognizing one or another normative deficiency in the project, or in symbolic flourishes intended to placate critics. Identity-building efforts are rarely explicitly labeled as such, and are often in fact only one part of broader initiatives that have multiple goals. Surely one purpose of Structural Funds, for example, is to engender a sense of loyalty to Europe, though this might not be explicitly stated in the justification for a given bridge, port, or school building, and may legitimately be a secondary purpose only. Moreover, the very idea of identity overlaps in certain important respects with other concepts such as citizenship, rights of citizens, and public programs of various stripes. The net result of these factors is that it is often difficult to distinguish European identity-building efforts from other programs and initiatives. There have nevertheless been efforts that were clearly intended to bring Europe and its body politic closer together, often under the rubric of "A People's Europe." Some of the more notable efforts (if not notable successes) have included the Tindemans Report of 1974 on institutional reform, the increasing powers of the European Parliament, the work of the Adonnino Committee of 1984, the Single European Act of 1986, and a series of citizenship rights, especially as articulated in the Maastricht Treaty of 1991. Several of these are reviewed briefly below.

Perhaps the most overt of efforts to raise levels of European identification, the Adonnino Committee (officially, the Ad Hoc Committee on a People's Europe) was one of two such bodies to emerge from the EU summit at Fountainebleau in June 1984, one of the most important meetings in the organization's history. Besides brokering a deal with Margaret Thatcher over British payments to the EU and thus ending a logjam in European affairs, the summit also created another ad hoc committee, this one on institutional affairs and known as the Dooge Committee, which was key to building a foundation for the Single European Act and the late 1980 *relance* of European integration. Given the historical importance of the Dooge Committee, the work of chair Pietro Adonnino and his colleagues on People's Europe matters is often overshadowed. But the latter's efforts were nevertheless useful. The Adonnino Committee was specifically charged with consideration of how the EU could enhance its identity and affect the everyday lives of European citizens. The first paragraph of the letter that established the committee reads: "The European Council considers it essential that the Community should respond to the expectations of the people of Europe by adopting measures to strengthen and promote its identity and its image both for its citizens and for the rest of the world" (Commission of the European Communities 1985: 5).

The Adonnino Committee generated a report, "Citizen's Europe," which made a series of minor recommendations (in the greater scheme of state affairs) that were nonetheless potentially important. These included simplification of border controls, mutual recognition of educational standards and diplomas, and establishment of the freedom of citizens to live and work in other member-states. Symbolic issues like a European flag and anthem were also addressed. Few recommendations of the Adonnino Committee were directly implemented as a result of its work, though many of them have since become key aspects of a unifying Europe. Whether they necessarily have had the intended effect of bringing Europeans closer to Europe is less clear. Many, especially among the young, take such mobility and standardization for granted, and thus their European consciousness may not necessarily be impacted. On the other hand, the very freedom to move, work, and live within expanded boundaries probably subtly but powerfully affects the psychological space within which individuals feel comfortable, and which they are willing to call home.

The Maastricht Treaty of 1991 (signed in 1992) was a huge milestone in the history of European integration, for a number of reasons. Among the less prominent of these are the treaty's provisions that codify and rationalize the rights of European citizens, in an attempt to bring the EU closer to the people of Europe. These provisions include: the right of citizens to live wherever in the Union they wish (Article 8a), the right to vote and stand for municipal and European Parliamentary elections in any part of the EU (Article 8b), diplomatic or consular protection abroad (Article 8c), the right to petition the European Parliament on EU matters (Article 8d), and the right to complain to an ombudsman concerning EU matters (Article 138e). The treaty also formalizes the notion of subsidiarity, which is the principle of locating decisionmaking at the lowest appropriate institutional level, and it guarantees citizens coverage by the European Human Rights Convention.

The historical development of the European Parliament has represented another effort to close the gap between Europe and its citizens, and especially to respond to the critique of Europe's "democratic deficit." The Parliament has been around in one form or another since the advent of the European Coal and Steel Community in 1952, but its representatives were not directly elected by European citizens until 1979. Its powers remain limited, but have grown over time, to the extent that it not long ago forced the resignation of an entire Commission. The Parliament cannot initiate legislation, but it must be heard before the Council can adopt any laws. Its powers vary according to which of several legislative procedures is employed, but it is now consulted in one fashion or another on almost all matters of EU legislation.

Whether the European Parliament has accomplished the goal of bridging the gap between Europeans and the EU—and, hence, enhancing European identification, however obliquely—is quite questionable at the moment. Voting patterns in elections for the Parliament tend to be far more reflective of national than European issues (the elections are frequently seen as popular confidence referenda on national governments), and turnout is generally low. To an extent, these conditions are to be expected, since the issues that face Europe tend not to be as great as those facing individual states, and since the Parliament is rightly seen as a place where such decisions would be unlikely to be taken anyway. Yet, should Europe's portfolio of important policymaking decisions expand, as the fallout from monetary union and recent rumblings about common defense structures certainly portend, the Parliament—possibly driven by the demands of citizens for influence on those decisions—may grow to occupy a meaningful role as a bridge between Europe and its citizens.

The many programs that fall under the rubric of EU cohesion policy constitute another major attempt at fostering an increased sense of European identity (among other things). As Desmond Dinan writes:

> Cohesion—the reduction of economic and social disparities between richer and poorer regions—is a fundamental objective of the EU. Not only do such disparities threaten the integrity of the single market and the prospects for Economic and Monetary Union (EMU), but their existence is incompatible with the sense of community and solidarity that, ideally, should infuse the movement for European integration. Indeed, an unusual blend of idealism and pragmatism has motivated the quest for cohesion, especially since the EC's Mediterranean enlargement in the 1980s. (1998: 46)

Cohesion efforts range widely across programs such as Structural-Fund projects for development of local infrastructure and support of poorer regions, social-fund projects aimed at vocational education and the reduction of unemployment, and rural development projects funded under the Common Agricultural Policy (CAP). All told, these programs account for a third of the EU's budget, and have—along with other developments—helped some of Europe's poorer countries, such as Ireland and Portugal, make a dramatic leap in their public standards of living (though other member-states have had less success). The programs are also among the most visible manifestations of the EU in many such places, especially in nonagricultural areas (CAP projects are extremely prominent among farming communities). Whether the programs have also been successful in fostering higher levels of European identification is much more doubtful. Richer (net-contributor) countries increasingly resent the large sums crossing their borders in transit for other lands, to the extent that even the formerly generous-to-Europe Germans have begun raising the issue in protest. Even more disappointing for Europhiles, however, may be the reaction (or absence thereof) engendered in those countries that have benefited most from European largess. If the Irish experience is indicative, even dramatic quality-of-life benefits that are clearly attributable to European efforts may produce little impact on levels of European identification.

Another significant EU project meant to enhance the sense of Europeaness felt by its citizens is the Union's substantial effort to promote educational exchange. A number of such programs exist, though the banner effort has been the Community Action Scheme for the Mobility of University Students (widely known as ERASMUS). More recently brought under the umbrella of SOCRATES, which now coordinates all EU educational exchange programs, ERASMUS has over the years made a quiet but substantial impact in Europe, funding study abroad in other member-states for college undergraduates, advancing the development of European language and culture curricula, and providing a system for the transfer of academic credits. From academic years 1987/1988 to 1999/2000 alone, some 750,000 students participated in the program, along with more than 1,800 institutions.

By its nature, a program like ERASMUS is not one that will show dramatic results in the development of identity transfers. But there are many reasons to believe that its successes may be as broad as they are subtle and slow. Of the European identifiers interviewed for this study, a vast proportion indicated that they were ERASMUS alumi, and many made reference to the program's significant impact in their hometowns, where, they reported, studying abroad is increasingly common for not only college but also high school students. Many European identifiers also noted, independent of the question of exchange programs, that educational experiences were a key part of the formation of their European identity. Especially given the lack of European "civics" content in secondary school classrooms, the capacity for a European government, culture, or history class to influence students is not surprising. But it is the exchanges themselves that are most noteworthy. Leaving the bounds of one's local homelands, perhaps for the first extended stay or the first time on one's own, meeting new friends, and experiencing other cultures—these are very likely to expand the sense of the individual's "home space" from the national boundaries to the continental. Many informants spoke in unequivocal terms of ERASMUS having had precisely this effect on them. It will certainly take time for the alumni of this program to increase as a percentage of the European population, but the effect on expanding the pool of European identifiers may in the end be quite profound. Thus Rob Kroes is probably correct in asserting that "this Brussels project is a shining example of Europe producing Europeans" (1995: 84).

Finally, the most recent—and as of this writing, failed—attempt at what might be described as "backdoor identity-building" may be imputed to the attempt at creating and ratifying a constitution for the European Union. It is clear that the language of that document (as well as the treaties it is meant to subsume) speaks to the unity and the shared characteristics, values, and aspirations of the would-be European people, all classic elements of a common identity. Though it is less clear the extent to which those who promulgated the document had the fostering of a European identity as a primary motivation, their rhetoric suggests that it was surely an important part of the mix. Ironically, it is probably fair to claim that the very absence of such shared values, aspirations, trust, and sense of commonality—in short, the absence of a shared identity—has been responsible, at least in substantial part, for sinking the ratification of the constitution to date. It appears that the citizens of France and the Netherlands still remain, at this time, too French and too Dutch, and not enough European, to make the formal leap of incorporating themselves under a common constitutional umbrella (the real effects of which would be—another irony—less legal than political and emotionally symbolic).

In any case, subsequent chapters will demonstrate in greater detail, and based on empirical findings, that such is the current state of shared identity in Europe, and that such are the challenges to its further development.

Notes

1. This discussion draws from Claude 1971, Dinan 1994, Hewstone 1986, Jacobson 1984, Lewis 1993, and especially Mikkeli 1998.

2. Though whether a popular political identity accompanied this geopolitical structure is unclear. Moreover, if such an identity did emerge at the time, it might as likely have taken the form of "Christian" as of "European."

3. Even before any European supranational institution was created, the division between "federalist" and "unionist" (or "intergovernmentalist") visions of Europe was already apparent. These differences continue to the present day and—if the American experience of federalism is any guide—may continue for the life of the European Union.

4. See also García 1993: 2.

5. Other scholars who are generally skeptical on the possibility of a European identity include Raymond Aron (1954: 313–316), E. J. Hobsbawm (1997: 274), Ariane Chebel d'Appollonia (1998: 66), Ali Kazancigil (1993: 123), Godfrey Hodgson (1993: 18), and Anthony Birch (1989: 223–224).

6. Other optimists on this question include Paul Howe (1995: 30), Gerard Delanty (1995: 32), and Furio Cerutti (1992: 148, 157, 159 fn.).

7. The nationalist reaction to the Battle of Jena by many in what would later become Germany is an exception.

8. For further discussion, see, for example, Schmidtke 1998: 47; Papcke 1992: 71–72; Mikkeli 1998; Wilterdink 1993: 121–122; Schlesinger 1994: 320; Giner 1994: 17.

9. See also Chebel d'Appollonia 1998: 69; Bloomfield 1993: 256.

10. For further discussion of the identity-forming function of the "Other" (including models that place the United States in that role vis-à-vis Europe), see García 1993: 13–14; Hobsbawm 1997: 271; Delanty 1998: 33–34; Papcke 1992: 62; Wilterdink 1993: 129.

11. For similar thinking on this question, see also Havel 1996; Schmidtke 1998.

3

Are There Any "Europeans" in Europe?

Completion of the internal market, a central element of European integration, will become really meaningful only if it brings balanced economic and social progress within the large frontier-free area. . . . [These] will not be enough to make Europe a tangible reality. Each and every Community citizen needs to feel bound by the links which unite European society.
—Jacques Delors (quoted in Lodge 1993: 303)

IN CHAPTER 2, THE question of whether a European identity is conceivable was addressed at a theoretical level, and various opinions from the literature on this topic were surveyed. This question can also (and arguably better) be addressed empirically, and it is the task of this chapter to do so. The chapter begins with a univariate analysis of European identity that presents response frequencies for each of the dependent-variable questions, in their respective formats, from each of the twenty-one surveys employed in this study. The remainder of the chapter looks at European identity in comparative perspective, along several dimensions including the temporal. First, the popularity of the identity is compared to that of other geopolities within which Europeans reside. Second, a single bivariate analysis breaks the identity data down along national lines. No causal relationship is inferred here, and the reader should bear in mind that no other effects are controlled for in this presentation.[1] Third, European identity itself is amenable to comparative analysis, given the existence of two World Values Surveys, which pose identity questions to respondents in all regions of the world, and that comparison is made in this chapter. Finally, an analysis of trends in identification with Europe over time rounds out the discussion.

The general task of this chapter is thus to describe basic levels of European identity and place the phenomenon in comparative context, prior to the examination of explanatory themes in subsequent chapters.

Basic Measures: The Extent of European Identity

"Are there any 'Europeans' in Europe?" The short answer to the question is yes. But a better and more nuanced response would be that it depends both on how European identity is defined, and on the form in which the question is posed. Table 3.1 presents percentage frequencies from responses to European identity questions across twenty extant datasets and one original dataset. The data are grouped according to the format of the dependent-variable question employed. Format One asked respondents to select the geographical/political entity with which they most closely identified. In each survey in which it was employed, this question was then immediately followed by another that asked respondents for their second choice.[2] Data from this question format are mostly available for the period 1971 through 1980, though the format was used again in the 1990–1993 World Values Survey and the 1999–2001 World and European Values Survey, and it is also one of the three question formats included in the Survey of European Identifiers (SEI) fielded in support of this study.

Apart from the latter survey—which draws from a completely biased sample and can only be compared to the other surveys accordingly—responses to this question format reveal a relatively stable pattern of what might be described as core-, secondary-, and non-European identifiers. Particularly because this zero-sum question format poses the starkest of choices for respondents, it is not surprising that it generates smaller numbers of European identifiers than do the other formats. At the same time, however, to the extent that respondents do choose Europe under such a demanding test of European identity, the question probably also provides the best proof to skeptics of the phenomenon's existence. Table 3.1 shows that something on the order of one in every twenty Europeans identify as such, first and foremost, over and above local, regional, national, and global identity alternatives. Moreover, for another 12 percent or so, Europe is the second strongest identity. For the remaining bulk of the population (about 80–85 percent), a European identity is their third or lower choice, or perhaps would not be chosen at all.[3]

In the second dependent-variable question format, respondents were asked, "Does the thought ever occur to you that you are not only [nationality] but also a European? Does this happen often, sometimes, or never?" This format is limited to the 1987–1992 period, but reveals a similarly stable pattern of core-, secondary-, and non-European identifiers, this time at about the 15, 35, and 50 percent levels, respectively. Thus, generally the public is evenly split between those who at least sometimes think of themselves as European and those who never do. The percentages of identifiers are considerably higher here than in the previous format, presumably because of the nonexclusivity of the European identity built directly into the question prompt for Format Two, as opposed to the zero-sum construction of Format One.

Table 3.1 Identification with Europe (percentages of respondents)

Survey and Year

Dependent Variable	ECS 1971	ECS 1973	EB6 1976	EB10A 1978	EB12 1979	WVS 1980–1984	EB27 1987	EB30 1988	EB31 1989	EB33 1990	WVS 1990–1993	EB36-0 1991	EB37-0 1992	EB41-1 1994	WEVS 1999–2001	SEI[a] 1998
Format one																
Europe 1st choice	8.1	5.9	6.2	4.1	5.1	4.3					4.9				3.9	27.1
Europe 2nd choice	12.2	13.0	11.8	11.8	13.5	9.0					12.8				11.9	46.9
Europe not chosen	79.6	81.1	82.0	84.1	81.4	86.7					82.2				65.9	26.1
Europe rejected															18.3	
Format two																
Often							14.2	16.2	14.8	15.8		15.9	14.4			68.1
Sometimes							35.3	38.3	35.6	31.4		33.6	33.0			27.9
Never							50.4	45.4	49.6	52.7		50.5	52.6			4.0
Format three																
9–10 (most European)														14.5		
7–8														22.6		
5–6														26.7		
3–4														17.5		
1–2 (least European)														18.8		

Dependent Variable	EB36-0 1991	ISSP 1995	EB51-0 1999	EB54-1 2000	EB56-3 2002	EB58-1 2002	SEI[a] 1998
Format four							
Very attached/close	13.1	14.6	19.0	17.3	9.9	10.6	39.7
Fairly attached/close	37.7	38.1	39.6	43.1	31.7	36.0	39.2
Not very attached/close	30.2	32.2	29.8	28.2	36.6	36.7	15.8
Not at all attached/close	18.9	15.1	11.6	11.4	21.8	16.7	5.3

Notes: Percentages are of valid cases only ("no answer" and "don't know" excluded). Datasets weighted by country population, and include respondents from EC/EU member-states only. EB = Eurobarometer; ECS = European Communities Study; ISSP = International Social Survey Program; SEI = Survey of European Identifiers; WEVS = World and European Values Survey; WVS = World Values Survey.

a. The SEI is not based on a random sample, and cannot be compared to the other survey data presented here.

Format Three utilized a virtually identical prompt to that of Format Two, asking respondents how close they felt to Europe, with the difference being in the design of the response structure.[4] In Format Three, an interval level response is required, ranging from 1 (least European) to 10 (most European); this format is employed in Eurobarometer 41-1 (1994) only. Table 3.1 shows a remarkably even response distribution to the question, where the choices have been collapsed into five groups of two intervals each. These values look much like those returned for Format Two, with about 15 percent core identifiers, about two to three times as many in the secondary group (those choosing responses 5–8 in this case), and roughly half the sample not really identifying with Europe much at all.

Format Four was deployed from 1991 through 2002, and asked respondents how attached they felt to Europe, requiring them to choose from four ordinal-level response choices, ranging from "not at all attached" to "very attached."[5] Once again, strong similarities to the proportions of identifiers found in the Format Two and Format Three surveys are manifest in Table 3.1, with the now familiar pattern of a core group of identifiers in the range of 15 percent (dipping closer to 10 percent in the two 2002 surveys), and a secondary group at around 35 percent or slightly more.

Overall, these data resist any simple conclusions with respect to the quantity of Europeans who identify as such. It is clear that measuring the degree of European identification depends first on how the question is phrased, and second on which responses one chooses to define as indicative of the identity (e.g., should those who responded "sometimes" to Format Two questions be considered European identifiers?). What certainly can be said, though, is that any argument suggesting that there is no such thing as a European identity would be extremely difficult to sustain in the face of these data. Indeed, beyond the just-described proof offered by findings from extant survey data, I personally interviewed and surveyed such individuals for purposes of this project. This is demonstrated by the SEI data shown in Table 3.1, according to which, for example, more than a fourth of respondents gave Europe as their first identity, nearly three-fourths picked it as either a first or second identity, 68 percent said they often thought of themselves as European, and nearly 40 percent felt very attached to Europe. In short, European identity and European identifiers clearly exist.

Beyond this minimalist claim that European identity exists, however, a further generalization may be safely advanced, as long as the above-discussed caveats about question format and response grouping are understood. Leaving aside responses to Format One questions—the most stringent and arguably the most unrealistic test (because of its exclusive nature) of European identity—it would seem reasonable to conclude that something on the order of 15 percent of Europeans (roughly one of every six or seven) strongly identifies with Europe, while perhaps another 35 percent (roughly every third person) also identifies with Europe, but to a lesser extent. This leaves about half of the population for whom a European identity is either irrelevant or actively rejected.

European Identity in Comparative Context

The preceding section has established that a European identity does, in fact, exist, but it has not provided a sense of how it might compare to other identities, how it breaks down within respective European countries, or how identity constellations in Europe compare to those of other parts of the world.

In order to address the first of these comparative questions, Table 3.2 presents data from three of the surveys employing Format One identity questions. For each of these surveys—Eurobarometer 6 and the two World Values Surveys—percentages of first and second identity choices are shown for each selection possibility, followed by a total of the two percentages. This last column represents the percentage of respondents who selected the respective identity as either a first or second choice. The data are quite consistent across the three surveys, and reveal some interesting patterns.

Perhaps the most surprising finding that emerges from the table is that the national (i.e., country) identity is not the most popular of the five choices. In each case, it is slightly eclipsed by the local town identity as the highest-ranked combined first or second choice. Thus, nearly 64 percent listed the local identity as either their first or second choices in the 1980–1984 World Values Survey, while about 60 percent chose the national identity. This relationship is even more prominent if one examines the ratio of first-choice selections instead of the combination of first and second. Here, we see that the local town provides the identity of choice for an overwhelming plurality of respondents. Again using the data from the 1980–1984 World Values Survey, one finds that 43 percent of respondents chose their town identity first, against 27.4 percent for the national identity. Indeed, in each of these surveys, half-again as many chose the town identity over those who selected their national identity, the next closest competitor. What is unclear—and this returns us to the Chapter 1 discussion of the liabilities of survey data in the measurement of subtle phenomena like political identity—is the relative depth of these identities. In this case, what is sorely missing from such datasets is a measure of salience. Would people be as willing to fight and die—to use a crude but resonant indicator—for Lyon as they would for France? This seems doubtful, and one wonders whether the data would have appeared differently if an element of depth had somehow been introduced into the measure. More specifically, there are still reasons to believe that for most people in most places the nation-state remains the locus of their deepest affect.

In any case, the second major observation to be made about the data in Table 3.2 is that the preponderance of political identification is "local"—that is,

Table 3.2 Identification Levels for Various Geopolities (percentages of respondents)

Geopolity	Eurobarometer 6, 1976			World Values Survey, 1980–1984			World Values Survey, 1990–1993		
	1st Choice	2nd Choice	Combined 1st and 2nd Choice[a]	1st Choice	2nd Choice	Combined 1st and 2nd Choice[a]	1st Choice	2nd Choice	Combined 1st and 2nd Choice[a]
Town	45.1	17.9	63.0	43.0	20.8	63.8	40.2	18.8	59.0
Region	13.8	30.1	43.9	15.5	30.1	45.6	19.2	29.5	48.7
Country	28.3	33.4	61.7	27.4	32.3	59.7	25.8	29.0	54.8
Europe	6.0	11.8	17.8	4.3	9.4	13.7	5.2	13.9	19.1
World	6.9	6.8	13.7	9.8	7.4	17.2	9.7	8.8	18.5
Number of respondents	8,924	8,644		12,323	11,866		15,072	14,606	

Notes: Percentages are of valid cases only ("no answer" and "don't know" excluded). Datasets weighted by country population, and include respondents from EC/EU member-states only.

a. Combined 1st and 2nd choices add to 200.0 percent.

at the national level or below. Clearly, there are those who possess a European and/or an international identity, and do so in numbers large enough not to be disregarded. In a relative sense, however, these identities are substantially less attractive than are those associated with local, regional, and national communities. Given the inertia of tradition, and the lack of established and powerful polities at either of these supranational levels, it should be of little surprise that identities are weakest here. This last factor—the role of polities in the structuring and deepening of identities—is particularly intriguing given the data in Table 3.2. Though the relationship cannot be developed within the scope of this study, it does seem likely that polities provide focal points for the projection of affective sentiments, if for no other reason than that they are in a position to offer people those goods and services that may animate instrumental identity effects. Perhaps this explains why the two geopolitical levels that command the highest levels of identification—town and country—are also the same two that tend to have the most highly developed institutional apparatuses.

A second form of comparison, between country samples, provides further useful information for constructing an initial overview of the nature of European identification. To get a sense of the distribution of European identity across EU member-states, data are presented in four tables, one for each of the dependent-variable question formats. Tables 3.3, 3.4, and 3.6 include data from selected surveys employing Formats One, Two, and Four, respectively. Table 3.5 includes the one survey that utilized the Format Three dependent-variable question. To facilitate easier comparison, each survey in each table includes a column that groups together core- and secondary-level identifiers, and presents the sum of these two percentages as standardized values around the EU-mean. Thus—looking at Eurobarometer 6 in Table 3.3, for example—dividing the sum of the 4.6 percent of French respondents who selected Europe first and the 10.6 percent who selected it second, by the sum of the respective percentages for all countries (6.2 plus 11.8), yields the proportion of European identifiers in France relative to those in all of Europe (i.e., 84.4 percent, or 15.2 divided by 18.0). All data presented in these four tables are the product of bivariate analyses, and hence do not control for other factors that may affect individual or even national tendencies to identify with Europe, such as wealth, religion, or duration of EU member-state status. These and other factors are included in the multivariate explanatory models developed in Chapter 4. Here, only an initial overview of national tendencies is sought.

The data presented in Tables 3.3 through 3.6 suggest some interesting patterns. One of these is that very few countries are consistently above or below the mean in combined levels of European identification. Italy and Luxembourg are consistently high in this sample of surveys, as is Austria, though it appears in only one survey. Ireland is generally well below the European mean, as is Sweden, though it also appears in only one survey. Between these extremes are those countries mostly higher than mean levels of European identity in any

Table 3.3 Identification with Europe, by Country, Format One Identity Questions (percentages of respondents)

	Eurobarometer 6, 1976				World Values Survey, 1980–1984				World Values Survey, 1990–1993			
	Europe Selected			1st and 2nd as Percentage of Mean	Europe Selected			1st and 2nd as Percentage of Mean	Europe Selected			1st and 2nd as Percentage of Mean
	1st	2nd	Neither		1st	2nd	Neither		1st	2nd	Neither	
France	4.6	10.6	84.9	84.4	4.1	8.3	87.6	95.5	7.8	16.3	75.9	136.2
Belgium	4.8	9.7	85.5	80.6	4.1	13.4	82.5	131.6	7.3	16.4	76.3	133.9
Netherlands	3.2	10.8	86.0	77.8	3.9	9.5	86.6	100.8	4.7	15.2	80.1	112.4
Germany	6.3	12.4	81.3	103.9	7.1	11.4	81.5	139.1	5.3	13.1	81.5	104.0
Italy	6.3	15.6	78.0	121.7	3.9	10.8	85.3	110.5	7.2	18.5	74.3	145.2
Luxembourg	1.8	21.5	76.7	129.4								
Denmark	2.1	7.6	90.4	53.9	2.0	9.8	88.3	88.7	1.6	8.8	89.6	58.8
Ireland	2.1	9.1	88.8	62.2	2.0	7.9	91.1	74.4	2.5	7.2	90.3	54.8
Britain	8.9	9.6	81.5	102.8	2.5	4.8	92.6	54.9	2.5	8.1	89.4	60.0
Spain									1.3	7.5	91.2	49.7
Portugal									3.7	12.1	84.1	89.3
All Countries	6.2	11.8	82.0	100.0	4.3	9.0	86.7	100.0	4.9	12.8	82.2	100.0
Number of respondents	8,618				12,387				15,762			

Notes: Percentages are of valid cases only ("no answer" and "don't know" excluded). Datasets weighted by country population, and include respondents from EC/EU member-states only.

Table 3.4 Identification with Europe, by Country, Format Two Identity Questions (percentages of respondents)

| | Eurobarometer 27, 1987 | | | | Eurobarometer 37-0, 1992 | | | |
| | Thinks of Self as European | | | | Thinks of Self as European | | | |
	Often	Sometimes	Never	Often and Sometimes as Percentage of Mean	Often	Sometimes	Never	Often and Sometimes as Percentage of Mean
France	17.1	36.0	46.9	107.3	16.6	36.3	47.1	111.6
Belgium	10.8	37.0	52.1	96.6	17.4	42.0	40.7	125.3
Netherlands	8.3	26.1	65.6	69.5	11.0	28.5	60.5	83.3
Germany	11.3	44.2	44.4	112.1	8.1	30.3	61.6	81.0
Italy	16.4	34.9	48.7	103.6	16.5	41.8	41.7	123.0
Luxembourg	20.8	44.3	34.8	131.5	23.4	40.9	35.8	135.7
Denmark	10.2	31.8	58.0	84.9	14.4	36.0	49.6	106.3
Ireland	7.5	31.2	61.3	78.2	14.9	20.0	65.0	73.6
Britain	9.6	23.8	66.5	67.5	10.4	17.9	71.7	59.7
Greece	20.8	33.8	45.4	110.3	22.8	37.8	39.3	127.8
Spain	21.9	40.2	37.9	125.5	25.4	35.5	39.1	128.5
Portugal	12.8	44.4	42.8	115.6	15.5	51.5	33.0	141.4
All Countries	14.2	35.3	50.4	100.0	14.4	33.0	52.6	100.0
Number of respondents				11,256				6,136

Notes: Percentages are of valid cases only ("no answer" and "don't know" excluded). Datasets weighted by country population, and include respondents from EC/EU member-states only.

Table 3.5   Identification with Europe, by Country, Format Three Identity Questions (percentages of respondents)

Eurobarometer 41-1, 1994

	Thinks of Self as European					7-10 as Percentage of Mean
	(Most) 9-10	7-8	5-6	3-4	(Least) 1-2	
France	17.0	22.4	27.3	17.2	16.1	106.2
Belgium	18.4	26.5	24.7	14.8	15.5	121.0
Netherlands	13.3	22.1	26.8	16.2	21.6	95.4
Germany	17.3	26.5	26.4	17.8	12.0	118.1
Italy	13.5	28.5	30.9	15.7	11.5	113.2
Luxembourg	19.7	17.8	28.1	15.5	18.9	101.1
Denmark	11.6	21.1	25.2	19.7	22.5	88.1
Ireland	9.7	19.7	24.9	20.4	25.2	79.3
Britain	8.2	12.2	18.6	19.9	41.0	55.0
Greece	12.0	13.4	29.5	17.7	27.4	68.5
Spain	15.2	23.4	31.2	17.7	12.6	104.0
Portugal	18.9	21.8	32.9	16.8	9.5	109.7
All Countries	14.5	22.6	26.7	17.6	18.7	100.0
Number of respondents						12,566

Notes: Percentages are of valid cases only ("no answer" and "don't know" excluded). Datasets weighted by country population, and include respondents from EC/EU member-states only.

Table 3.6 Identification with Europe, by Country, Format Four Identity Questions (percentages of respondents)

	Eurobarometer 36-0, 1991					Eurobarometer 58-1, 2002				
	Attachment to Europe				Very and Fairly as Percentage of Mean	Attachment to Europe				Very and Fairly as Percentage of Mean
	Very	Fairly	Not Very	Not at All		Very	Fairly	Not Very	Not at All	
France	10.9	44.3	26.5	18.4	108.7	13.2	40.7	31.7	14.4	115.7
Belgium	11.7	38.9	28.6	20.8	99.6	10.3	39.7	37.2	12.8	107.3
Netherlands	5.2	26.9	47.2	20.7	63.2	6.0	23.5	47.6	23.0	63.3
Germany	12.0	37.0	36.8	14.2	96.5	10.8	37.4	39.8	12.1	103.4
Italy	21.3	44.8	18.3	15.6	130.1	14.7	48.2	29.6	7.4	135.0
Luxembourg	16.7	40.6	26.9	15.9	112.8	29.9	46.3	19.2	4.6	163.5
Denmark	15.1	46.6	27.6	10.7	121.5	8.2	38.0	38.6	15.2	99.1
Ireland	8.8	27.2	33.9	30.2	70.9	14.6	37.4	33.6	14.4	111.6
Britain	7.8	29.9	32.3	30.0	74.2	5.3	23.6	36.8	34.3	62.0
Greece	16.4	37.2	25.9	20.5	105.5	7.1	30.7	43.1	19.0	81.1
Spain	19.2	36.9	29.6	14.3	110.4	10.8	33.2	38.9	17.0	94.4
Portugal	8.7	34.8	33.3	23.3	85.6	12.9	36.9	37.6	12.6	106.9
Finland						2.5	22.4	53.7	21.4	53.4
Austria						15.1	35.3	37.8	11.7	108.2
Sweden						6.5	28.2	42.0	23.3	74.5
All Countries	13.1	37.7	30.2	18.9	100.0	10.6	36.0	36.7	16.7	100.0
Number of respondents					11,928					15,622

Notes: Percentages are of valid cases only ("no answer" and "don't know" excluded). Datasets weighted by country population, and include respondents from EC/EU member-states only.

given survey, including France, Belgium, Germany, Spain, and Portugal; and those countries generally below the mean, including the Netherlands, Denmark, and Britain. The pattern thus revealed is immediately suggestive of at least two deeper divides that may affect levels of European identification. Those countries manifesting the highest levels of European identity are both more southern and more Catholic than the group of countries that tend to fall below the mean. In Chapter 4, these and other hypothesized effects are substituted for raw country designations, in an attempt to determine cross-national effects that produce varying levels of European identity within individuals.

A final form of initial comparison is permitted by the World Values Surveys, which, as their name implies, include data from countries across the globe. Table 3.7 groups these countries into seven geocultural continents, and displays Format One identity-question data for each. Interestingly, the table shows that the nation-state, expected to be a strong locus of identity, in fact does much better in some parts of the world than others. Asian, African, and Middle Eastern countries included in the sample tend to manifest substantially higher national identities, while Western, Latin American, and especially Eastern European countries evince lower levels of identification with the nation.

Turning to a comparison of European identity with its continental analogues elsewhere, the tendency might be to expect that the former is far more popular, given the advanced state of the EU relative to any other supranational regional polity. In fact, this is generally true, though not to the extent that might be expected. In the 1980–1984 survey, the 12.4 percent of Europeans who selected a continental identity either first or second precisely equals the mean for the entire dataset (in part, no doubt, because Europe accounts for two-thirds of the respondents surveyed). In that survey, there is about half Europe's level of continental identity in North America and Asia, but also about double Europe's level in the Latin American sample of two countries and in the single African country surveyed. In the 1990–1993 survey, Europe's 15.9 percent of continental identifiers exceeds both the overall survey percentage, and every other continental subset except Africa (now two countries included). Though Europe does generally manifest higher levels of continental identity than do other regions of the globe, these findings nevertheless are somewhat mystifying in that Europe does not trump *all* other continents in this regard, as might be expected, and does not lead those it does surpass by larger margins than those shown.

One plausible explanation for these findings is that the role of an institutionally developed polity as a focal point for identification has been overstated, and that the factors that drive political identities are largely to be found elsewhere. A further extension of this notion would posit that, in fact, the existence of such polities not only doesn't advance levels of identification, but instead actually produces the opposite effect, alienating potential identification tendencies. If true, substituting "the European Union" for "Europe," "the

Table 3.7 Identification Levels for Various Geopolities, by Continent (percentages of respondents)

Continent/Polity	World Values Survey 1980–1984[a]			World Values Survey 1990–1993[b]		
	1st Choice	2nd Choice	Combined 1st and 2nd Choice[c]	1st Choice	2nd Choice	Combined 1st and 2nd Choice[c]
Western Europe						
Town	45.1	21.1	66.2	43.1	18.9	62.0
Region	14.9	29.7	44.6	17.9	28.7	46.6
Country	28.4	33.6	62.0	26.3	32.5	58.8
Continent	3.9	8.5	12.4	4.3	11.6	15.9
World	7.7	7.1	14.8	8.3	8.3	16.6
Number of respondents	20,404	19,737		20,529	19,884	
Eastern Europe						
Town				40.5	27.8	68.3
Region				27.8	29.7	57.5
Country				22.2	23.6	45.8
Continent				2.9	9.6	12.5
World				6.6	9.3	15.9
Number of respondents				13,742	12,033	
North America						
Town	46.8	17.5	64.3	34.7	22.6	57.3
Region	19.2	42.7	61.9	14.1	30.7	44.8
Country	25.0	23.3	48.3	34.3	27.3	61.6
Continent	2.2	4.2	6.6	3.3	7.3	10.6
World	6.8	12.3	19.1	13.6	12.1	25.7
Number of respondents	2,945	2,858		3,664	3,581	
Latin America						
Town	43.5	21.4	64.9	35.8	18.3	54.1
Region	13.1	27.3	40.4	13.6	29.6	43.2
Country	29.2	27.5	56.7	32.7	30.8	63.5
Continent	6.4	17.0	23.4	4.8	9.2	14.0
World	7.8	6.7	14.5	13.1	12.1	25.2
Number of respondents	2,642	2,539		4,664	4,508	

continues

Table 3.7 Continued

	World Values Survey 1980–1984[a]			World Values Survey 1990–1993[b]		
Continent/Polity	1st Choice	2nd Choice	Combined 1st and 2nd Choice[c]	1st Choice	2nd Choice	Combined 1st and 2nd Choice[c]
Asia						
Town	36.8	26.1	62.9	37.6	21.2	58.8
Region	18.5	35.3	53.8	17.8	42.1	59.9
Country	42.4	30.3	72.7	40.6	27.6	68.2
Continent	1.6	3.7	5.3	0.9	3.8	4.7
World	1.0	4.6	5.6	3.0	5.3	8.3
Number of respondents	3,589	3,337		7,167	5,706	
Africa						
Town	26.5	18.7	45.2	38.1	16.5	54.6
Region	8.0	18.4	26.4	16.9	27.1	44.0
Country	44.0	34.9	78.9	32.5	35.9	68.4
Continent	12.9	16.1	29.0	7.0	12.5	19.5
World	8.7	11.9	20.6	5.4	8.1	13.5
Number of respondents	760	663		2,149	2,059	
Middle East						
Town				33.6	31.0	64.6
Region				11.7	22.0	33.7
Country				45.5	34.5	80.0
Continent				1.2	3.9	5.1
World				8.0	8.7	16.7
Number of respondents				1,011	984	

continues

Table 3.7 Continued

	World Values Survey 1980–1984[a]			World Values Survey 1990–1993[b]		
Continent/Polity	1st Choice	2nd Choice	Combined 1st and 2nd Choice[c]	1st Choice	2nd Choice	Combined 1st and 2nd Choice[c]
Entire sample						
Town	43.7	21.3	65.0	40.1	21.7	61.8
Region	15.4	31.1	46.5	19.6	30.5	50.1
Country	30.2	31.7	61.9	28.9	29.4	58.3
Continent	3.9	8.5	12.4	3.5	9.5	13.0
World	6.9	7.4	14.3	7.8	8.8	16.6
Number of respondents	30,339	29,135		52,927	48,755	

Notes: Percentages are of valid cases only ("no answer" and "don't know" excluded). Datasets weighted by country population, and, for Europe, include respondents from EC/EU member-states only.

a. In the 1980–1984 dataset, Western Europe includes France, Britain (with Northern Ireland), West Germany, Italy, Netherlands, Denmark, Belgium, Spain, Ireland, Norway, Sweden, Iceland, and Finland; North America includes the United States and Canada; Latin America includes Mexico and Argentina; Asia includes Japan and South Korea; Africa includes South Africa.

b. The 1990–1993 dataset includes all of the countries from the 1980–1984 dataset, as well as the following: Western Europe also includes Switzerland, Portugal, and Austria; Eastern Europe is added to the list of continents, with data collected from Hungary, Poland, Belarus, Czechoslovakia, East Germany, Slovenia, Bulgaria, Romania, Moscow, Lithuania, Latvia, Estonia, and Russia; Latin America also includes Brazil and Chile (but not Argentina); Asia also includes India and China; Africa also includes Nigeria; and the Middle East is added to the list of continents, with data collected from Turkey.

c. Combined 1st and 2nd choices add to 200.0 percent.

African Union" for "Africa," and so forth, in these survey questions, might result in depressing levels of continental identification. As the successive discussion suggests, this may be precisely true for Europe and its often unpopular polity, the European Union.

European Identity over Time

This chapter has so far been concerned with the character of European identity in the geographical context of competing regional and state identities. We now turn to an examination of the identity across another dimension—that of time. A return to Table 3.1 allows a quick apprehension of the difficulty associated with such a task. As discussed above, European identity has been measured by means of four separate and largely incompatible question formats employed by the various opinion surveys examined. Worse still, with a couple of key exceptions, each of these formats is concentrated in a single period of time, before and after which they do not appear, rendering those formats useless for longitudinal analysis. These exceptions therefore provide the only viable quantitative options for examining how European identity has changed over significant periods of time. Fortunately, the Format One question appears intermittently across nearly the entire thirty-two-year period for which there are identity survey data (1971 through 2002). Format Four data range from 1991 to 2002.

A brief glance at the Format One data in Table 3.1 suggests little change at all during the period 1971–2001. About 4–8 percent of the sample in every survey chose European as their first identity, while about 12 percent quite consistently chose it second, and 80–85 percent did not choose it as either first or second. Figure 3.1 presents these findings graphically, using data (as available) for all countries surveyed. Each country's set of five vertical bars in the figure represent data from, respectively, the 1971 European Communities Study (five countries only), the 1976 Eurobarometer 6 survey, and the 1980–1984, 1990–1993, and 1999–2001 World (and European) Values Surveys. These national breakouts tell much the same story as Table 3.1 does for the entire sample. That is, there is some variation between states along the pattern of attitudes toward Europe that is typical for a host of questions, such that the "Six" (France, Germany, Italy, the Netherlands, Belgium, and Luxembourg) are generally higher in identification with Europe than the "Three" (Britain, Ireland, and Denmark), for example. Within countries, however, it is difficult to locate sustained patterns of movement. Belgium appears to gradually grow in European identification over time, and Germany perhaps shrinks a bit.

In fact, though, the real story of Figure 3.1 and the data from Table 3.1 is stasis, not movement. Not much changes over time in levels of European identification. This conclusion will also be supported by the finding in Chapter 4 that

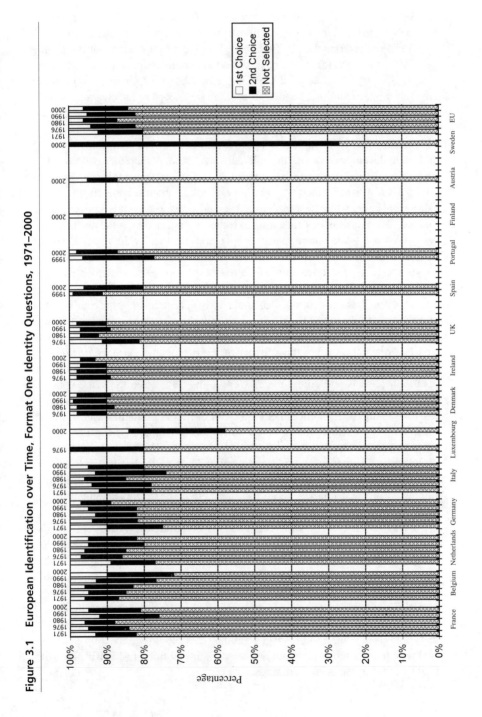

Figure 3.1 European Identification over Time, Format One Identity Questions, 1971–2000

age does not predict European identity levels, a conclusion that would probably not be expected if there were growth over time in the general population.

The Format Four data in Table 3.1 also evidence a similar pattern for the years 1991 through 2002. Generally, something on the order of 15 percent of the sample is "very close/attached" to Europe/the EU, while about 35–40 percent are "fairly attached/close," about 30 percent are "not very attached/close," and about 15 percent are "not at all attached/close." There does appear to be some downward trending in the latter two surveys, Eurobarometers 56-3 and 58-1. This could possibly be explained by the fact that they were both fielded in 2002 and some development (e.g., the enlargement debate, perhaps) drove down Europhile sentiments at that time. More likely, however, this small change is accounted for by the fact that these two surveys asked about sentiments toward the European Union, while the others asked about Europe per se. It is safe to assume that the Union itself is less endearing to some Europeans than is the abstract concept of Europe—the culture, place, people, and community. In any case, this is a minor trend, if it is a trend at all.

If there is any conclusion to be reached about European identification over time (and any such conclusions must be tempered by the gaps in data available for these purposes), it is that it has *not* changed appreciably in the years since public opinion surveying of Europeans began in earnest. Interviewed informants tend to tell a similar story, but with two related caveats. The first is a distinction often made between the personal experience of younger informants and that of their parents. When asked if they are closer to Europe than their parents and communities were at the time when they (the younger generation) were growing up, a very typical response was that "Europe didn't exist for them" (the parent generation). But this is a comment on visibility as much as it is on affect, and in that sense reflects the potential for identity development more than, necessarily, its actual growth. The second caveat is, as discussed in Chapter 4, the widespread belief among informants that European identity is far more prevalent among the young. But the quantitative empirical findings from that chapter show little age effect on European identity, and what effect is found is not always in the predicted direction.

Perhaps the best way to reconcile this contradiction is to consider the character of European identity for those who possess it, which will be discussed in Chapter 5. Should it be found—as, by way of preview, it will—that this identity is of a less emotional quality than national identities, a possible explanation begins to take shape. Europe is not much available—as a polity, or a place of unrestricted travel, study, and work—for older generations, and thus by comparison, the younger appear "more European" to informants. In fact, though, for these younger generations, this mobility and "Europeaness" are taken for granted, and do not necessarily stir emotion or identification with Europe—hence the survey findings.

Young Europeans, in sum, are probably considerably more *comfortable* than their parents and grandparents with Europe as a social and political space in which to exist, but they have not been drawn to identify with Europe more than previous generations (and may in fact do so less than their elders). As Elizabeth Haywood, director of the Wales Confederation of British Industry, put it in an interview: "For younger people, it's not an issue—they are European and expect to be able to move about freely" and enjoy the other advantages of European integration.

Perhaps these subtle attitudinal distinctions explain why qualitative data indirectly predict increasing levels of European identification that don't, in fact, show up. In any case, what is clear is that the available quantitative evidence for longitudinal change in levels of European identification strongly suggests that there has not been any.

Conclusion

This chapter has sought to provide an overview of the absolute and relative extent of European political identity. It has established that a European identity clearly exists, though—depending on the phrasing of the question and the classification of the responses—it is generally a minority sentiment. The analysis has shown that the extent of such an identity varies across European countries, but not yet why (though at least two explanatory patterns are suggested by the data). It has demonstrated that, while a continental identity is hardly unique to Europe, it is the region of the world where such an identity is generally most prevalent, though not by much. And, finally, it has established—to the limited extent permissible from the data available that are amenable to comparison— that levels of European identification have shown little movement over time.

With the establishment of the fact that there are, indeed, "Europeans" in Europe, we turn now to a series of four additional empirical questions that further explore the identity in greater detail. The phenomenon will be examined in terms of its character, its depth, and its meaning. First, though, we approach in Chapter 4 the core question "Who are the 'Europeans'?" and test a series of hypotheses that offer explanatory purchase on the varying levels of European identity found among individuals there.

Notes

1. Chapter 4 measures the effect of nationality on European identity, while controlling for other effects, and arguably there is no reason to present bivariate findings here. However, given the salience of countries as units of study for political scientists,

it is worth preceding the causal analysis of succeeding chapters with the juxtaposition of this single variable against identity variables, in order to help sketch a general overview of the phenomenon.

2. Question text: "Among the following geographic units, to which one do you feel you first belong? And, secondly?" Response choices were: "the locality or town where you live," "the region, province or county where you live," "your country as a whole," "Europe," and "the world as a whole" (except for the 1971 European Communities Study, for which the choices were "city," "locality," "canton," "department or province," "region," "country," "Europe," and "other").

3. With the exception of the 1999–2001 World and European Values Survey, it is impossible to disaggregate those for whom Europe is a distant identity choice from those who actively reject it. In that survey, however, respondents were given a third prompt not offered in the other surveys, which followed the first and second identity-choice couplet. The third question allowed respondents to choose an identity that they most actively rejected. If this one data point were to represent a general tendency, we might then view the distribution of European identifiers in roughly the following proportions, according to the Format One formulation: about 5 percent of Europeans are core identifiers, about 12 percent are secondary identifiers, about 65 percent feel the identity distantly or not at all, while about 18 percent are clear nonidentifiers with Europe who actively reject the identity.

4. Format Three text: "As well as thinking of themselves as [nationality] or (add if appropriate [nationality] and/or [subnationality]), or whatever, some people think of themselves also as European. Others do not do so. How about you? Please choose between the two ends of the scale. If you fully agree with the opinion on the left hand side, you give a score of 1. If you fully agree with the opinion on the right hand side, you give a score of 10. The scores in between allow you to say how close to either side you are."

5. Format Four text: For Eurobarometer surveys: "People may feel different degrees of attachment to their town or village, to their region, to their country, to the European Community or to Europe as a whole. Please tell me how attached you feel to . . . Europe as a whole [or] Europe." Response choices were: "very attached," "fairly attached," "not very attached," "not at all attached." For the ISSP: "To begin, we have some questions about where you live: your neighbourhood or village, your town or city, your (county, state, etc.) and so on. (By 'neighbourhood' we mean the part of the town or city you live in. If you live in a village, we take this as your 'neighbourhood.') How close do you feel to . . . Europe?" Response choices were: "very close," "close," "not very close," "not close at all." Importantly, Eurobarometers 56-3 and 58-1 used "the European Union" in place of "Europe as a whole" or "Europe" when asking respondents for their degree of attachment at the continental level.

4

Who Are the "Europeans"? Explaining Variance in Levels of European Identity

The evidence of the past 25 years seems to show that publics can be won over to a European perspective under favorable conditions. The publics of the original six member nations are now solidly pro-European. Significant progress in this direction has taken place among the Irish and the Greek publics, but not among the Danes. The British remain a mixed case, emotionally favourable to European unification but divided in their pragmatic assessments. What will happen in Spain and Portugal remains to be seen. It is readily conceivable that, given more favorable economic conditions than those that shaped the past decade, the development of a European identity would resume. But the process seems to reflect a complex interaction of economic, political and psychological factors.

—Ronald Inglehart (1986: xvi)

MEET JEAN-PAUL. HE is a European, as are Mary and Eef. But there are Europeans, and then there are Europeans. All three of these archetypal (and fictionalized) individuals are EU citizens, inheritors of the European cultural tradition, and residents living within the geographical boundaries of the continent. But they vary considerably in terms of the degree to which they identify themselves as European. How can we explain these variances? Is there something about the characteristics possessed by individual Europeans that would allow us to use those factors to predict their identity sentiments? Are men "more European" than women? Belgians more than Greeks? Rich more than poor, left more than right, highly educated more than less so?

Statistical data, guided and enhanced by qualitative observations, permit us to specify the impact that various characteristics possessed by people and the countries to which they belong will typically produce on the propensity of a given individual to identify as a European. This chapter examines each of these characteristics in some detail, ultimately quantifying the strength, direction, and probability (statistical significance) of these effects. We then return, at the end of the chapter, to our three composite Europeans, to see through constructed examples how these independent variables shape the levels of European identification possessed by individual Europeans.

Explanatory hypotheses for the variance in levels of European identification have been drawn principally from the literatures on nationalism, nation-building, social psychology, and regional integration theory, from empirical studies of identity and integration support, and from original contributions presented in this book. For organizational purposes, these hypotheses have been grouped into four broad categories (though certain hypotheses could arguably fit as well in alternative categories). The first of these categories is constituted by hypotheses related to individual-level (largely demographic) *attributional* factors. In the second category are *attitudinal* factors that are thought to be associated with varying levels of European identification. Hypothesized explanations broadly related to *social-psychological* processes form the third category. And those factors associated with notions of *political-culture* are grouped together in a fourth category. These latter include, first, nationality, followed then by a series of variables that seek to substitute cross-national attributes for nationality designations.[1]

Findings from the original Survey of European Identifiers (SEI) and from field interviews are presented throughout this discussion. Data from extant surveys appear in Tables 4.1A, 4.1B, 4.2, 4.3, 4.5A, and 4.5B.[2] SEI findings are shown in Table 4.4.

Attributes

"I definitely describe myself as a European," twenty-six-year-old businessman Jean-Marc Routiers is quoted as saying in a front-page *New York Times* article of December 24, 1998. The *Times* goes on to describe Routiers as

> at the vanguard of a new generation of Europeans who do not have to brace themselves for a shock [from the euro] in the new year. Mobile, fluent in several languages and aggressively non–nationalistic, they are already living the kind of borderless, cosmopolitan existence that the single European currency is supposed to advance. They do not share their parents' memories of World War II or their parents' sense of national identity. (Stanley 1998: A1)

According to the *Times* article, these new Europeans are still relatively small in number, but disproportionately influential within their respective societies. The article is only one of the more recent of many, both academic and journalistic, that strongly suggest that attitudes toward the European project are at least in part a function of certain key demographic attributes.

Among the most prominent of these attributes is socioeconomic status, with European integration having been described from its inception as an elite project (Hodgson 1993; Haas 1971; Howe 1995: 28). Indeed, it was originally so by design, according to neofunctionalist theory (Haas 1958: 17–18), and by practice, according to Kevin Featherstone's description (1994) of Jean Monnet's construction of the ECSC and its High Authority. Both Philip Schlesinger (1994: 321) and Soledad García (1993: 1) observe that European identifiers are overrepresented among elites, while Max Haller (1994: 252) finds a deep split in many countries between the elites and masses on integration issues. And Bernhard Wessels (1995b: 141) suggests that empirical support for Ernst Haas's original argument is as clear as it has been long-standing: Wessels argues that Eurobarometer data show that elites in Europe have always led the masses in both the breadth and timing of their support for integration.

Four measures are employed in this study to operationalize socioeconomic status and test the hypothesis that elites are more prone to identify with Europe: income, generally in quartiles; class, generally as self-described by survey respondents, but sometimes by interviewer observation; occupation, as recoded for purposes of this project into one of three broad, ordinal levels ranking the degree of social esteem generally associated with the occupation; and education, generally as indicated by the respondent's age when leaving school. As Tables 4.1A, 4.1B, and 4.2 indicate, there is considerable evidence supporting the broad hypothesis that status is positively related to European identification tendencies, though not for all four of the specific measures.

Class, perhaps the best indicator of socioeconomic status, also has historical precedent as an important factor in identity formation. In her influential work on nationalism, for example, Liah Greenfeld (1992) argues that the identity was everywhere driven by the *ressentiment* of a certain class of individuals chafing at their status inequality in the social order. In the empirical findings presented here, class is consistently significant across every survey in which it appears. Table 4.3 indicates that its potential effect on the dependent variable is moderate but nevertheless notable, with the capacity to shift responses nearly half a point on the 10-point identity scale. The occupation variable also produces the hypothesized effect, but is only significant in about half the surveys examined, an outcome that is perhaps not surprising given that it is a somewhat crude measure. As Sophie Duchesne and André-Paul Frognier (1995: 209–213) also found, income similarly produces significant associations herein for about half the surveys examined, and is always positively associated with higher levels of European identification.

These authors had also discovered that education was the strongest identity predictor among their sociodemographic variables, and it again proves to be highly significant in each of the surveys examined in the present broader study except one, with Table 4.3 demonstrating that moving from the lowest to the highest level of education can shift European identity outcomes more than half a point on the 10-point scale. While education is traditionally a measure of status, it also has wider implications with respect to attitudes toward the European project in general. The notion that Europe is an alien and there-

Table 4.1A Effects on European Identification, Using Member-State Variables, Format One and Format Two Identity Questions (ordered probit analysis, multiple surveys)

Category *Hypothesis* Measure	Most / Next Most Attached Format								Think Self European Format					
	ECS 1971	ECS 1973	EB6 1976	EB10A 1978	EB12 1979	WVS 1980–1984	WVS 1990–1993	WEVS 1999–2001	EB27 1987	EB30 1988	EB31 1989	EB33 1990	EB36-0 1991	EB37-0 1992
Attributional hypotheses														
Elite hypothesis														
Income	.07**	< .00	.04**	.02*	.03	.01	.02**	.02***	.08**	.02	.01	.02	.01	.04*
Class	.06*	.13**	-.06	.06	.04	.10**	.05**	.05***			.09**	.08**	.06**	.08**
Occupation	.14**	.03**	-.01	.07**	.03**	.05	.08**	.04***		.06**	.02	.08**	.07**	.09*
Education	.04**	.07**	.12**	.04*	.11**	.14**	.04**	.04***	.07**	.04**	.06**	.06**	.06**	.04**
Cosmopolitan hypothesis														
Town size									.10**	.01	.02	.09**	.08**	.02
Frontier zone										-.06*	.02			
Travel frequency	.23**		.08**											
Number of languages			.19**											
Interested in other countries			.16**											
Trust other Europeans			.07*									.29**		
Attitude toward immigrants														
Foreigner okay for neighbor						.05	.09**							
Other peoples in country okay									-.11**					
Number of other peoples neighborhood										.03				
Number of other peoples as friends										.31**				
Presence of other nationals okay														.11
Presence of other races okay													.03	
Presence of other religions okay														-.03
Parents citizens of country okay														
Where childhood spent														

continues

Table 4.1A Continued

Category / Hypothesis / Measure	Most / Next Most Attached Format								Think Self European Format					
	ECS 1971	ECS 1973	EB6 1976	EB10A 1978	EB12 1979	WVS 1980–1984	WVS 1990–1993	WEVS 1999–2001	EB27 1987	EB30 1988	EB31 1989	EB33 1990	EB36-0 1991	EB37-0 1992
Years spent in current town														
Time spent in other countries														
Preference for own country														
Other countries should be like mine														
Generational hypothesis														
Age 15–24	.14**	—	—	.19**	-.02	—	.11**	.01	-.03	-.09**	-.12**	-.16**	-.10**	—
Age 25–34	—	-.02	.17**	—	-.02	<.00	-.02	<.01	-.07*	—	-.10**	-.10**	-.04	-.08
Age 35–44	.04	-.04	.10	.04	-.04	.15*	.04	—	.05	.03	—	-.07	—	.03
Age 45–54	.10	<.01	.08	.11*	—	.08	.10*	.05*	.10**	.11**	<.00	—	-.07	.07
Age 55–64	.02	-.02	.16**	.06	-.02	.07	.13**	-.05	.05	.05	.07	.08	-.06	.05
Age 65–74	.01	-.12*	-.11	.09	-.13*	.03	-.08	-.06	.03	.03	.09*	.09*	-.08	.11*
Age 75–84			.09	.17	-.10	-.33*	.18	-.03	.12	-.03	-.11	-.09	-.10	-.01
Age 85–94			-.29	.10	-7.34	.35		.10	-.51*	.24	-.28	-.56**	-.09	.09
Gender hypothesis														
Gender	-.14**	-.09**	-.21**	-.20**	-.19**	-.13**	-.18**	-.11**	-.13**	-.15**	-.15**	-.13**	-.11**	-.15**
Attitudinal hypotheses														
Postmaterialism hypothesis														
Postmaterialism		.16**	.20**		.14**	.17**	.14**	.09**	.15**	.13**	.18**	.19**	.16**	.19**
Ideological hypothesis														
Left		.22**	-.05	—	—	-.01	-.06*	.07**	—	.07	.06*	.05	.03	.11**
Broad center		.16**	.15**	.01	.01	—	—	—	-.09**	—	—	—	—	—
Right		—	—	-.10	.12*	.08	.12**	-.12**	.01	.01	-.07	-.11**	-.08*	-.18**
Nontraditionalism hypothesis														
No religious association	.38**	.01	.07	.07	.08	.06	.01		-.04	-.07*	-.06	.05	-.10**	-.04
Living as married			.09	-.08	-.20	.16	<.01		-.06	.16*	-.06	.02	-.05	-.24**
Left ideology				see above	see above					see above	see above			
Attitude to societal change	< .01		< .01	.05	.05	.03	.01		-.01	.08**	.08**	.04		
New or old ideas best							.02**							

continues

Table 4.1A Continued

			Most / Next Most Attached Format							Think Self European Format					
Category *Hypothesis* Measure	ECS 1971	ECS 1973	EB6 1976	EB10A 1978	EB12 1979	WVS 1980–1984	WVS 1990–1993	WEVS 1999–2001	EB27 1987	EB30 1988	EB31 1989	EB33 1990	EB36-0 1991	EB37-0 1992
Attitude to new things		.04**												
Sexual freedom attitude						.01	-.01							
Marriage attitude						<.00	.08**							
Willing to fight for country						-.01	<.00							
Marijuana use okay						<.00	.03**							
Homosexuality okay						.01	.02**							
Prostitution okay						.02**	-.01							
Abortion okay						-.01	.02**							
Divorce okay						.02*	-.01							
National pride						.09**	.09**							
Integration support hypothesis														
Integration support	.23**	.30**	.18**	.05**	.22**				.41**	.44**	.44**	.32**	.38**	.38**
Normative hypothesis														
EU = peace, cooperation									.23**					
Social-psychological hypotheses														
Efficacy hypothesis														
Tries to influence others	.11**	.07**	-.01		.03*	.03	.07**	.02**	.13**	.11**	.16**	.16**	.12**	.12**
Feels respected		-.12**												
Can change nation		.08**												
Powerful try to gain from me										.13**				
Control over life						<.00	.01							
Party member						.25**	.02							
Party activist						-.21	-.06							
Instrumentalism hypothesis														
EU good for country	.08**	.05	.08**		.15**				.27**	.40**	.40**	.32**	.30**	.31**
EU good for me personally		.07*												
EU good for my job			.03											
EU good for economy			.08**											
EU good for lowering prices			-.04											

continues

Table 4.1A   Continued

	Most / Next Most Attached Format								Think Self European Format					
Category *Hypothesis* Measure	ECS 1971	ECS 1973	EB6 1976	EB10A 1978	EB12 1979	WVS 1980–1984	WVS 1990–1993	WEVS 1999–2001	EB27 1987	EB30 1988	EB31 1989	EB33 1990	EB36-0 1991	EB37-0 1992
EU good for development			.01											
Region's EU dependency									.60**					
EU advantage/disadvantage scale				.09**										
Minority refuge hypothesis														
Religious minority	.51**	-.01	.06			-.04			.14*	-.10	.17**	.13*	-.08	.02
Racial minority						-1.00*	.17**							
External factor hypothesis														
US positive role for peace														
Socialization hypothesis														
No measure available														
Leadership hypothesis														
No measure available														
Political-cultural hypotheses														
By member-state														
France	-.06	—	-.19**	.11*	—	.08	.20**	-.28**	.06	.29**	.12**	.24**	.45**	.12*
Belgium	-.21**	.07	-.31**	-.02	<.00	.37**	.15*	—	-.22**		-.09	.19**	.19**	.13
Netherlands	-.05	.14*	-.48**	.14	.06	—	-.24**	-.21**	-.66**	-.54***	-.62***	-.55***	-.19**	-.44***
Germany	.16**	.17**	—	—	-.06	.22*	—	-.34**	—	.27**	—	-.16*	—	-.33***
Italy	—	.15**	.22**	.27**	.30**	.33**	.29**	-.27**	-.08*	.18**	-.10**	.19**	.26**	—
Luxembourg		-.12	-.22	.62	-.03			.39	.24	.12	-.01	.14	.36	.20
Denmark		-.31**	-.60**	-.25	-.34*	-.16	-.49**	-.34**	.10	.17	-.23*	-.10	.01	-.11
Ireland		.01	-.10	-.32	.24	.01	-.27*	-.49**	-.30**	-.22	-.36**	-.40**	-.23**	-.40*
Britain		.11*	.25**	-.04	.21**	-.12	-.34**	-.76***	-.35**	-.22**	-.46**	-.40**	-.13**	-.42***
Greece								-.75***	.19**	.14	.15*	.28**	.31**	.19*
Spain							-.40**	.21**	.45**	.32**	.35**	.20**	.51**	.35***
Portugal							.07	-.37***	.17*	<.01	.15*	.01	.41**	.21*
Finland								-.34**						
Sweden								1.26**						
Austria								-.17*						

continues

Table 4.1A Continued

Model	Most / Next Most Attached Format								Think Self European Format					
	ECS 1971	ECS 1973	EB6 1976	EB10A 1978	EB12 1979	WVS 1980–1984	WVS 1990–1993	WEVS 1999–2001	EB27 1987	EB30 1988	EB31 1989	EB33 1990	EB36-0 1991	EB37-0 1992
Observations	8,645	12,273	8,655	8,310	8,471	9,730	18,779	17,432	11,233	11,344	11,232	11,421	12,578	6,329
Chi-square	921	1,641	1,081	421	529	696	1,658	1,255	2,396	2,765	2,756	2,728	2,554	1,515
Probability > Chi-square	.0000	.0000	.0000	.0000	.0000	.0000	.0000	.000	.0000	.0000	.0000	.0000	.0000	.0000
Pseudo R-square	.08	.11	.11	.05	.05	.08	.08	–.70	.11	.12	.12	.12	.10	.12
Cut 1	2.82	3.60	3.36	2.02	2.69	2.80	2.51	1.29	2.72	2.82	2.67	3.43	2.61	3.04
Cut 2	3.45	4.38	4.07	2.80	3.48	3.47	3.30	2.10	3.94	4.11	3.91	4.52	3.74	4.20
Cut 3														

Notes: All independent variables (other than nominal variables) are coded in the direction of the hypothesized relationship. Positive effects shown in the table thus support the hypothesized relationship, and negative effects support its inverse. Categorical/nominal variables (age, nationality, ideology, geographical location) are yes (1) / no (0) dummy variables; the directional sign in the table indicates a positive or negative effect on the dependent variable relative to the omitted baseline category. EB = Eurobarometer; ECS = European Communities Study; WEVS = World and European Values Survey; WVS = World Values Survey.

  — = Baseline (omitted) category.

  * p ≤ .05
  ** p ≤ .01

Table 4.1B Effects on European Identification, Using Member-State Variables, Format Four Identity Questions (ordered probit analysis, multiple surveys)

Category Hypothesis Measure	Attachment to Europe Format					
	EB36-0 1991	ISSP 1995	EB51-0 1999	EB54-1 2000	EB56-3 2002	EB58-1 2002
Attributional hypotheses						
Elite hypothesis						
Income	.01	.02	.05**	.04**	.04**	.02**
Class	.04**	.04*				
Occupation	< .00	.01				
Education	.03**	.01**	.01**	.02**	.02**	.01**
Cosmopolitan hypothesis						
Town size	.05**	.03			−.01	−.01**
Frontier zone						
Travel frequency						
Number of languages		.08**				
Interested in other countries						
Trust other Europeans						
Attitude toward immigrants						
Foreigner okay for neighbor						
Other peoples in country okay						
Number of other peoples neighborhood						
Number of other peoples as friends						
Presence of other nationals okay						
Presence of other races okay						
Presence of other religions okay						
Parents citizens of country		.05				
Where childhood spent		.01				
Years spent in current town		< .01				
Time spent in other countries	.08**					
Preference for own country		−.02				
Other countries should be like mine	−.03*					
Generational hypothesis						
Age 15–24	−.03	−.19**	−.09**	.10**	−.09**	−.01**
Age 25–34	−.06	−.15**	−.05**	.06*	−.04	< .01**
Age 35–44	—	—	—	—	—	—
Age 45–54	.11**	.10**	−<.01**	.07*	.04	.14**
Age 55–64	.17**	.17**	.09**	.18**	.15**	.15**
Age 65–74	.24**	.13**	.04**	.12**	.17**	.16**
Age 75–84	.04	.16*	.15**	.21**	.15**	.11**
Age 85–94	−.08	.09	.17**	.25*	.04	−.06**
Gender hypothesis						
Gender	−.05**	.03	.07**	.06**	−.15**	−.05**

continues

Table 4.1B Continued

Category *Hypothesis* Measure	| Attachment to Europe Format					
	EB36-0 1991	ISSP 1995	EB51-0 1999	EB54-1 2000	EB56-3 2002	EB58-1 2002
Attitudinal hypotheses						
Postmaterialism hypothesis						
Postmaterialism	.10**					
Ideological hypothesis						
Left	−.01	—	−.02**	−.06**	.04	−.10**
Broad center	—	.12*	—	—	—	—
Right	−.06	−.33*	−.12**	−.12**	−.14**	−.17**
Nontraditionalism hypothesis						
No religious association	−.12**	.02				
Living as married	−.09	.01				
Left ideology			see above			
Attitude to societal change						
New or old ideas best						
Attitude to new things						
Sexual freedom attitude						
Marriage attitude						
Willing to fight for country						
Marijuana use okay						
Homosexuality okay						
Prostitution okay						
Abortion okay						
Divorce okay						
National pride						
Integration support hypothesis						
Integration support	.40**	.47**				
Normative hypothesis						
EU = peace, cooperation						
Social-psychological hypotheses						
Efficacy hypothesis						
Tries to influence others	.05**		.08**	.05**		.08**
Feels respected						
Can change nation						
Powerful try to gain from me						
Control over life						
Party member						
Party activist						
Instrumentalism hypothesis						
EU good for country	.39**	.47**	.79**	.70**	.29**	.54**
EU good for me personally					.41**	.44**
EU good for my job						
EU good for economy						
EU good for lowering prices						
EU good for development						
Region's EU dependency						
EU advantage/disadvantage scale						
Minority refuge hypothesis						
Religious minority	−.03	.26**				
Racial minority		−.06				

continues

Table 4.1B   Continued

Category *Hypothesis* Measure	Attachment to Europe Format					
	EB36-0 1991	ISSP 1995	EB51-0 1999	EB54-1 2000	EB56-3 2002	EB58-1 2002
External factor hypothesis						
US positive role for peace						−.06**
Socialization hypothesis						
No measure available						
Leadership hypothesis						
No measure available						
Political-cultural hypotheses						
By member-state						
France	.04		−.28**	−.12*	.16**	.17**
Belgium	−.12		—	—	—	—
Netherlands	−.39**	−.22**	−.46**	−.32**	−.55**	−.58**
Germany	—	—	−.06**	−.03	.03	.01**
Italy	.17**	.18**	−.04**	.04	.34**	.35**
Luxembourg	.08		.24**	.41	.59*	.53**
Denmark	.26**		.09**	−.02	−.11	−.27**
Ireland	−.52**	−.40**	−.38**	−.44**	−.15	−.28**
Britain	−.23**	−.80**	−.59**	−.44**	−.30**	−.50**
Greece	−.14*		−.63**	−.55**	−.19**	−.37**
Spain	.13**	.36**	.17**	.17**	−.21**	−.29**
Portugal	−.38**		−.18**	−.03	.28**	.03**
Finland			.06**	.06	−.39**	−.46**
Sweden		−.30**	.46**	.44**	−.15	−.29**
Austria		.65**	.17**	.23**	.14	.12**
Model						
Observations	12,213	9,835	15,565	15,321	15,155	15,622
Chi-square	2,209	2,517	2,161	2,114	3,244	4,238
Probability > Chi-square	.0000	.0000	.000	.000	.000	.000
Pseudo R-square	.07	.10	.15	.13	.19	.24
Cut 1	1.11	.05	−.39	−.27	.23	.80
Cut 2	2.07	1.20	.70	.77	1.37	2.05
Cut 3	3.34	2.48	1.90	2.06	2.58	3.38

Notes: All independent variables (other than nominal variables) are coded in the direction of the hypothesized relationship. Positive effects shown in the table thus support the hypothesized relationship, and negative effects support its inverse. Categorical/nominal variables (age, nationality, ideology, geographical location) are yes (1) / no (0) dummy variables; the directional sign in the table indicates a positive or negative effect on the dependent variable relative to the omitted baseline category. EB = Eurobarometer; ISSP = International Social Survey Program.

— = Baseline (omitted) category.

* p ≤ .05

** p ≤ .01

Table 4.2 Effects on European Identification, Using Member-State and Political-Cultural Variables, Format Three Identity Questions (ordinary least squares analysis, Eurobarometer 41-1, 1994)

Category Hypothesis Measure	Using Member-State Variables			Using National Attribute Variables		
	Parameter	Standard Error	Sig T	Parameter	Standard Error	Sig T
Attributional hypotheses						
Elite hypothesis						
Income	.003	.008	.709	.003	.008	.671
Class	.109	.024	.000	.106	.024	.000
Occupation	.152	.048	.002	.153	.048	.002
Education	.074	.010	.000	.074	.010	.000
Cosmopolitan hypothesis						
Town size	−.003	.028	.927	−.013	.028	.639
Trust other Europeans	.460	.042	.000	.467	.042	.000
Attitude toward immigrants	.260	.050	.000	.234	.051	.000
Generational hypothesis						
Age 15–24		baseline			baseline	
Age 25–34	.049	.069	.480	.052	.070	.453
Age 35–44	.233	.071	.001	.233	.071	.001
Age 45–54	.134	.073	.067	.133	.073	.070
Age 55–64	.180	.076	.018	.185	.076	.015
Age 65–74	.114	.079	.148	.114	.079	.148
Age 75–84	.037	.113	.740	.061	.113	.590
Age 85–94	−.680	.340	.045	−.664	.341	.052
Gender hypothesis						
Gender	−.353	.043	.000	−.352	.043	.000
Attitudinal hypotheses						
Postmaterialism hypothesis						
Postmaterialism		no data			no data	
Ideological hypothesis						
Left		baseline			baseline	
Broad center	−.288	.058	.000	−.305	.059	.000
Right	−.203	.078	.009	−.236	.078	.003
Nontraditionalism hypothesis						
No religious association	.062	.053	.246	.096	.053	.072
Living as married	.017	.107	.878	−.001	.107	.992
Left ideology		see above			see above	
Integration support hypothesis						
Integration support	1.010	.031	.000	1.004	.031	.000
Social-psychological hypotheses						
Efficacy hypothesis						
No measure available		no data			no data	
Instrumentalism hypothesis						
EU good for country	.760	.052	.000	.747	.052	.000
Minority refuge hypothesis						
Religious minority	.207	.107	.054	.192	.107	.073
External factor hypothesis						
US positive role for peace		no data			no data	
Socialization hypothesis						
No measure available		no data			no data	
Leadership hypothesis						
No measure available		no data			no data	
Political-cultural hypotheses						
By member-state						
France	.040	.077	.604			

continues

Table 4.2　Continued

Category Hypothesis Measure	Using Member-State Variables			Using National Attribute Variables		
	Parameter	Standard Error	Sig T	Parameter	Standard Error	Sig T
Belgium	.296	.132	.025			
Netherlands	−.641	.119	.000			
Germany	.430	.071	.000			
Italy	baseline					
Luxembourg	−.430	.567	.448			
Denmark	−.581	.183	.002			
Ireland	−1.229	.225	.000			
Britain	−1.345	.084	.000			
Greece	−.939	.137	.000			
Spain	.144	.086	.094			
Portugal	.271	.140	.053			
By national attribute						
Length of EU membership				−.010	.003	.003
Size (population)				−.013	.002	.000
GDP per capita				4.2 e-05	1.3 e-05	.001
Catholic country				.006	.001	.000
World War II side				.375	.042	.000
Northern country				−.317	.131	.015
Central country				.808	.116	.000
Southern country				baseline		
Constant	.467	.190	.014	.307	.234	.190
Model						
R-square		.25393			.24766	
Adjusted R-square		.25200			.24596	
Standard error		2.37491			2.38449	
Regression DF		33			29	
Residual		12,766			12,770	
F		131.6687			144.9589	
Significance of F		.0000			.0000	

fore intimidating thing for many of its citizens was a common theme articulated by interviewed informants. Education, with particular emphasis on European "civics," was an equally commonly expressed remedy for the breach between the EU and its body politic. Nor is it difficult to imagine the implications of this relationship for European identity, since a polity that appears dark and foreboding to its public is unlikely to attract the latter's affective sentiments. None of the interviewed informants mentioned having been taught "civics" content (a well-proven strategy of identity-building) with respect to Europe in secondary school. But many said they were inspired by their elective educational experiences to adopt a European identity.

There is also good reason to believe that those who possess various cosmopolitan[3] characteristics, like the individuals described in the aforementioned *New York Times* article, may also tend to identify with Europe, and this concept was mentioned repeatedly by informants during field interviews (see below). To measure this relationship, a variety of indicators are available, though most appear in only one or two surveys, and only one appears in most of the twenty extant surveys examined. That latter variable is size of the re-

Table 4.3 Effects of Independent Variables on European Identification (10-point scale, mean = 5.40), Using Member-State and Political-Cultural Variables, Format Three Identity Questions (Eurobarometer 41-1, 1994)

Category Hypothesis Measure (highest)	Using Member-State Variables		Using National Attribute Variables	
	Lowest Value	Highest Value	Lowest Value	Highest Value
Attributional hypotheses				
Elite hypothesis				
Income	not significant		not significant	
Class	−.15	.29	−.14	.28
Occupation	−.13	.18	−.13	.18
Education	−.22	.37	−.22	.37
Cosmopolitan hypothesis				
Town size	not significant		not significant	
Trust other Europeans	−.81	.57	−.82	.58
Attitude toward immigrants (not problematic)	−.09	.17	−.08	.15
Generational hypothesis				
Age 15–24 (baseline)	−.10		−.11	
Age 25–34	not significant		not significant	
Age 35–44	.13		.13	
Age 45–54	not significant		not significant	
Age 55–64	.07		.08	
Age 65–74	not significant		not significant	
Age 75–84	not significant		not significant	
Age 85–94	−.79		−.77	
Gender hypothesis				
Gender (male)	−.17	.18	−.17	.18
Attitudinal hypotheses				
Postmaterialism hypothesis				
Postmaterialism	no data		no data	
Ideological hypothesis				
Left (baseline)	.21		.23	
Broad center	−.07		−.08	
Right	.01		−.01	
Nontraditionalism hypothesis				
No religious association (no religion)	not significant		not significant	
Living as married	not significant		not significant	
Left ideology	see above		see above	
Integration support hypothesis				
Integration support	−2.04	.99	−2.03	.98
Normative hypothesis				
No measure available	no data		no data	
Social-psychological hypotheses				
Efficacy hypothesis				
No measure available	no data		no data	

continues

Table 4.3 Continued

Category *Hypothesis* Measure (highest)	Using Member-State Variables		Using National Attribute Variables	
	Lowest Value	Highest Value	Lowest Value	Highest Value
Instrumentalism hypothesis				
EU good for country (yes)	−.46	.30	−.45	.30
Minority refuge hypothesis				
Religious minority (minority)	−.02	.19	not significant	
Socialization hypothesis				
No measure available	no data		no data	
Leadership hypothesis				
No measure available	no data		no data	
Political-cultural hypotheses				
By member-state				
France	not significant			
Belgium	.46			
Netherlands	−.48			
Germany	.60			
Italy (baseline)	.17			
Luxembourg	not significant			
Denmark	−.42			
Ireland	−1.06			
Britain	−1.18			
Greece	−.77			
Spain	.31			
Portugal	.44			
By national attribute				
Length of EU membership (shortest)			−.09	.25
Size: population (smallest)			−.39	.72
GDP per capita			−.51	.73
Catholic country			−.28	.24
World War II side (Axis power)			−.36	.39
Northern country			−.56	
Central country			.56	
Southern country (baseline)			−.25	
All significant variables	**−6.11**	**4.18**	**−7.12**	**6.53**
Added to mean of 5.40 =	−.72	9.58	−1.72	11.93

Notes: Unless indicated, all highest-value outcomes shown are produced using the highest value of the independent variable. For example, for the "Education" variable, the results listed under the two highest-value columns represent the effect of the highest level of education. Likewise, those figures under the lowest-value outcome columns are produced using the lowest value of the independent variable. Where this is not the case, the independent-variable value corresponding to the highest outcome is in parentheses (e.g., for the "Attitude to immigrants" variable, the coding for those respondents seeing immigrants as not problematic generates the highest European identity value). The effect of categorical variables is shown in centered columns.

spondent's community, a somewhat tenuous operationalization of cosmopolitanism, but one that tends to be quite significant and positively associated with European identity in the majority of surveys (see Tables 4.1A, 4.1B, and 4.2). Two surveys include variables indicating whether respondents live in areas near a national frontier, but the relationship between this variable and European identity is decidedly mixed. Variables measuring frequency of travel, number of languages spoken, interest in what happens in other countries, and trust in other Europeans probably represent the best operationalizations of cosmopolitanism, and are also quite significant in the few instances where they appear. As Table 4.3 shows, moving from the lowest to the highest levels of trust has the capacity to shift the predicted level of European identity nearly one and a half points.

A number of other indicators of cosmopolitanism are found scattered throughout the survey datasets, including those measuring the respondents' feelings toward people of different types, those measuring the degree of movement in the respondents' personal history, and those indicating respondents' attitudes toward other countries as compared to their own. These indicators tell a mixed story, as seen in Tables 4.1A, 4.1B, and 4.2, and it would be difficult to assess this hypothesis on the basis of these relationships alone. However, those indicators that arguably represent the most valid operationalizations of cosmopolitanism—frequency of travel, number of languages spoken, interest and trust in other peoples—do suggest that cosmopolitan attributes and attitudes are associated with European identity. Comparisons between respondents to the Survey of European Identifiers and respondents to the mass surveys are also revealing. In the SEI, 82 percent said they went abroad several times per year or more, and another 12 percent said they traveled at least once per year. In contrast, just over half of the respondents to Eurobarometer 6 said they had not been abroad at all in the preceding five years.[4] And, among the SEI respondents the mean number of languages spoken was 3.45, while for respondents to the 1995 ISSP survey it was 1.22.

Finally, among interviewed informants, the continual exposure to other cultures and languages (for many, starting in their youth) was an experience frequently invoked in explaining their attachment to Europe. Many had studied abroad, an experience that they believed had changed their lives. Said one, mentioning one of the EU's increasingly ubiquitous exchange programs, "ERASMUS *is* European integration, more than anything else." Interestingly, as well, a disproportionate percentage of targeted interview informants came from mixed-nationality marriages, and for these people, a European identity brought to a potentially problematic situation not only a psychological solution, but sometimes a very pragmatic one in addition. One French informant reported (before the accession of Poland in 2004), "My mother is French, my father is Italian, and my girlfriend is German; if these nationalities were Turkish, Polish and French, these relationships would be impossible." And a Portuguese woman who described her European identity as a solution to the mixed nationality of her parents said that, as a result of her unconventional background, "it is quite natural for me to think like a European." Many others noted the increasing frequency of exchanges, the many cross-national relationships that ensue, and the results these are likely to have on current and future generations' identity constructs. Whatever the philosophical merits of integration with respect to achieving peace and cooperation, in a very real sense behavior on the ground—certainly for elites, but increasingly for all—is now bursting the seams of formerly limiting national identities.[5]

Turning next to a third attributional hypothesis, there are excellent reasons to suspect a generational effect on the tendency to possess a European identity. Ronald Inglehart (1977) long ago posited constellations of multiple attitudinal differences between generations, identities included. More recently, Mattei Dogan (1994: 51) arrived at the same conclusion, arguing that young people were, among other things, clearly less nationalistic than older generations; and Paul Howe (1995: 42) also notes a generational difference with respect to national and European identities. Indeed, given the magnitude of changes that have swept across Europe over the past six decades alone, it is almost unimaginable that there would not be profound generational effects with respect to many attitudes, including identities. The grandparents of today's twenty-year-olds were born into a Europe that dominated most of the globe, and that was characterized by rigid borders and powerful national rivalries. Tens of millions of this generation would lose their lives in a devastating final exercise of those rivalries, with all the bitterness attendant to such a conflict remaining for the survivors. But their grandchildren have grown up in a very different Europe, where armed conflict has been replaced by cooperation and integration, where the single market and Schengen Agreement have largely erased the meaning of national boundaries other than as linguistic markers, and where travel and study abroad is vastly more commonplace than it was even one generation prior. According to Alessandra Stanley (1998: A10), in 1998 alone the EU's SOCRATES program (which is not its only exchange program) permitted 200,000 university students to study in another EU country—the equivalent of 5 percent of the EU's entire university population. One is therefore tempted to agree with former British foreign minister Robin Cook's remarks, at the People's Europe Conference on June 7, 1998, that "younger people are warmer toward Europe [than their elders] because it is rare to find one who has not traveled there and does not do so regularly. Europe's ease of travel regulations is building affinities and changing public opinion about Europe."

Moreover, such beliefs manifested themselves repeatedly in interviews conducted in the field. Informants—young and old—described time and again the richness and density of their cross-national experiences, and the generational contrasts along this dimension. According to a very large proportion of interviewed informants, the effects of these changes have been profound. As one—a Liverpool businessman in his late fifties—explained it, because the youth of today are freer of the bitterness of past rivalries, and because they have experienced other people and cultures directly, they are far more able and likely to form their own ideas about those people and cultures, and far more likely to view both in a positive light.

An anecdote from the College of Europe puts this effect in very real terms. According to informants there, dorm-mates from France and Germany in the earliest years (beginning in 1950) could not bring themselves to talk to one another—the College's very mission of unification notwithstanding—so bitter were their feelings about World War II. Today, of course, nearly all such sentiments have disappeared at the College. In discussing age effects on European attitudes, some informants described two generational groups (the World War II generation versus those younger), while others saw the existence of three distinct groups (the World War II generation, the "1968" or baby boom generation, and the "Internet" generation). All agreed, however, that the young were far more attached and open to Europe than their elders.

It comes as something of a surprise, then, when survey data strongly reject this hypothesis. Two fairly clear patterns emerge from the generational data presented in Tables 4.1A, 4.1B, and 4.2. First, age doesn't matter, as indicated by the relative infrequency with which levels of statistical significance allow the groups[6] to be distinguished from one another (though this is somewhat less true for the Format Four surveys of Table 4.1B). But, second, when significant differences are apparent, it is (along with the older cohorts) the *younger* who are actually less likely to possess a European identity. There are certainly plausible explanations for these findings, not least of which would point to rising levels of unemployment, especially among the young, and the possible association of economic hardship with European integration in the popular mind. It may also be that holidays abroad and educational exchanges are impacting the elites only, yet removing the four socioeconomic status variables from the Eurobarometer 41-1 model does not appreciably change the age-cohort parameters.

Input from interviewed informants on this question was recurrent and unequivocally supportive of the hypothesis, yet one might describe the survey data, on the other hand, as equally insistent—especially given the number of datasets examined—in its refutation of the generational explanation. This puzzle was also discussed in Chapter 3, and a possible solution can be further developed in light of this additional empirical evidence. It seems likely that young Europeans *are* more open to Europe, more experienced of it, and more likely to take it (and even to take it for granted) as the best definition of the cultural and political space in which they operate and exist. This may be what informants are referring to when invoking generational divides. But these attitudes and practices do not necessarily equate to identification, nor especially to the emotive qualities normally associated with political identities.

Finally for the attributional hypotheses, just the opposite conundrum is manifest in the relationship between gender and European identification. Here, there was virtually no mention of a relationship by interviewed informants, nor is the variable given a lot of attention in empirical research on European identity or support for integration. Duchesne and Frognier (1995: 212) note a gender-based difference in their bivariate analyses of European identification, but find the effect to be weak other than in Mediterranean countries, while Mathieu Deflem and Fred Pampel (1996: 131) discover a similarly weak relationship in their multivariate analysis of support for integration. In both cases, men are found to be more Europhile in their attitudes than women. In a study devoted entirely to the question of gender differences in attitudes toward European integration, Brent Nelsen and James Guth (2000) also identify a continentwide tendency for men to be more supportive of the project, though both the statistical significance and even the direction of gender differences varies from country to country. Positing a variety of theoretical explanations for this tendency and then testing their ideas empirically, Nelsen and Guth conclude that "distance to integration, women's values, ideology, economic vulnerability and national tradition" (2000: 286) account for about one-fourth of the variation observed on attitudes toward integration.

The data in Tables 4.1A, 4.1B, and 4.2 reaffirm the general findings of these prior studies with great consistency. With only three exceptions (one of which is not statistically significant), the relationship in every survey examined is always strongly significant and always shows higher European identification levels among men. But the effect is not large, as Table 4.3 shows: being male moves one's response about a fifth of a point higher on the 10-point identity scale, while being female has just the opposite effect.

Attitudes

Of the possible attitudinal associations with European identity that might be hypothesized, Ronald Inglehart's notion of postmaterialism (1977) is the most developed. Inglehart argued that a constellation of certain values are particularly prevalent within younger generations. Included among these attitudes—which may be characterized as generally rejecting certain traditional values—are new constructions of political identity. In Europe, this translates into a tendency to embrace both supranational and regional identities, with a corresponding loss of affect toward the nation-state. Tables 4.1A and 4.1B show the supranational identity aspect of Inglehart's hypothesis to be supported, as postmaterialism is very much statistically significant and positively related to European identity in every survey in which it appears. Given that it is an academic theory, informants were understandably silent on the question of postmaterialism during interviews, nor did they have much to say about postmaterialist ideas in lay terms.

However, a comparison of SEI data with data portraying the European general public provides further support for the hypothesis. Among the SEI sample, 7.6 percent were materialists, 50.0 percent were mixed, and 42.4 were postmaterialists, while for all Europeans (as represented by 1991's Eurobarometer 36-0) the figures were 26.7, 58.9, and 14.4, respectively.

It might also be imagined that ideology and European identity are related in some fashion, and Deflem and Pampel (1996: 132) find a slight relationship between rightist ideology and support for integration, while Duchesne and Frognier (1995: 217) generally find no statistically significant relationship between ideology and identity. In any case, there are several ways in which such a relationship might be hypothesized. Painting the spectrum with broad strokes, we might describe the left as having universalistic aspirations tending toward supranationalism on the one hand, while simultaneously leaning away from it because of European integration's association with neoliberal economics. The right, meanwhile, may reject Europe as anathema to its nationalist project, or it could embrace Europe on the same economic grounds on which the left might be expected to reject it. In the end, it was hypothesized for purposes of the present analysis that mistrust on both sides of the ideological spectrum would trump positive perceptions, and that European identity would thus be stronger for those in the ideological center than for those at either the left or the right.

To measure this effect, responses on the surveys' 10-point self-locating ideological scales have been divided into three parts, the left (1–3), the broad center (4–7), and the right (8–10). The results shown in Tables 4.1A, 4.1B, 4.2, and 4.3 paint a rather mixed picture of the relationship between ideology and European identity. In several cases, neither of the remaining categories manifest a statistically significant difference from the baseline. In others, one category is significantly different, while in yet a third set of surveys both remaining categories are significantly different. These data are not easy to interpret, though some tentative conclusions might be offered. First, in most of the cases where the differentiation is significant, being on the right produces a negative effect on identity relative to the baseline category. Leftist ideology, on the other hand, has a split effect on European identity relative to the baseline among the surveys in which it can be significantly differentiated. The broad center, meanwhile, appears to be just that with respect to European identity as well, to the extent that can be determined. Thus, mostly concurring with the hypothesized relationship, European identification seems to have a mixed association with a leftist ideology, but is negatively associated with rightist attitudes, while those in the center fall between. A comparison of the SEI sample's ideological mean of 4.43 with Eurobarometer 41-1's mean of 5.22 offers some further marginal support for this finding. Somewhat similarly, Table 4.3 shows that for Eurobarometer 41-1, at least, those on the left increase their level of European identification by a fifth of a point on the 10-point scale, those in the center decrease theirs by less than a tenth of a point, and those on the right essentially show no change.

A third attitudinal hypothesis, not unlike the previous two, suggests that the rather unconventional attitude of European identification (relative to more traditional identities) may be associated with a larger constellation of nontraditional attitudes. This notion is certainly at the core of Inglehart's postmaterialist construct, and Mattei Dogan (1994: 51) makes a similar argument with regard to a series of attitudes that he finds concomitant with the rejection of nationalism. But Tables 4.1A, 4.1B, and 4.2 provide little evidence to support this hypothesis. For example, those who claim no religious association and those who are living together but not married—the two most ubiquitous indicators across the surveys examined—are not significantly different from others in their degree of identification with Europe. Or, in the few instances where they are different, the relationship is as likely to be opposite what is predicted as not. To the extent that a leftist ideology, discussed above, implies substantial or radical societal change, it may also be considered a measure of nontraditionalism.

A more direct, if rather awkwardly structured, measure is provided by the frequently appearing question regarding attitude toward societal change, which allows respondents to choose between defending the existing order, gradually changing it, or radically upending it.[7] As might be expected, most respondents choose the gradual change category, and in any case the relationship between this measure and European identity is rarely significant. Responses to questions asking whether new things and ideas are generally preferred over old do have a significant relationship with attitudes toward European identity, but the effect seems minor and the measures are infrequent. Finally, a look at two of the World Values Surveys produces a very mixed picture of the relationship between European identification and a series of attitudes toward specific moral issues. These relationships are mostly not significant in the 1980–1984 survey, and then rather sporadically so in the 1990–1993 fielding, with the parameters in any case suggesting little effect. To sum, there is little overall support for the hypothesis linking nontraditionalist attitudes with a tendency to identify as a European.

On its face, there is clear reason to believe that European identification would be positively related to support for the integration project, and Richard Flickenger and colleagues (1997: 13), for instance, find that it is the most potent predictor of their measure of European citizenship. Indeed, it may be tempting to believe that this measure[8] taps the same sentiment as do measures of European identity, but Nico Wilterdink (1993: 126) demonstrates that they are different, with large majorities of Europeans supporting integration, but far fewer emotionally identifying with Europe. Moreover, an analysis of the relationship between the two variables in Eurobarometer 41-1 produces a correlation (r) of .41, indicative of a substantial relationship, but far less than one would expect from roughly synonymous measures.

What is less clear, however, is the causal directionality of the relationship. Are those who support European integration more likely to identify with Europe, as the hypothesis suggests, or do those who identify with Europe therefore tend to support integration? Or are the two concepts not causally related to each other at all, with both perhaps the product of some third factor? While it is difficult to know the answers to these questions, regression analysis in any case demonstrates that support for integration is a powerful predictor of European identity. Across Tables 4.1A, 4.1B, and 4.2, the parameters are large and always highly significant. Moreover, Table 4.3 suggests that this measure has the greatest capacity to influence the respondents' level of European identification, knocking two full points off the identity mean for those least supportive of integration, and adding a full point for those most supportive. Additionally, a comparison of Eurobarometer 41-1 models—with and without the support variable—demonstrates that this factor accounts for about a fourth of the change in European identity explained by the model (which itself accounts for about a fourth of the total change to be explained), dropping the adjusted R-squared from .246 with the variable, to .183 without it.

A final attitudinal hypothesis argues that European identification is a function of a normative belief in the unity of peoples, with particular reference to the idea of replacing conflict with peace and cooperation. Indeed, when asked to explain their attitudes toward European integration, informants interviewed in the field rather frequently invoked these notions. One German interviewee noted, for example, that "the EU has a great deal of potential to pacify and democratize countries on the continent." And nearly a fifth (19.1 percent) of the SEI respondents mentioned war- or peace-related concerns in response to the open-ended question asking them to describe the factors that accounted for their feelings toward Europe. The data in Eurobarometer 27 permit a test of this hypothesis. The variable operationalizing this notion was created from responses to the question: "When you hear about the European Community, what does that bring to your mind?" Those whose response referred to "positive basic values and goals" such as peace, freedom, and understanding among people, or to "positive internal political process" such as cooperation among governments or democratization, were coded "1," those who mentioned both were coded "2," and those who mentioned neither were coded "0." The model indicates a strong and significant relationship between this variable and European identity, even when controlling for other effects, including support for integration.

Social Psychology

Theories of political identification—and especially of its most prominent manifestation, nationalism—are abundant. But as Donald Horowitz notes (1985), many fail to account for the depth of emotive power often associated with such sentiments. Both Horowitz and Richard Koenigsberg (1977: 51–52) are among those who believe that group identities, and their vehemence, are explained by the psychological insecurities of individuals living in an overwhelmingly vast and foreboding world. Attachment to a group enterprise and group destiny thus offers meaning and worth where little may be otherwise available. Michael Hogg and Dominic Abrams (1988: 23) describe a similar phenomenon, making an even more explicit link between self-esteem and imputed group characteristics, and reviewing experimental and empirical evidence for the significance of that link. Theories such as these thus require, by definition, multiple and divisive group identities, since relatively cosmopolitan alternatives—such as the continent-wide European model—offer little of the psychological satisfaction provided by feelings of superiority over immediate neighbors. The construct must therefore be inverted in this case, producing the hypothesis that those low in political efficacy would be unlikely to adopt the comparatively diffuse European identity, while, conversely, those with higher levels of efficacy would be more likely to do so.

Here the evidence is mixed, though more supportive of the hypothesis than not. The most frequently appearing measure is the ubiquitous Eurobarometer question asking: "When you, yourself hold a strong opinion, do you ever find yourself persuading your friends, relatives or fellow workers to share your views? If so, does this happen often, from time to time or rarely?" Though not the best operationalization of the efficacy concept—since one could certainly be highly efficacious and yet reserved (or, for that matter, even friendless!)—the question nevertheless offers some purchase on the relationship between efficacy and European identity. As Tables 4.1A and 4.1B indicate, that relationship is quite consistently positive and significant. And among the SEI respondents, 6.6 percent chose "rarely" in response to this question, 49.3 percent "from time to time," and 44.1 percent "often," in contrast to Eurobarometer 37-0 respondents (who also had a "never" response choice), 18.4 percent of whom said "never," 24.1 percent "rarely," 41.1 percent "from time to time," and 16.4 percent "often." These figures suggest substantially higher levels of efficacy among the sample of European identifiers relative to the general public.

Four other measures provide arguably more valid operationalizations of the efficacy concept: these are the degree to which respondents believe that (1) "people give you the respect which you deserve," (2) "if things are not going well in [your country] people like yourself can help to bring a change for the better," (3) "most people in positions of power try to gain something out of people like you," and (4) respondents have "freedom of choice and control . . . over the way your life turns out." Unfortunately, however, these questions only appear on one or two surveys each, and provide mixed, though more positive than not, support for the hypothesis.

The last efficacy variables in Table 4.1A measure party membership and activism—fairly tenuous operationalizations of efficacy—providing completely mixed evidence concerning the validity of the hypothesis. However, a final piece of evidence offers more support. A comparison of responses to the question "Some people say they sometimes feel that what they think doesn't count very much. Do you yourself ever happen to think that?" shows that only 38.5 percent of the SEI sample answered yes, while 60.0 percent of those queried in Eurobarometer 30 answered affirmatively.

A second social-psychological explanation for European identification is provided by the instrumentalism hypothesis, which argues that identity is driven in part by perceptions of personal and group benefit from membership in the polity. A variety of studies of support for European integration, for example, have found just such a relationship,[9] and the role of instrumentalism has been noted in studies of nationalism as well, such as Linda Colley's analysis of the making of a British identity (1992: 371), and Richard Merritt's discussion of the rise of American nationalism (1966: 59–60). The most frequently applied measure of instrumentalism takes the form of asking the respondent whether his or her country "has on balance benefitted or not from being a member of the European Community." Tables 4.1A, 4.1B, and 4.2 show that the association between this variable and European identification is always in the predicted direction, is highly significant in sixteen of the seventeen survey models developed, and appears to mostly grow in strength over time. Table 4.3 shows that this variable can move identity levels up to three-fourths of a point, ranging from least- to most-perceived national benefit.

Even better measures of instrumentalism probe personal benefits perceived by respondents, but curiously, however, only two are available in the survey data—one asking whether EC/EU membership is good for the respondent personally, and the other asking whether EU membership has had a good or bad effect on his or her job—and both appear rather infrequently. The three manifestations of the former question are all in the predicted direction and all statistically significant, while the single appearance of the latter is directionally as predicted, but not significant.

Other measures provide more of a mixed picture, but again are more supportive of the hypothesis than not. Those who believed that the EC was good for their country's economy, that their region was dependent on other EC countries for its prosperity, and who scored high on a composite scale of advantages and disadvantages of EC membership[10] all tended to possess statistically significant higher levels of European identification. Relationships between European identity and perceptions of the EC's effect on both prices and on underdeveloped areas of the respondent's country were not significant, however. Of those responding to the SEI survey, fully 99.1 percent said that their country had benefited from EU membership either "extensively" or "to some extent," compared to the 58.4 percent (choosing between "benefitted" or "not benefitted" only) from 1994's Eurobarometer 41-1 who said that their country had benefited. Additionally, 93.0 percent of SEI respondents said that they had personally benefited "somewhat" or "extensively" from European integration, compared to the 49.8 percent from the 1973 European Communities Study who said that their country's EC membership was a good thing for them personally, and compared to the 31.0 percent from 2002's Eurobarometer 58-1 who claimed that Europe had provided them with either "more" or "many more" advantages than disadvantages.

Not surprisingly, then, there was much positive sentiment among interviewed informants with respect to both the personal and national benefits of EU membership. "Definitely," "absolutely," and "enormously" were fairly typical initial responses evoked by questions asking whether the informant and his or her country had benefited from EU membership. Said one young Irish informant with regard to Europe's effects on Ireland: "I was in Poland recently and saw the Ireland my parents talked about from the 1950's—conservative, church-dominated, and backwards." Others claimed that Europe has helped to democratize, unify, and modernize Italy; made the Netherlands fifth worldwide in trade; legitimized postwar Germany and allowed its reunification; given postimperial Britain a role in the world and discouraged its inward-looking tendencies; brought modern social values to Portugal; allowed France to maintain influence in the world; consolidated democracy and human rights in Spain; given Denmark leverage to spread its social and environmental values; and generally raised economic standards in rich and poorer member countries alike. Personal benefits that were repeatedly mentioned included freedom to travel,[11] study and work abroad, friends from other countries, cultural enrichment, student exchange programs, and professional opportunity. Said one informant of the benefits Europe provides, "I can't imagine life without it."

A third social-psychological hypothesis is derived from the existence of minority cultures within European national communities. Might members of these minority groups, to the extent that they feel excluded from the dominant culture, adopt a European identity as an inclusive, universalistic alternative? Michael Wintle (1996: 21) has suggested both that there is ample precedent for this sort of behavior at the state level—for example, Catholics in northern Europe building a niche in order to locate themselves within the larger national identity—and that the "Europe of the Regions" idea is reflective of the same dynamic at the continental level, with regional groups turning toward Europe as a means of escaping the politics of hegemonic majorities at the state level. Moreover, the social-psychology literature on identity-building is replete with experimental data demonstrating that little distinction is often necessary in order for strong group identities to emerge, often with highly consequential behaviors directly in tow (Tajfel 1982: 23–24).

For European identification, however, evidence supporting this hypothesis at the individual level is weak. For religious minorities,[12] less than half the models indicate that statistically significant relationships with European identity exist. Similarly, racial identification[13] is only captured in two of the surveys, is only significant in one of them, and in both cases produces coefficients in the opposite direction from that which the hypothesis predicts. However, a comparison of the mean European identification levels of five regions with prominent autonomous identities against the remainder of their respective national samples does offer some support for the hypothesis from the regional perspective. The figures reveal that, in most cases, regional samples are considerably higher in European identity: 6.29 in Lombardy versus 5.81 in the rest of Italy; 4.31 in Scotland versus 3.83 in the rest of Britain (including Wales); 4.28 in Wales versus 3.86 in the rest of Britain (including Scotland); but only 5.27 in northeastern Spain versus 5.73 in the rest of the country.[14]

When asked to define what it means to be European, quite a number of interviewed informants included in their response an allusion that ran something along the lines of "not American," a concept that gives rise to a fourth social-psychological hypothesis for explaining European identity, and one that emanates from a literature describing the identity-building process as rooted in making distinctions between an in-group and the "Other" (compare Said 1979; Colley 1992). Such an external factor driving European identity is perhaps likely to be especially operative today, as Europeans and Americans have grown further apart recently due to disagreements over issues such as global warming, the International Criminal Court, the Anti–Ballistic Missile Treaty, and the US-led invasion of Iraq. The one measure available for examining this relationship (in Eurobarometer 58-1, 2002) is in fact statistically significant, but in the opposite direction of that hypothesized. Thus, those who believe that the United States plays a positive role for peace in the world are more, not less, likely to be European identifiers. The imperfection of this question prompt as an operationalization of the distinction between European and American identities—that is, one might simultaneously hold that the United States is a force for peace in the world while still seeing it as very different from Europe—may explain its failure to move European identities as hypothesized. In any case, this singular bit of evidence nevertheless suggests that whatever else drives the identity, Europeans are not being forged in the United States.

A fifth hypothesized explanation of European identity in the social-psychological category argues that it is the product of socialization processes. A Swedish informant, for example, told the story of his grandfather in Greece, who every year makes a horrible-tasting soup from goat intestines, to remind himself of the hard times during World War II, when there was little else to eat. This left a deep impression on the informant, who adopted many of his attitudes toward Europe from his grandfather. Unfortunately, there are no data from existing surveys to address this issue, though the general and persistent lack of significant differences between age cohorts at least allows for the possibility of generational socialization of attitudes toward Europe.

Both the SEI data and the responses from interview informants offer some insight into the question, however. Table 4.4 presents responses to a series of

Table 4.4　Comparative Levels of Attachment to Europe (Survey of European Identifiers, 1998; percentages of respondents)

		Compared to . . .		
Respondent is . . .	Coworkers	Parents	People from Home Community	Schoolmates	Admired Political Leaders
Much less attached	3.4	7.7	6.4	5.4	5.6
Somewhat less attached	7.8	7.2	6.4	9.3	10.2
About the same	31.2	21.5	17.3	23.0	50.8
Somewhat more attached	34.1	31.6	31.7	37.7	21.8
Much more attached	23.4	32.1	38.1	24.5	11.7
Number of respondents	205	209	202	204	197

Notes: Percentages are of valid responses. Missing data are excluded.

five questions that attempt to determine whether a prima facie case exists for socialization effects at work on European identification tendencies. With the exception of the case concerning political leaders (discussed below), the remaining data suggest that these processes do not generally account for such tendencies. That is, among the European identifiers surveyed, well more than half are more attached to Europe than are their coworkers, parents, people from their home community, and their secondary schoolmates, while another 10–15 percent are actually less attached in each of the comparisons. Only the remaining 17–31 percent are about as attached to Europe as are the comparison groups—the relationship that implies the possibility of socialization processes at work. SEI respondents were also asked to identify the factors that they believed most shaped their level of attachment to Europe, and as many as five responses were coded for each of the 173 people who answered this open-ended question. Of the 356 total responses, 27 (7.6 percent) referenced family background or home culture/socialization, 6 (1.7 percent) made reference to educational programs (excluding exchanges, which are counted separately), 6 to various forms of the media, 1 (less than 1 percent) to peer-group influence, and 1 to political leaders.

To probe the possibility of various socialization relationships, interviewed informants were asked to compare their level of attachment toward Europe to that of various other groups within their social orbit. Some described their attachment to Europe as equal to that of their parents during the time when they (the informants) were growing up, but the vast majority said they felt far closer to Europe than had their parents. Reasons cited included wartime memories, exchange programs and travel experienced by the younger generation only, and greater levels of knowledge about the EU. A fairly typical comment was that Europe literally just "didn't exist" for their parents and was hardly discussed during the informant's childhood. Not surprisingly, informants told the same story of their home communities from the time they were being raised. For most, Europe simply wasn't an issue (and often still isn't), at best. At worst, community members might have harbored hostility from the war, or were fearful and mistrustful of European institutions about which they knew little. Even today, one informant described the difference between his attitudes and those of people in his home community of Stockholm (hardly an unsophisticated hinterland) as being like "night and day," saying, "I feel like a crusader when I go home."

As for their friends in secondary school and at university, there was more of a split in comparative sentiment, but most respondents still described themselves as closer to Europe than their peers. This seemed to be especially the case in secondary school, and less so for university peers, either because the latter crowd was more elite in character, had accumulated more life experience, especially from travel and exchanges, because peer groups became more specialized around interest areas, or perhaps because general feelings toward Europe had evolved over time for all concerned. Finally, most informants reported that they were the same or closer in their European attachments compared to their coworkers or fellow graduate students. Overall, then, the evidence supporting socialization relationships as the mechanism of European identity-building is weak at best. European identifiers appear instead to be a "vanguard" whose sentiments are derived from other sources. Indeed, they would seem more likely to be "crusaders" attempting to socialize others, rather than being socialized themselves.

Finally, it is quite plausible that there exists a Thatcher-, Mitterrand-, or even Delors-effect, such that leadership figures may influence attitudes toward Europe, including identities. Again, existing survey data offer no help here, but the fact that there is only one reference to a leadership figure among the 356 SEI responses to the question about factors influencing attitudes toward Europe suggests very little effect (or at least little effect that is consciously understood by respondents). The 50.8 percent match-up from Table 4.4 is more supportive of the possibility of the hypothesized relationship, but here the reverse scenario is at least as plausible: that is, individuals may select leaders to admire on the basis of shared views, rather than having their views influenced by admired leaders.

In an attempt to see whether responses would heavily favor influential advocates of European integration, SEI respondents were also asked the open-ended question "Can you name one or several political leaders whom you've very much admired in your lifetime?" In fact, a remarkable variety of figures were named; the 185 respondents who answered this question named 142 admired politicians (up to three were coded for each respondent, for a total of 425 mentions), a list that included Enoch Powell and Fidel Castro, as well as both Lyndon Johnson and Barry Goldwater, to name just a few of the more surprising selections. Jacques Delors had the highest number of mentions, with 29 (or 15.7 percent of respondents), clearly an endorsement of a figure closely associated with European integration. Similarly, among those with the highest number of mentions were such other prointegration individuals as Helmut Kohl (17, or 9.2 percent), Robert Schuman (16, or 8.7 percent), François Mitterrand (14, or 7.6 percent), Jean Monnet (12, or 6.5 percent), and Vaclav Havel (11, or 6.0 percent). Also high on the list, however, were individuals with mixed European credentials, such as Winston Churchill (22, or 11.9 percent) and Tony Blair (13, or 7.0 percent); those little associated with any position on Europe, such as Nelson Mandela (21, or 11.4 percent) and Mohandas Gandhi (13, or 7.0 percent); and those clearly thought to be hostile to integration, such as Margaret Thatcher (11, or 6.0 percent).

Interview data paint a similar picture, though there is clearly more emphasis here on figures who have led the fight for deeper integration (Kohl and Mitterrand were mentioned quite frequently, but it should also be noted that many informants responded by saying there were no political figures whom they admired). Most described their attachment to Europe as about the same as what they perceived the admired politician's attachment to be, but only a few gave hints that the latter influenced the former. For example, one (relatively uncommon) remark was, "I was pretty much influenced by Delors [and also Mitterrand] . . . he really influenced my vision of Europe." But another informant explicitly said that leaders had not influenced her attitudes toward Europe (also an uncommon remark). Somewhat more typical was a comment such as, "The politicians I admire are definitely pro-European," or "I would never vote for an anti-Europe politician," but here again the directionality of the effect is highly suspect—who, that is, is influencing whom? In the end, the possibility of a leadership effect remains open, as well as intuitively compelling, but beyond the scope of this analysis to investigate further. It is possible that the tracking of national poll data or perhaps an experimental research design might uncover more evidence regarding the nature and level of such an effect, though this would presumably be trickier for the question of identities than for, say, support for integration, or positions on a policy question. Still, according to one middle-aged British informant, such an effect is potentially profound; he claimed that the effect of a government campaign for continuing UK membership in the EC prior to the 1975 referendum was to invert the two-thirds ratio of public sentiment against into two-thirds in favor, all within the space of just three months.

Political Culture

Finally, there is the effect of political culture. There is every reason—anecdotal as well as scholarly—to believe that attitudes toward Europe vary as one crosses national frontiers. Previous work on this topic has identified such differences

(Inglehart 1977; Hewstone 1986; Duchesne and Frognier 1995), and others have offered explanations for differing national traditions toward Europe (Dogan 1994: 46; Fulbrook 1993: 9; Hewstone 1986: 4–8; Eichenberg and Dalton 1993: 524–525).[15] The data presented in Tables 4.1A, 4.1B, and 4.2 confirm that such differences clearly exist. Those countries that tend to be significantly higher in levels of European identification include France, Italy, Luxembourg, Spain, and Austria. Conversely, significantly lower levels of European identity are found in the Netherlands, Denmark, Ireland, Britain, Greece, and Finland. The remaining cases are more ambiguous, either because of variability in the direction of the effect, or because of a lack of statistically significant differentiation from baseline countries (thus suggesting that these countries are toward the center of the distribution). These are Belgium, Germany, Portugal, and Sweden. Table 4.3 demonstrates that the political-cultural effect on identity can be substantial; Irish or British respondents, for example, will tend to drop more than a point on the 10-point European identity scale (relative to Italians—the baseline category in this model), wholly apart from the effects of any additional attributional or other causal factors on identity.

Nationality clearly affects tendencies to identify with Europe, but it would be preferable if conceptual measures could be substituted for nominal nation-state categories in analyses of political culture. That is, are there cross-national attributes that might account for varying levels of European identity and thus provide more explanatory purchase than simply saying Italians identify with Europe more, and Danes less? Several possibilities—some well established in the literature on attitudes toward Europe—present themselves. For most of these political-cultural measures the evidence is mixed, with relationships to European identity varying across the multiple surveys examined. Nevertheless, certain tendencies appear to arise from the data.

The first of these may be formulated as a sort of "primordialist" hypothesis, which suggests that the longer one's country has been an EU member-state, the deeper the roots of the European project will have sunk into the political culture, and the more likely the respondent will therefore be to identify with Europe. Empirical evidence for this relationship has been uncovered by Ronald Inglehart (1977: 331), Richard Eichenberg and Russell Dalton (1993: 519–520), Bernard Wessels (1995b: 152), Oskar Niedermayer (1995: 59), and Carol Glen (1995: 230–232, 243–247, 252), though Sophie Duchesne and André-Paul Frognier (1995: 201) find no such effect, and Martin Slater (1982: 158–159) finds the opposite relationship. Tables 4.2, 4.5A, and 4.5B do indeed indicate that there is a significant relationship between European identification and length of EU membership. The directionality of the relationship is somewhat mixed, but the preponderance of evidence points to a relationship exactly opposite of that hypothesized, such that respondents in newer member-states are actually more likely to be European identifiers. This finding might be explained in the same way varying levels of support for European integration

Table 4.5A Effects on European Identification, Using Political-Cultural Variables, Format One and Format Two Identity Questions (ordered probit analysis, multiple surveys)

Category / Hypothesis / Measure	Most / Next Most Attached Format								Think Self European Format					
	ECS 1971	ECS 1973	EB6 1976	EB10A 1978	EB12 1979	WVS 1980–1984	WVS 1990–1993	WEVS 1999–2001	EB27 1987	EB30 1988	EB31 1989	EB33 1990	EB36-0 1991	EB37-0 1992
Political-cultural hypotheses														
By national attribute														
Length of EU membership e-02	n/a	1.54**	−1.01	1.43*	.56	−.52	2.96**	.01**	−2.55**	−1.74**	−1.92**	−.70**	−.55**	−.73**
Size (population) e-03	4.06	2.83	17.0**	1.06	2.99	8.34**	−.82	<.01**	−.69	2.18*	−.36	1.88*	−.22	−2.93*
GDP per capita e-05	−.96	−4.15**	1.81	−1.22	−4.58	6.99**	−4.91**	.06	5.43**	5.24**	3.43**	4.09**	1.96**	2.47**
Catholic country (%) e-03	−3.13*	−2.02	6.35	−2.24	−.07	9.16**	−1.85	<.01**	4.88**	6.01**	6.23**	6.64**	3.33**	3.03**
World War II side	.02	.02	.13**	−.09*	−.05	.18**	−.10**	.12**	.03	.01	<.01	−.14**	−.19**	−.16**
Northern country	a	.12	.60*	−.05	.09	.51**	−.31**	−.10*	−.27**	−.14	−.18	−.24**	−.44**	−.41**
Central country	a								.13*	.16**	.29**			
Southern country	a	−.01	.01	.36**	.24**	−.19	.15**	−.24**				.18**	.15**	.19**
Model														
Observations	8,645	12,273	8,655	8,310	8,471	9,730	18,779	17,432	11,233	11,344	11,232	11,421	12,578	6,329
Chi-square	921	1,640	1,079	417	527	696	1,614	934	2,379	2,737	2,734	2,709	2,543	1,495
Probability > Chi-square	.0000	.0000	.0000	.0000	.0000	.0000	.0000	.000	.0000	.0000	.0000	.0000	.0000	.0000
Pseudo R-square	.08	.11	.11	.05	.05	.08	.08	.05	.11	.12	.12	.12	.10	.12
Cut 1	2.69	3.27	4.92	1.96	2.17	4.93	2.13	−.29	3.29	3.65	3.24	4.36	2.56	3.17
Cut 2	3.32	4.05	5.64	2.74	2.96	5.60	2.92	1.69	4.52	4.94	4.48	5.45	3.68	4.33
Cut 3								2.47						

Notes: Values shown represent a portion of the total model only. Remaining values are virtually identical to those shown in Table 4.1A, less the nationality variables. Independent variables (other than nominal variables) are coded from low to high. Positive effects shown in the table thus indicate a positive relationship between the independent and dependent variables, with negative parameters indicating an inverse relationship. Categorical/nominal variables (geographical location) are yes (1) / no (0) dummy variables; the directional sign in the table indicates a positive or negative effect on the dependent variable relative to the omitted baseline category.

— = Baseline (omitted) category.

a. Omitted due to collinearity.

* p ≤ .05

** p ≤ .01

Table 4.5B   Effects on European Identification, Using Political-Cultural Variables, Format Four Identity Questions (ordered probit analysis, multiple surveys)

Category *Hypothesis* Measure	Attachment to Europe Format					
	EB36-0 1991	ISSP 1995	EB51-0 1999	EB54-1 2000	EB56-3 2002	EB58-1 2002
Political-cultural hypotheses						
By national attribute						
Length of EU membership e-02	−.76**	.38**	−.70**	−.01**	< .01*	.01**
Size (population) e-03	1.78*	−12.7**	−<. 01**	−<.01**	< .01	−< .01**
GDP per capita e-05	5.95**	−.43	1.95**	1.53	3.83**	4.68**
Catholic country (%) e-03	−.21	−3.01*	< .01**	3.00**	< .01**	< .01**
World War II side	−.07**	−.05	.20**	.15**	.02	.03**
Northern country	−.16**	−1.20**	−.14**	−.12**	−.27**	−.36**
Central country	—	—	—	—	—	—
Southern country	.45**	.05	−.12**	−.12**	.13**	.10**
Model						
Observations	12,213	9,835	15,565	15,321	15,155	15,622
Chi-square	2,176	2,521	1,530	1,911	3,028	3,987
Probability > Chi-square	.0000	.0000	.000	.000	.000	.000
Pseudo R-square	.07	.10	.14	.12	.18	.23
Cut 1	2.16	−1.07	.22	.20	1.38	2.21
Cut 2	3.11	.07	1.30	1.23	2.51	3.45
Cut 3	4.38	1.35	2.48	2.52	3.71	4.77

Notes: Values shown represent a portion of the total model only. Remaining values are virtually identical to those shown in Table 4.1B, less the nationality variables. Independent variables (other than nominal variables) are coded from low to high. Positive effects shown in the table thus indicate a positive relationship between the independent and dependent variables, with negative parameters indicating an inverse relationship. Categorical/nominal variables (geographical location) are yes (1) / no (0) dummy variables; the directional sign in the table indicates a positive or negative effect on the dependent variable relative to the omitted baseline category.
— = Baseline (omitted) category.
* $p \leq .05$
** $p \leq .01$

sometimes are, namely by arguing that a European identity provides an alternative to national identities where state institutions have somehow been discredited. Such an approach could explain why Spain and Italy produce high levels of identification, though by this logic one might also expect to see Greece and Belgium among the high identifiers. Perhaps a better explanation is that membership in the EU actually alienates Europeans from Europe. If true, this is not exactly good news for would-be identity-builders on the continent.

Europe might also be seen to provide more benefits and an enhanced international profile to smaller member-states than would otherwise be available to them. Keith Middlemas (1995: 622) has identified state size as one of the four main cleavages in Europe, and Mathieu Deflem and Fred Pampel (1996: 123) argue that smaller states will be more likely to support European integration because of the enhanced leverage and stature it provides them. It is thus hypothesized that respondents from small (population) states would also be more likely to identify with Europe. However, Tables 4.2, 4.5A, and 4.5B reveal that the relationship is not statistically significant about half the time, and is negative nearly as often as it is positive in the remaining models. The hypothesis therefore is not supported.

Societal wealth provides a third potential cross-national explanation for variance in European identity. Economic condition is also one of Middlemas's defining European cleavages (1995: 621), and Eichenberg and Dalton (1993: 521–522) find that it is influential in determining levels of support for European integration. For Matthew Gabel (1998), the relationship is more complex. He finds a strong relationship between economic interests and support for integration, though—oddly—such support is positively related to perceptions of improved personal and national economic conditions, yet negatively related to actual economic improvements. In any case, Tables 4.2, 4.5A, and 4.5B generally confirm the hypothesized relationship, at least in a comparative sense, that links actual national economic standing to European identification tendencies. Per capita gross domestic product relates positively and significantly to identity in most of the surveys examined, and Table 4.3 shows that the effect of national wealth from its lowest to highest levels can move European identity more than a point on the 10-point scale.

Associations between Catholicism and the European integration project have often been remarked upon, and there are reasons to believe that Europe's universalistic appeal may resonate better in those countries dominated by a Catholic social and political culture. Both Haller (1994: 245–246) and Nelsen and Guth (2003), for example, suggest that EU institutions—launched by a group of Catholic founding fathers—have been strongly influenced by Catholic social thinking, and that Catholics tend to be more pro-Europe, while Protestants are wary of its centralizing tendencies. The data from Tables 4.2, 4.5A, and 4.5B generally support this hypothesis, though here the relationship appears to be a function either of the dependent-variable question format or of the period during which respondents were surveyed.[16] When the Format Two and Format Four dependent-variable questions were asked, the relationship to the national percentage of population that is Catholic was quite consistently positive and strongly significant. For models employing Format One, however, the relationship was far more mixed (only one instance of Format Three exists).

More than half a century has now passed since the final chapters of World War II were written, and yet its repercussions are still clearly manifest in discussions with even young Europeans, and in understanding the impetus behind European integration projects as recent as monetary union. Particularly given the delegitimization of nationalist sentiments within the countries that formed the Axis alliance, it would be logical to surmise that levels of European identification would be higher in those countries. However, Tables 4.2, 4.5A, and 4.5B do not provide much support for this hypothesis. The relationship is not statistically significant in many of the models, and the directionality of the parameter in the remainder is almost evenly mixed. This is perhaps because the categories for this variable include a substantial mix of sentiment toward Europe: both France and Britain are among the Allies, for example, with Spain and Ireland both neutral, and Germany, Italy, and Austria forming the Axis category. The World War II–side variable cannot account for these national differences in identification with Europe.

Finally, Europeans frequently refer to a geographical division of the continent that is at once economic, cultural, and historical in character. This north-south division constitutes the third of four main cleavages within Europe according to Middlemas (1995: 618), and is also discussed at some length by García (1993). While differentiating attitudes among Europeans along the lines of geographical divisions is somewhat dissatisfying in much the same way that purely categorical national differentiation is, such distinctions may nevertheless point to broad cultural (but as yet otherwise undefined) tendencies of interest. That is, to the extent that there are subregional differences in European political culture that are autonomous from other variables such as religion or wealth, identifying these effects at least initiates a process of inquiry that may ultimately lead to greater understanding of the identity puzzle. For purposes of this analysis, Europe was divided into three geographical groups: north (Britain, Ireland, Belgium, Netherlands, Denmark, and Sweden), central (France, Germany, and Luxembourg), and south (Italy, Spain, Portugal, Austria, and Greece). Results, shown in Tables 4.2, 4.5A, and 4.5B, are not entirely consistent, but nevertheless do substantially point to a north-to-south gradient of increasing European identity, even while controlling for all the other indicators built into the model.

Conclusion

The foregoing analysis has shown that there are indeed European identifiers in Europe, and that we can ascribe certain characteristics to those who tend to possess such an identity. In very general terms, it is evident that the categories most efficacious in explaining European identity are those containing attributional and attitudinal hypotheses, within each of which the large majority of hypotheses are supported. Some of the social-psychological and political-cultural hypotheses also work, but several others within these categories do not. Thus, nationality, political efficacy, and instrumentalism are clearly factors in explaining identification with Europe, but the bulk of the purchase on this question derives from attitudes (especially toward all things European), and particularly from relatively fixed characteristics like socioeconomic status, cosmopolitanism, and gender.

Specifically, European identifiers may be said, with relatively high levels of confidence, to be overrepresented among elites (as measured by class and education, and to a lesser extent by occupation and income), the more cosmopolitan, men, postmaterialists, centrists and leftists, those who perceive instrumental benefits accruing from EU membership, those who possess a normative belief in the idea of European integration, and those from richer, more Catholic, and southern member countries (notwithstanding certain contradictions inherent in these categories). With somewhat less assurance, we may also say that such European identifiers are high in political efficacy, and are members of a religious and/or regional minority in a country that is also a relatively recent member of the EU. Conversely, the respondent's age and degree of nontraditionalist attitudes do not affect levels of European identity, nor does the size of his or her country or its historical legacy from World War II. There is also little evidence that European identifiers tend to be the products of socialization processes or leadership effects, though the latter remains a theoretical possibility.

As noted at the beginning of this chapter, it is possible to put a human face on these findings by applying predicted probabilities equations to Eurobarometer 41-1—the outcomes of which are shown in Table 4.3—and then modeling composite Europeans possessing combinations of the various explanatory characteristics.[17] "Jean-Paul," for example, is an upper-class, well-educated, left-leaning French government official (France is geographically central,[18] wealthy, Catholic, and—contrary to this ideal type—an original EU member). He is cosmopolitan in character and belief, and both supports European integration and believes it is good for his country. The predicted probabilities calculations suggest that were he to respond to the European identity question posed in Eurobarometer 41-1, he might well place himself at about 9 (9.30, to be mathematically precise) on the 10-point scale.

"Mary," on the other hand, is an Irish shop clerk (Ireland being a poorer—formerly, at least—northern country of middling length of EU membership and—again contrary to this ideal type—predominately Catholic) who possesses little formal education or cosmopolitan background or attitude. She is conservative and she neither prefers EU involvement over traditional Irish neutrality nor sees EU membership as beneficial to her country. Her predicted response to Eurobarometer 41-1's identity question would be about a 1 (0.85, per the calculation).

Finally, somewhere in-between is "Eef," a middle-class saleswoman of moderate income and educational background. She is a Protestant living in predominately Catholic Belgium (a northern country of moderately high national wealth, and an original EU member), whose ideological views are center-right, and whose attitudes toward Europe are fairly moderate. Given these characteristics, she would be predicted to select 6 (6.08, per the calculation) on the European identity scale, not far from the real-world mean of 5.40 for the survey sample.

These illustrations are obviously fictional composites. However, they demonstrate powerfully the significant degree of explanatory purchase that is collectively provided by the variables introduced in this chapter. On a 10-point scale of European identification, archetypal combinations of values for these variables can drive the predicted response from one end of the scale (or even a bit beyond, since .85 is less than 1, the lowest choice actually available to respondents), nearly all the way to the other (9.30).

Notes

1. This follows W. Phillips Shively's strategy of "enriching measurement" (1974: 71–76) in the modeling of social phenomena by substituting hypothesized underlying conceptual dimensions for nominal designations.

2. Table 4.1A presents parameter and statistical significance data from all dependent-variable Format One and Format Two extant surveys, using national dummy variables to represent differences in political culture. Table 4.1B does the same for the Format Four surveys. The (sometimes constructed) dependent variables from each of these surveys are of an ordinal type, and the ordered probit regression procedure is therefore employed to analyze the data. For Tables 4.5A and 4.5B, the same models have been run, respectively, but with cross-national attributes substituted for the national dummy variables. In these tables, only the substituted variables (from the political-cultural category) are reported, since neither the parameter values nor the statistical significance of the other variables remaining in the models changed appreciably from what is reported in Tables 4.1A and 4.1B. Table 4.2 presents the results of an ordinary least squares regression analysis of Eurobarometer 41-1, the only dataset with an interval-level measure of European identity (Format Three). Finally, parameter values and variable means from Eurobarometer 41-1 were used to generate predicted probabilities using the lowest and highest values of each statistically significant independent variable. The results of these calculations, which indicate each independent variable's range of possible impact on the dependent variable, measured in terms of movement on the latter's 1–10 scale, are presented in Table 4.3.

For all tables, variables have been (re)coded so that positive parameter values indicate agreement with the hypothesized relationship, with the exception of dummy variables (e.g., for country, age group, gender), which have not been coded according to predicted outcome. For the various related dummy-variable series (country, age group, ideology, and geographical location), model variations were run with each variable in each of the series as the omitted baseline category. Based on these tests, the configuration that yielded the most information was selected for reporting in the tables (i.e., the baseline choice that produced the greatest balance between positive and negative parameters for other variables in the series, and the greatest number of statistically significant differences between the baseline and other variables in the series).

3. Cosmopolitanism can be an attitude as well as an attribute, and the indicators employed to operationalize it in this book's analyses reflect both aspects of the concept. Nevertheless, for convenience, the entire discussion of this notion is presented under the single attributional hypothesis.

4. Admittedly, the data from Eurobarometer 6 are three decades old.

5. Moreover, from a normative perspective, this may be producing precisely the consequences intended by such exchange programs. One informant commented, "Once you have friends in another country, you are really unwilling to start a fight with them."

6. The continuous age variables were recoded into essentially nominal-level age-group dummy variables because of expectation that the relationship between age and identity might not be linear.

7. Question text: "On this card are three basic kinds of attitudes towards the society we live in. Please choose the one which best describes your own opinion: 1. The entire way our society is organised must be radically changed by revolutionary action; 2. Our society must be gradually improved by reforms; 3. Our present society must be strongly defended against all subversive forces."

8. "In general, are you for or against efforts being made to unify Western Europe? Are you . . . 1. For—very much; 2. For—to some extent; 3. Against—to some extent; 4. Against—very much?"

9. For example, see Gabel and Whitten 1997; Gärtner 1997; Smith and Wanke 1993; Gabel and Palmer 1995. William Bloom (1990: 51) also argues the theoretical case for the centrality of instrumentalism to identity. And the aforementioned *New York Times* article on the new European identifiers describes how Europe's freedom of movement allows a highly valued "cherry-picking" approach to career and other goals, facilitating possibilities that would otherwise be precluded to these individuals. On the other hand, *The Economist* (1995b: 46) notes the ironic fact that respondents from the very member-states that most benefit from EU membership are among the least-European in attitude, according to its review of survey data.

10. This scale represents the mean of certain responses to the open-ended question, "When you hear about the European Community, what does that bring to your mind?" The composite variable includes mentions of positive agricultural effects, positive effects in other, nonagricultural areas, positive and negative effects for the respondent's country, and miscellaneous advantages and disadvantages.

11. A British informant said, for example, "It is as easy, if not more, to go from London to Brussels as to Scotland."

12. This variable was coded "0" if the respondent was member of the dominant religious confession of his or her country, and "1" if a member of another faith. Those who chose "none" for their religious association were excluded, as were respondents from Germany and the Netherlands, where there is no dominant confession. Predominantly Catholic countries are Austria, Belgium, France, Ireland, Italy, Luxembourg, Portugal, and Spain. Protestant-dominated countries are Britain, Denmark, and Sweden. Greece is predominantly Orthodox.

13. Non-Caucasians were coded as minorities.

14. Figures are from Eurobarometer 41-1. Corsica was also checked, but had no respondents in this survey.

15. See also Kaase and Newton 1995: 117, however, for the conclusion that national variances are idiosyncratic and cannot be simply explained.

16. Given the way question formats were deployed across the various surveys examined, it is unfortunately not possible the disaggregate the two possible effects.

17. Since Eurobarometer 41-1 is anomalous in some regards, mean values have been used for the following variables: country size, income, and town size.

18. In Eurobarometer 41-1, central countries are higher in European identity than are southern countries.

5

What Does It Mean to Be "European"? The Nature and Content of European Identity

Europe is something that rings a bell in your mind, but not in your heart. It doesn't have a spirit.

—Interviewed European identifier

IDENTITIES ARE NOTORIOUSLY DIFFICULT to measure and to understand substantively. Just what does it mean to be—or, more accurately, to feel—French? What distinguishes a sense of being Austrian from being German, when the language and much of the culture and history are shared? Are national identities qualitatively different conceptual beasts than regional or supranational identities? And, perhaps most difficult of all, does specifying the substantive content of an identity (say, love of mountains and music) actually get one very far toward understanding its dynamism and emotional content? To cite a recently prominent example, is it possible to believe that a battle fought by Serbs *600 years ago* (and one they lost, at that) on the Field of Blackbirds provided sufficient content to animate Serbian sentiment and behavior in the Balkan wars of the 1990s?

These and related questions highlight the obstacles endemic to the study of political identities. These impediments simultaneously suggest limitations on what may be discernible with respect to such phenomena, as well as the healthy caution that should accompany any findings developed even within those boundaries. Notwithstanding such obstacles, however, the understanding of a given political identity is not complete by virtue of measuring its extent and explaining its variance, the topics of the prior two chapters. One must minimally also explore both the content and the depth of the identity in question. The latter issue is the subject of the next chapter. This chapter focuses on the substantive content of a European identity, with particular attention to its meaning among those who feel its call most acutely.

Fortunately, there are some empirical resources available for purposes of addressing this topic, though they are limited in scope. The discussion in this chapter is built around evidence derived from five Eurobarometer surveys—numbers 27 (1987), 33 (1990), 38-0 (1992), 50-0 (1998), and 52-0 (1999)—plus the 1990–1993 World Values Survey; the Survey of European Identifiers (SEI), fielded in 1998 in support of this project; and interviews of European identifiers and elites conducted in 1998, 2002, and 2004. This multisource, multimethodological approach produces some broad outlines of the content and *meaning* of European political identity, a question that has been heretofore little addressed in the literature, and perhaps never empirically.

Rather than simply expressing findings in the form of univariate frequencies (e.g., the percentage defining European identity in terms of culture, or the percentage defining it as a commitment to democracy), the identity content variables have, where appropriate, been arrayed against another variable in bivariate cross-tabulations that provide more detailed information.[1] Any number of demographic or other variables might have been selected for these purposes in order to determine the extent to which European identity content is affected by the respondent's religion, gender, ideology, and the like. In order to keep the analysis manageable, however, the measures of identity content presented in this chapter are arrayed only against the two most prominent variables of those that might possibly be examined: nationality and (where available) measures of European identity level. These cross-tabulations thus not only indicate the extent to which European identity is held to entail one or another meaning, but also the degree to which such interpretations vary across national boundaries, or between strong identifiers, weak identifiers, and nonidentifiers. Such variances are expressed in the individual percentage figures shown in each cell of each table presented here, and the overall relationship is also given as a Cramer's-V standardized measure of association between the two variables.[2]

Before turning to the content and meaning of European identity, it is worth asking whether there is such a thing, at least in the minds of the potential identifiers themselves. That is, do Europeans themselves believe that there exists a singular, unified, European identity, apart from any particular meaning they might then assign to that identity were it conceivable for them? Fortunately, the question can be addressed by means of survey data collected in 1998 and 1999. These iterations of the Eurobarometer survey (50-0 and 52-0, respectively) included a prompt that asked respondents, "Do you completely agree, slightly agree, slightly disagree or disagree completely with the following statement? [show card with scale] There is a European cultural identity shared by all Europeans." One can certainly quibble with the concept of whether a cultural identity is the same thing as a political identity. And, further, assuming the analyst interprets these to be conceptually distinct, there is the second-order matter of whether respondents also do so when presented with this prompt.

But, these caveats noted, the question responses probably provide a reasonable approximation by which to judge the extent to which Europeans perceive the existence of a unifying identity. The data in Table 5.1 demonstrate

Table 5.1 Is There a Shared European Cultural Identity? (by country, percentages of respondents)

	Eurobarometers 50-0, 1998					Eurobarometers 52-0, 1999				
	Disagree Completely	Disagree Slightly	Slightly Agree	Completely Agree	Percentage of Mean Agreeing	Disagree Completely	Disagree Slightly	Slightly Agree	Completely Agree	Percentage of Mean Agreeing
France	22.7	34.6	34.9	7.8	97.5	27.5	34.5	30.5	7.5	86.8
Belgium	25.3	30.1	37.3	7.2	101.6	24.1	35.7	30.6	9.7	92.0
Netherlands	38.3	22.8	34.1	4.8	88.8	36.5	25.5	34.0	4.0	86.8
Germany	16.3	33.7	39.8	10.2	114.2	19.1	30.2	41.1	9.6	115.8
Italy	18.5	33.6	38.4	9.5	109.4	18.1	34.3	40.4	7.2	108.7
Luxembourg	23.5	29.4	35.3	11.8	107.5	25.0	31.3	31.3	12.5	100.0
Denmark	32.9	26.4	34.3	6.5	93.2	34.6	27.5	31.3	6.6	86.5
Ireland	22.6	21.8	46.0	9.7	127.2	26.0	25.2	40.2	8.7	111.6
Britain	42.5	24.8	26.9	5.7	74.4	42.4	23.4	28.1	6.2	78.3
Greece	24.7	21.3	41.0	12.9	123.1	21.2	24.3	36.7	17.8	124.4
Spain	18.9	41.0	35.3	4.8	91.6	18.6	37.4	39.0	5.0	100.5
Portugal	16.1	32.6	45.0	6.4	117.4	12.2	32.4	51.1	4.3	126.5
Finland	30.7	32.2	31.2	5.9	84.7	37.1	30.7	28.3	3.9	73.5
Sweden	42.3	20.9	31.9	4.9	84.0	39.6	16.8	33.2	10.4	99.5
Austria	20.3	27.9	36.6	15.2	118.3	26.0	26.0	34.4	13.5	109.4
All countries	24.6	31.6	35.8	8.0	100.0	25.6	30.6	36.0	7.8	100.0
Number of respondents	13,890					13,796				
Cramer's V	.14					.14				

Notes: Percentages are of valid cases only ("no answer" and "don't know" excluded). Datasets weighted by country population, and include respondents from EC/EU member-states only.

that the answer to this question is quite mixed, with about a quarter of all respondents (to both surveys—the data are rather consistent from one to the other, as would be expected for surveys from back-to-back years) completely disagreeing with this notion, roughly a third each disagreeing slightly and slightly agreeing, and about 8 percent completely agreeing. In other words, though there is a broad distribution of sentiment, it is worth noting that the samples are almost evenly split overall between those who believe in the idea of a singular European identity and those who don't, but with the preponderance of the sample leaning against. A slightly greater percentage of respondents disagree than agree with the proposition overall, and three times as many completely disagree compared to those who completely agree.

The table also demonstrates some degree of response variance associated along national lines, as evidenced first by the moderate Cramer's V of .14 for both surveys, and second by the "Percent of Mean Agreeing" column, which gives the combined percentage of national respondents either slightly or completely agreeing, as a percentage of the EU-wide total who slightly or completely agree. Some of the usual suspects appear here, with the Netherlands and Britain falling considerably below the total sample, and Italy and Austria placing above it. On the other hand, there are some anomalies from the general pattern as well, especially with respect to the extent to which both Irish and Greek respondents seem to agree with this idea, perhaps in part because they champion Catholic and Hellenic visions of that shared identity, respectively. In any case, the evidence available suggests that even the idea of a unified European identity—let alone its content—is far from universally accepted.

Turning next to the content of any such identity, Table 5.2 presents a first look, based on those surveyed in Eurobarometer 27. Respondents were given the following prompt:

There are different ways of feeling European. Among the following [show list], which ones come close, as far as you are concerned, to the fact of being European? [Several responses possible.] And still looking at this list, which one appears to you the most important? [Only one response.]

1. Putting past rivalries behind us and living in peace with the people of neighboring countries;
2. Belonging to similar cultural traditions and sharing more or less the same way of life and thought;
3. Having in common the same basic religious and philosophic values;
4. Being involved in a great adventure: the formation of a United States of Europe;
5. The ability to travel without difficulties or too many regulations at least within Western Europe;
6. It is only the expression of a geographical fact: I live in Europe and that's all;
7. Other;
8. None of these things.

Table 5.2 Content of European Identity, by Nationality (Eurobarometer 27, 1987)

Percentage Choosing (multiple choices permitted) (first row) / Percentage Choosing as Most Important (second row)

	France	Belgium	Netherlands	Germany	Italy	Luxembourg	Denmark	Ireland	UK	Greece	Spain	Portugal	EU	Cramer's V
End rivalries/Peace	62.8	36.3	34.1	58.0	56.4	70.0	54.8	45.8	42.9	55.4	42.2	47.0	51.7	.18***
	45.9	25.7	35.3	51.4	32.0	62.2	38.3	35.6	43.5	42.1	35.5	35.8	41.4	.12***a
Shared cultural traditions	25.3	19.0	14.6	24.4	28.3	18.9	34.4	26.4	17.2	16.4	23.8	26.6	23.3	.11***
	9.9	8.8	8.7	6.8	14.4	6.9	15.4	11.1	7.5	5.7	16.3	15.8	10.3	
Religious philosophic values	8.5	6.0	5.5	13.5	13.4	11.5	11.1	13.7	7.1	11.4	10.2	15.5	10.5	.10***
	1.3	4.7	3.7	3.7	4.6	1.8	2.1	4.4	2.0	4.1	5.8	7.0	3.4	
Adventure of European integration	32.5	28.9	14.9	17.0	34.0	20.9	15.5	16.8	7.6	22.1	16.6	17.8	21.3	.24***
	17.3	22.3	10.6	5.2	18.7	8.0	8.3	8.5	3.9	16.9	11.9	12.7	11.6	
Freedom of travel	43.6	35.7	41.5	53.4	45.8	41.8	49.7	47.6	39.5	31.5	27.0	34.4	42.5	.16***
	16.4	28.5	23.5	22.8	20.5	13.4	23.5	28.1	19.5	16.2	18.3	21.8	20.2	
Geographical fact only	20.1	15.1	22.2	23.5	14.2	15.3	14.5	21.0	28.5	14.7	13.1	9.2	19.9	.14***
	6.7	7.2	8.3	6.8	6.2	2.6	7.2	6.5	10.5	7.8	8.6	4.9	7.6	
Other than these	.9	.7	1.3	2.1	0	1.1	1.4	.6	1.3	0	.5	1.3	1.0	.07***
	.4	.7	1.5	.3	0	0	.5	.7	.2	0	.5	1.2	.4	
None of these	2.3	1.6	6.6	2.1	3.4	4.9	3.3	7.1	7.5	5.9	1.8	.6	3.6	.12***
	2.1	2.2	8.4	2.9	3.7	5.1	4.7	5.1	12.9	7.2	3.1	.9	5.1	
Number of respondents														10,497

Notes: a. This Cramer's-V value applies to all second-row ("most important") entries in this table.
*** p ≤ .001

For each of these responses, the table presents two rows, with the first showing the percentages who chose the response at all (that is, as one of their as-many-as-three possible selections), and the second showing the percentages who chose the response as their "most important." The second-to-last column, marked "EU," gives the overall response percentages from the survey, while the preceding columns break down the percentages country. The last column provides the Cramer's-V measure of association for each cross-tabulation, thus indicating—in this case—the degree to which there are national differences in interpretations of European identity content.

One initial interpretation of the data in this table is that they are strongly suggestive of a rather instrumental approach to the meaning of Europe for Europeans. This is all the more remarkable because the question prompt asked about the meaning of "being European," not about the integration process or the European polity (though that distinction may not have been made by many or most respondents). In any case, being European would appear to be mostly about freedom of travel, and especially peace, for those responding to this question. More than half picked peace as one of their choices, and more than 40 percent called it the most important aspect of being European. On the other hand, the qualitative, noninstrumental aspects of European identity that might be supposed to be prominent are not. For example, little support is given for the notion of shared religious and philosophical values being at the core of Europeaness. Shared culture and way of life does attract more agreement, but only at approximately the same levels as what might be described as the minimalist and maximalist definitions of being European, respectively: only a geographical fact, and an adventure in integration. This latter choice also provides the most variance in response across national frontiers (V = .24), just as might be expected, more or less mirroring tendencies portrayed in Chapter 4. Only 7.6 percent of British respondents think that being European means taking part in the adventure of integration, for example, whereas a third (or nearly five times the British level) of Italians and the French do so.

Table 5.3 presents the same identity-meaning data as shown in Table 5.2,[3] but this time arrayed against the variable in the dataset that measures the level of European identification. This cross-tabulation allows us to see that levels of identification with Europe do indeed affect interpretations of the meaning of being European, much as might be expected. The first indicator of this effect is the quite substantial .20 Cramer's-V value, which applies to all second-row ("most important" descriptor) entries in the table. Since respondents could choose only one item of the many presented in response to this question, the second-row percentages are more easily comparable than the first-row entries, for which multiple simultaneous choices could be selected. The peace characteristic is rather impervious to levels of European identification, with roughly 40 percent of those who never identify with Europe, and about the same proportion of those who sometimes and often do so, all saying that this is the most

Table 5.3   Content of European Identity, by European Identity Level (Eurobarometer 27, 1987)

| | Percentage Choosing (multiple choices permitted) (first row) / Percentage Choosing as the Most Important (second row) | | | | |
| | Thinks of Self as European | | | | |
	Never	Sometimes	Often	EU	Cramer's V
End rivalries/Peace	43.7	60.6	60.8	52.1	.17***
	39.0	44.4	41.1	41.3	.20***a
Shared cultural traditions	15.4	30.8	34.6	23.6	.20***
	7.5	12.5	13.8	10.3	
Religious philosophic	7.1	13.4	15.5	10.5	.11***
values	3.1	3.6	3.8	3.4	
Adventure of European	12.1	28.3	39.4	21.7	.25***
integration	7.2	14.7	18.9	11.7	
Freedom of travel	37.4	50.9	42.7	42.9	.12***
	23.3	18.5	14.9	20.3	
Geographical fact only	25.3	14.9	14.3	20.1	.13***
	10.2	4.9	5.5	7.6	
Other than these	.4	1.4	2.1	1.0	.06***
	.2	.4	.9	.4	
None of these	6.7	.5	.6	3.7	.16***
	9.5	1.0	1.2	5.1	
Number of respondents					10,241

Notes: a. This Cramer's-V value applies to all second-row ("most important") entries in this table.

*** $p \le .001$

important aspect of being European. The same is true for the few respondents who see shared religious or philosophical values as most important.

For those choosing the remaining categories, however, the relationship between the two variables is far more articulated. The proportion of those picking shared cultural traditions or the adventure of European integration rises with the level of European identification. At the same time, the proportion of those selecting freedom of travel, geographical fact only, or none of the offered choices is inversely related to levels of European identity. The latter two relationships are probably indicative of a general lack of European identity for those choosing these responses. But the remaining relationships suggest an interesting pattern. Overall, it appears that peace is the universally most popular meaning attributed to being European, and shared religious and philosophical values is the universally least popular, but that beyond agreement on these, definitional meanings of the identity are affected by degree of identification, such that the instrumentalism effect alluded to above means that non- and sometime-identifiers mention freedom of travel more often than do frequent identifiers. Among identifiers, on the other hand, the less material concerns of culture and politics become more prominent. With some exceptions, the first-row percentages follow the same pattern. Since these figures are reflective of up to three choices from the small handful of options, they are less readily interpretable. Nevertheless, they point in the same general direction as the second-row ("most important") figures.

Tables 5.4 and 5.5 provide another look at this same question, from the same data source, but utilizing a different question prompt and a more narrow response structure.

> What things, in your opinion, bring the countries of the European Community together most? Could you tell me by choosing from this list those which appear to be the most important ones? [Show list, several responses possible.]
>
> 1. The economic links which they have developed with one another;
> 2. The efforts these countries make for peace in the world;
> 3. The wish to form a counter-balance faced with domination by the superpowers;
> 4. The democratic and humanitarian values they share;
> 5. The need to unite their efforts in order to master the technologies of the future;
> 6. Their culture and their ways of life;
> 7. The need to defend themselves against outside threats;
> 8. Other.

The responses to this question are cross-tabulated with nationality and European identity level, as was the previous survey question. In this case, however, respondents were asked only to pick multiple responses (up to three), not also to specify the single most important of the options; hence only one row of data is presented for each response choice on these two tables.

As in the previous case, the data in Table 5.4 suggest a remarkably instrumental or utilitarian attitude toward the meaning of being European.[4] The big-ticket items are economic links and peace efforts—peace and prosperity—each mentioned by about 41 percent of respondents. Next come superpower counterbalance, defense against outside threats, and the need to master technologies of the future. Even this seemingly oblique latter choice is selected considerably more often than the two least-popular items on the list: common democratic/humanitarian values, and especially shared culture. These latter two items also manifest the least degree of differentiation across national boundaries, as evidenced by Cramer's-V scores of .06 for each. That is, Europeans see values and culture as the least-significant aspects uniting the Community, and they do so with relative unanimity. Indeed, though there is more variance on the other selections, any sort of pattern of responses by nationality is difficult to discern from these data. A final comment on Table 5.4 requires noting its historical timing. This survey was conducted in 1987, both before the West had come to trust Soviet leader Mikhail Gorbachev (and certainly before the conclusion of the Cold War), and before European integration

Table 5.4 Factors Linking EC Countries Together, by Nationality (Eurobarometer 27, 1987)

	France	Belgium	Netherlands	Germany	Italy	Luxembourg	Denmark	Ireland	UK	Greece	Spain	Portugal	EU	Cramer's V
	Percentage Choosing (multiple choices permitted)													
Economic links	46.9	33.2	52.1	42.6	42.2	54.3	39.2	45.2	35.1	45.2	32.5	38.9	40.9	.11***
Peace efforts	40.4	22.7	29.6	50.7	43.9	53.0	36.2	50.5	40.9	43.6	30.1	31.5	40.9	.15***
Counterbalance to superpowers	42.9	24.8	35.5	26.0	30.0	35.6	29.1	13.4	21.9	30.2	19.7	18.0	28.3	.17***
Democratic and humanitarian values	19.4	11.2	19.8	23.3	20.2	30.4	19.5	19.7	20.6	18.0	19.5	17.2	20.2	.06***
Need to master technology	35.8	18.5	22.9	24.2	29.4	20.6	15.9	27.9	25.7	21.6	22.8	24.3	26.8	.11***
Culture and ways of life	12.7	9.5	9.4	15.2	13.4	9.0	13.0	20.9	11.5	8.5	12.2	10.6	12.7	.06***
Defend against outside threats	34.5	19.1	21.6	22.4	18.5	39.7	18.9	35.8	36.2	29.1	14.0	16.6	25.2	.19***
Other	.4	.1	.3	1.1	0	.4	1.1	1.1	1.0	.2	.9	.2	.6	.06***
Number of respondents														11,651

Note: *** p ≤ .001

Table 5.5   Factors Linking EC Countries Together, by European Identity Level (Eurobarometer 27, 1987)

| | Percentage Choosing (multiple choices permitted) | | | | |
| | Thinks of Self as European | | | | |
	Never	Sometimes	Often	EU	Cramer's V
Economic links	35.2	47.4	47.9	41.6	.13***
Peace efforts	39.0	42.6	46.5	41.4	.05***
Counterbalance to superpowers	22.7	33.7	38.0	28.8	.14***
Democratic and humanitarian values	14.1	23.9	33.6	20.3	.17***
Need to master technology	21.9	32.5	32.8	27.2	.12***
Culture and ways of life	9.6	15.9	16.4	12.8	.10***
Defend against outside threats	25.7	26.0	24.7	25.7	.01
Other	.5	.6	.5	.6	.01
Number of respondents				11,256	

Note: *** p ≤ .001

had fully reemerged from the doldrums of the prior decades. Especially given the selection of choices offered by the question, therefore, the distribution of responses might have been substantially different had the question been posed at another time.

Table 5.5 presents data from this same prompt, this time cross-tabulated with the variable measuring the strength of European identification. Here it appears that the substantive nature of the content choice is virtually irrelevant to the near-universal effect of identity strength. That is, in every case except defense against outside threats and "other," choice of the characteristic is positively related to strength of identification, such that strong European identifiers always select the characteristic in greater proportions than do weak identifiers, who in turn choose it in greater proportions than do nonidentifiers.[5] There may be several possible explanations for this phenomenon, which is driven in part by the higher response rate among stronger identifiers. One possibility is that weak identifiers tend to find less on the list that they associate with Europe, possibly because their attitudes toward Europe do not include many positive characteristics. Another is that strong identifiers simply have a more developed sense of the content of a European identity, while for weak identifiers the notion of Europe is a benignly empty vessel. In any case, the differentiated instrumentalism effects across identity-level categories that were manifest in Table 5.3 do not appear in Table 5.5. Rather, virtually *all* of the characteristics of

European identity in the latter table are subject to identity-level effects, not just those related to instrumental and cultural/political characteristics.

Eurobarometer 33 (1990) offers a different approach to exploring the content of European identity, but one similar in form to that presented in Tables 5.2 and 5.3. Here, the prompt to respondents was:

> There is a certain way of life, a standard of behavior and values, that may be considered more specifically European than others. To which of the following aspects of Europe are you personally most attached? [Maximum 3 replies possible. Show card.]

Prompted responses included "culture," "peace," "democracy," "way of life (customs and habits, etc.)," "standard of living," and "quality of life." Unprompted responses coded in the dataset included "I don't think specifically European values exist" and "don't know." Tables 5.6 and 5.7 present the response frequencies to this question, arrayed against nationality and European identification levels, respectively. As in previous cases, the permitted (but not required) multiple possible responses make interpretation more difficult.

Data in Table 5.6 show that peace is once again the most defining characteristic of Europeaness for Europeans—this is a finding that has emerged with the greatest consistency from data examined in this chapter. Inconsistent with previous data, on the other hand, is the high selection rate of democracy, compared to the unpopularity of religious/philosophical and democratic/humanitarian values for the previously examined survey questions. Perhaps the difference is that, here, democracy stands alone, where in the other formats it is either not directly mentioned at all, or is associated with another attribute. In any case, culture is the next most popular choice overall, which is again contradictory to the previously examined data, for which culture tended to be quite low on the list of selected characteristics. Another explanation that might account for all of these anomalies is the fact each question prompt (stem) is different but, even more important, each presents a different array of responses from which to choose, which could dramatically affect responses.

Standard of living and quality of life are perhaps the two choices best associated with an instrumental outlook on Europe. Both are among the least-popular choices, yet they still are each mentioned by roughly a fourth of the sample. Only 6.5 percent claim that no specifically European values exist, but this value may have been somewhat higher had it been a prompted response. Finally, national variances certainly exist on any given response choice, but no discernible pattern emerges from the data. This is particularly true if one tries to track the tendencies of respondents from a given country across the datasets. As just one example, German respondents select peace as a characteristic of Europeaness more often than do those in the general EU sample in the first two formats (Tables 5.2 and 5.4), but not in the third (Table 5.6).

Table 5.6 Aspects of Europe Most Attached To, by Nationality (Eurobarometer 33, 1990)

	France	Belgium	Netherlands	Germany	Italy	Luxembourg	Denmark	Ireland	UK	Greece	Spain	Portugal	EU	Cramer's V
	Percentage Choosing (up to three choices permitted)													
Culture	29.4	30.8	24.2	38.8	42.3	38.7	32.6	26.7	22.7	39.1	33.5	37.0	33.2	.15***
Peace	56.7	53.3	61.7	45.5	48.3	48.3	52.6	37.0	37.5	57.8	33.6	47.2	46.6	.17***
Democracy	39.0	36.6	49.0	49.0	38.8	33.0	55.2	23.3	24.5	48.6	33.1	38.1	38.5	.18***
Way of life	23.3	30.9	27.0	24.0	31.9	30.1	21.4	29.6	31.6	17.3	17.3	21.8	26.0	.12***
Standard of living	24.0	25.7	26.5	26.1	9.0	29.5	25.5	40.5	38.7	17.5	11.4	13.5	22.8	.24***
Quality of life	37.3	33.0	37.4	25.3	25.0	20.6	35.7	33.6	34.3	22.8	10.7	13.0	27.8	.19***
No European values exist	9.1	5.4	2.2	7.1	3.8	4.7	2.8	8.3	4.6	3.2	12.8	5.4	6.5	.12***
Don't know	2.0	3.1	1.2	4.8	4.6	3.5	2.8	8.9	6.4	11.0	11.6	17.2	5.7	.16***
Number of respondents														11,580

Note: *** p ≤ .001

Table 5.7   Aspects of Europe Most Attached To, by European Identity Level (Eurobarometer 33, 1990)

	Percentage Choosing (multiple choices permitted)				
	Thinks of Self as European				
	Never	Sometimes	Often	EU	Cramer's V
Culture	24.5	40.1	49.5	33.4	.21***
Peace	45.1	49.1	47.1	46.7	.04***
Democracy	30.2	45.8	51.1	38.4	.18***
Way of life	24.3	29.0	27.0	26.2	.05***
Standard of living	24.4	21.9	20.0	22.9	.04***
Quality of life	24.9	29.3	35.2	27.9	.08***
No European values exist	9.2	4.1	2.4	6.5	.12***
Don't know	8.3	2.5	1.0	5.3	.14***
Number of respondents					11,231

Note: *** p ≤ .001

When identity-characteristic choices are arrayed against the identification levels of respondents, as seen in Table 5.7, a pattern with some similarities to that of Table 5.3 emerges. That is, both the most- and some of the least-popular responses appear relatively impervious to levels of identification. Thus, peace is selected by 45–50 percent of respondents (V = .04) and way of life by 24–29 percent (V = .05), no matter how often they think of themselves as European. Standard of living also yields a low Cramer's V, of .04, though it manifests a slight inverse linear relationship to identity level. Culture and democracy, on the other hand, and to a lesser extent quality of life, are more likely to be selected the more one identifies with Europe, while both those who don't know and those who claim that no European values exist are less likely to be found among European identifiers. As in Table 5.3, then, peace is the solid choice of European identifiers at all levels, but level of identity affects the extent to which respondents view the content of Europeaness in instrumental or attributional terms. Those who least-frequently identify with Europe are more likely to characterize it in instrumental terms (e.g., standard of living) or not at all, while those highest in European identity tend more often to characterize its content in terms of culture and political values (e.g., democracy).

Further evidence of this relationship is presented in Table 5.8, which displays responses to a Survey of European Identifiers (1998) question using a prompt similar to that employed in Eurobarometer 33, but different in three respects. First, the SEI sample is composed almost entirely of strong Europhiles; second, the survey instrument was presented in written form, not orally; and

Table 5.8   Ways of Life, Standards, and Values That Are Specifically
European (Survey of European Identifiers, 1998; percentages
of respondents)

Value	Not Very Important	Somewhat Important	Very Important	Percentage Listing	Number of Respondents
Prompted responses					
Culture	6.1	22.2	71.7		212
Peace	6.7	10.5	82.8		209
Democracy	1.9	10.0	88.2		211
Way of life	13.6	47.1	39.3		206
Standard of living	10.0	51.7	38.3		209
Quality of life	5.2	37.6	57.1		210
No specifically European values exist				5.7	227
Open responses					
Social security/solidarity				8.4	227
Diversity/tolerance				7.4	227
Political ideas/ideals				9.1	227
History/heritage				2.1	227

third, respondents were asked to rank the importance of all the choices, rather
than to select among them. The question asked:

> There is a certain way of life, a standard of behavior and values, that may be
> considered more specifically European than others. Please indicate the de-
> gree to which you think each of the following are important aspects of being
> European: "Culture," "Peace," "Democracy," "Way of life," "Standard of liv-
> ing," and "Quality of life."

Respondents were also given two blank lines, labeled "other (please specify)," in which to fill in their own choices. They were asked to check boxes indicating whether each of the items was "not very important," "somewhat important," or "very important." Respondents could also check a box labeled "I
don't think specifically European values exist."

As in previous findings, peace is extremely highly ranked, with nearly 83
percent labeling it a very important aspect of European identity, and less than
7 percent believing that it is not very important. Among the SEI group, however, democracy ranks even higher than peace, with more than 88 percent believing it very important, and less than 2 percent finding it not very important.
Culture is also considered very important, as is—to a lesser extent—quality of
life. Standard of living and way of life are considered the least important of the
named qualities. The volunteered responses covered a wide range of notions,
though they cannot fairly be compared in magnitude to those that were
prompted, since the former required the small but important extra effort of
conceiving a response and writing it in. Table 5.8 lists four of the most popular and substantively significant responses, which largely lean toward political
values. Finally, 5.7 percent of the entire survey indicated their belief that no

specifically European values exist. Overall, these findings suggest an apprehension of Europeaness among European identifiers that again appears less rooted in instrumental qualities and more in normative (perhaps even postmaterialist) characteristics.

A second approach on the SEI toward understanding the content of European identity took the form of a series of open-ended questions directly addressing this topic. The questions, posed in succession, were:

> What does being European mean to you? What words, ideas or feelings come to mind when you think of being European?
>
> What does being part of your nation mean to you? What words, ideas or feelings come to mind when you think of being French, Italian, etc.?
>
> What does being part of your regional or provincial community mean to you? What words, ideas or feelings come to mind when you think of being Scottish, Bavarian, etc.?

Each was followed by several blank lines upon which respondents could list whatever thoughts were triggered by the prompts. For each respondent, as many as three themes were coded from each of the three question responses. Tables 5.9, 5.10, and 5.11 list the most favored and/or substantively significant responses to each of the above questions regarding Europe, the nation, and the region/province, respectively. For each table, the three resulting variables have

Table 5.9   Meaning of Being European—Open Response Question (Survey of European Identifiers, 1998; up to three responses coded)

Response	Percentage of Respondents Mentioning
Nothing/None (active answer—not blank response)	3.6
Solidarity/Collectivism/Socialism	7.1
Security/Peace/European defense	14.2
Similar lifestyles/culture	21.3
Similar or common morals/ethics/values	4.6
Part of a great idea, project, or organization/Necessary for future	7.6
Human rights/Humanitarianism/Humanism	5.6
European civilization/Cultural heritage/Tradition/Destiny	13.2
History	8.6
Diversity/Multiculturalism/Difference/Tolerance/Exchange	27.4
Openness/Open-mindedness	7.6
Liberty/Freedom	7.1
Democracy	8.1
Shared space/Living in Europe/Geographical proximity	2.0
Cooperation/Collaboration/Lack of conflict	7.6
Multilingual culture	4.6
Togetherness/Unity/Love/Harmony/Union/Community/Social relations	14.2
Friends/Contacts/Family	6.6
Economic progress, benefits, or development/Euro	5.6
Standard of living	3.0
Number of respondents	197

124

Table 5.10 Meaning of Being Part of Nation—Open Response Question (Survey of European Identifiers, 1998; up to three responses coded)

Response	Percentage of Respondents Mentioning
Nothing/None (active answer—not blank response)	9.0
Culture/Cultural identity	26.5
Tradition/Heritage	7.9
European ties/Cooperation/Part of Europe/Europeaness	4.8
Language	12.7
Diversity/Tolerance/Cultural variety	4.8
Politics/Political system/Constitution/Political culture/Institutions	7.4
History/Common experiences	13.2
Democracy	4.2
Emotion/Pride/Self-esteem/Love/Nationalism/Patriotism	14.3
Home/Lifestyle/Peacefulness	8.5
Shame/Embarrassment/Blame for national history	5.8
Solidarity/Welfare state/Socialism/Social security	3.2
Natural/urban beauty	3.2
Number of respondents	189

Table 5.11 Meaning of Being Part of Region—Open Response Question (Survey of European Identifiers, 1998; up to three responses coded)

Response	Percentage of Respondents Mentioning
Nothing/None (active answer—not blank response)	30.4
Home/Where I live	6.5
Common concerns, experiences, values, or habits/Shared idea	6.0
Beautiful landscape/Nature	3.6
Urban/Cultural opportunities/Energy	6.0
Warmth/Shelter/Security/Acceptance/Comfort/Reassurance	5.4
Friends	5.4
Multiculturalism/Diversity/Cosmopolitanism/Tolerance	8.3
Wealthy region/Economic dynamism	4.2
Where I was born or grew up/Personal history/School/Upbringing	4.2
Pride/Pride in history of region/Something special	7.7
Traditions/Heritage	3.6
Culture/Cultural identity/Cultural integration	9.5
Identity	5.4
Multilingualism	.6
Number of respondents	168

been collapsed, so that the tables show the percentages of all respondents answering the question who mentioned each theme, regardless of the order of mention.

Table 5.9 includes what is perhaps the most fascinating finding of this chapter. Here, the most popular characteristics of European identity—by a considerable margin—are notions of diversity, multiculturalism, and tolerance. More than a fourth of all respondents included this as key to their definition of Europeaness, while 4.6 percent also referred to the related concept of multilingualism, and 7.6 percent listed open-mindedness.[6] This is striking, above all, because diversity and tolerance have heretofore been the very antithesis of content in the structuring of political identities. With the exception of the American celebration of the "melting pot" (which, in any case, implies only a brief transition to a nondiverse end-state, from separate to blended, from multiple solids to melted singular), identities have historically been centered on the ideology of communal-wide monolithic characteristics, however false the premise or stretched the actual reality. But here, alternatively, is a case in which the seemingly oxymoronic notion of diversity is celebrated as a core unifying concept of a political identity.

This finding becomes more intriguing and complicated as one moves to the next most popular item on the list, in which more than a fifth of all respondents make reference to similar lifestyles and culture as key to their notion of being European, with 4.6 percent also mentioning common morals, ethics, and values. This, of course, appears to contradict the celebration of diversity just described, though that is not necessarily the case. Respondents could form two camps, embracing diversity and uniformity, respectively, but it is also possible to embrace both notions simultaneously, perhaps appreciating cultural diversity and shared normative/political values at the same time. In any case, the next most popular characteristics referenced include security/peace (mentioned by 14.2 percent of all respondents), togetherness/unity (14.2 percent), and common civilizational heritage (13.2 percent). A number of respondents mentioned specific normative/political characteristics, such as solidarity (7.1 percent), human rights (5.6 percent), liberty/freedom (7.1 percent), and democracy (8.1 percent). Only a small percentage mentioned either economic development (5.6 percent) or standard of living (3.0 percent). Finally, 7.6 percent of respondents mentioned the great adventure/future necessity theme, while 2.0 percent saw Europeaness as merely a geographical fact and 3.6 percent felt it had no content at all.

While these findings are difficult to summarize internally, they do present a striking contrast to responses given by the same individuals concerning the content of their national and regional identities. Table 5.10 presents the main responses given for national identity content, in which more than a fourth of respondents referenced culture characteristics. If the categories of language (12.7 percent), tradition and heritage (7.9 percent), history (13.2 percent), and negative historical attributes (5.8 percent) are added to this choice to form a broad cultural category, its definitional dominance becomes even more prominent. Another large contingent (14.3 percent) referred to the emotional character of their national identities, or to the sense of being at home (8.5 percent), that they associated with those identities. A respectable portion of respondents (7.4 percent) also mentioned their national political systems, institutions, or political cultures as key to their sense of national identity. As was the case for Europeaness, national identification brought forward normative/political references, but not to the same extent. Democracy was mentioned (4.2 percent), as was solidarity (3.2 percent) and even diversity (4.8 percent). But nearly one in ten respondents (9.0 percent) said their national identity had no meaning or content at all.

Referring to their regional identities, more than 30 percent described them as vacant of meaning and content. This represents by far the most popular comment on regional identities. Otherwise, perhaps the next most significant constellation of responses focused on the comforts and pleasures of home. The identity was described in precisely those terms by 6.5 percent of respondents, while others referred to common habits/values (6.0 percent), beautiful environs (3.6 percent) or urban opportunities (6.0 percent), warmth and acceptance (5.4 percent), friends (5.4 percent), or personal history (4.2 percent). Culture was less conspicuous (9.5 percent) than in the national case, as was the category of traditions/heritage (3.6 percent). There was again mention of pride of identity (7.7 percent) and, surprisingly, even diversity generated a healthy response at the regional level (8.3 percent).

As Tables 5.9, 5.10, and 5.11 make clear, European, national, and regional identities possess substantially divergent content for SEI respondents. Among this group of mostly Europhiles, European identity appears to stand, in important respects, for a set of shared values, chief among which is the seemingly contradictory celebration of diversity, but which also includes solidarity, human rights, freedom, and democracy. Peace is also a substantial component of the identity, as prior analyses in this chapter have shown. If—as appears to be the case—European identity is largely constituted by normative notions that are the product of cerebral calculation, national identities tend instead to reflect cultural commonalities, historical experiences, and even political institutions, all woven into a tapestry of a more emotive pattern. Regional identities, finally, are noteworthy first for their weakness among SEI respondents, nearly a third of whom ascribe no content to them whatever, and second for the degree to which themes of home, comfort, familiarity, and friends characterize the identity for the remainder of those surveyed.

A final and further illuminating data source on the content of European identity emerges from interviews with Europeans.[7] Informants were asked the same question that appears on the SEI, namely: "What does being European mean to you? What words, ideas or feelings come to mind when you think of being European?" Many were quite taken aback just by the question, and most at least required a moment of puzzled reflection to produce an answer. This fact alone may be indicative of the degree to which Europeans' sense of their Europeaness is amorphous and unsettled. On the other hand, political identities have historically been associated with internal processes having at least as much to do with affective and emotive sensibilities as with cognitive ratiocination, and it may thus be too much to expect a fluent, developed answer to a question sprung on any informant, regarding any identity.

In any case, many of the same factors drawn from the above discussion of quantitative sources were also manifest in the qualitative data. Themes related to diversity, tolerance, and multiculturalism were again the most frequently invoked, mentioned by about half of those interviewed. As with those captured by the quantitative data, a very large number of informants also made reference to commonalities of culture, values, and traditions. But—to a much greater extent than survey respondents—even more saw history and historical heritage as key to their sense of what it means to be European. Here, references were made to a range of specific events and developments, as well as to the general notions of history and historical heritage. Among the specific references were classical inheritances from Greece and Rome, Christianity, the Renaissance, Romanticism, and the Enlightenment, as well as more temporally proximate developments such as colonialism and World War II. A substantial number of informants made reference to the normative/political ideas of democracy, human rights, and freedom, though to a lesser extent than they invoked the dominant themes of diversity, culture, and history. Even more popular in this group was the notion of solidarity or the welfare-state model, which several informants argued was the key defining concept of Europeaness.

Three remaining themes appeared with some frequency, but each only about a fourth as often as diversity, the characteristic most often mentioned. One of these, interestingly, is peace, the notion that dominated the meaning of Europeaness in most of the quantitative data. One informant described being European as the prevention of pointless killing, or "what people in the battlefield graveyards would want," but this theme was actually slightly less frequently invoked than was solidarity, and substantially less so than diversity, culture, and history. Second, roughly the same proportion of informants described European identity as either nonexistent, or simply a geographical fact, with comments such as, "We don't have one culture, and God forbid we should try to create one," and "I see what is Italy, I see what is German, but I don't see what is European." Meanwhile, third, about the same number again saw Europe as vaguely distinct (especially from the United States), but did not specify the nature of the distinction. Said one informant, "It is so much a part of you, you don't even think of it."

Whatever the specific content constituting a European identity for those interviewed, however, the tone of their affect was typically similar to that manifested in the SEI data. A European identity appears to be less an emotional expression or primordial passion than an intellectual commitment to a set of principles rationally derived from personal experience and knowledge of history. As such, it tends not to possess the emotive current that national identities have previously evoked, and sometimes continue to evoke today, occasionally even among strong European identifiers. The Portuguese informant whose comment opened this chapter is perhaps a bit too stark in the description of her European identity to be generally representative of all those interviewed, but her take on the subject nevertheless provides a good sense of the flavor of Europeaness, even among those generally strongly committed to the identity. As noted, for her, "Europe is something that rings a bell in your mind, but not in your heart. It doesn't have a spirit."

Conclusion

If the discussion of the meaning and content of European identity in this chapter were a painting, it would clearly be an impressionist piece. As such, its broad contours would be recognizable, but beyond that, most of its representational clarity would cease. That is, a sense of what it means to be European does emerge from the foregoing analyses, but it is neither precise nor consistent across data sources examined. Nevertheless, we can safely adumbrate some significant themes that emerge from the investigation in rough but unambiguous form. To stretch the art analogy one step further, we may not be able to recognize specific plant species or individual human characters in our painting, but we can see the clear outlines of mountains, lakes, trees, and people. Moreover, if we step back a few paces, we can sense a general mood that the piece conveys.

Where European identity is concerned, the notion of peace seems most prominent and universal within that general mood. A shared sense of culture is variably invoked too, as are important normative/political commitments such as democracy, human rights, and socioeconomic solidarity. And, perhaps especially for those who least identify as European, instrumental benefits related to standard of living or economic gains may also define what it means to be European. Last, two other themes emerge powerfully from the qualitative data and from the SEI quantitative data collected expressly for purposes of this study. First, the idea of common history and heritage is especially prominent among interviewed European identifiers. That this theme doesn't show up in extant surveys (it does emerge in the SEI) may in part be a function of the Europhilic bias of interviewees, or their tendency to have more advanced educational backgrounds. But surely the main reason is that extant surveys did not prompt for it or include it among response choices (see Tables 5.2–5.7).

The second theme is that of diversity, multiculturalism, and tolerance, which among SEI respondents and interviewed informants trumps every other notion of the meaning of European identity. Again, this option did not appear in extant survey questions, so it is difficult to know how generalizable this most intriguing of identity components is. But it is probably safe to conclude that this is the most important dimension of Europeaness for those who feel the identity's call most powerfully. Finally, the evidence among SEI respondents and interviewed informants suggests that European identity may be more the product of cognitive calculation than are other identities. For these same respondents, national identity stirs pride and other emotions, and focuses on cultural distinctiveness, while their regional identities are primarily characterized by a sense of comfort and familiarity in the context of being "home." Being European, on the other hand, stirs considerably less emotion, but reflects instead more of a rational analysis of necessary or preferable political structures and identities.

Notes

1. Cross-tabulations array two variables against each other to produce a table, or two-dimensional matrix. Table entries in each respective cell may indicate either the percentage of the total for that row, the percentage of the total for that column, or the percentage of the total of all cells in the matrix.

2. Cramer's V is a measure of strength of association between two variables that can be employed when examining nominal or categorical variables (that is, unranked or nonordinal variables—such as nationality and religion). The product of a cross-tabulation analysis, this statistic summarizes the entire relationship between the two variables, rather than any single row, column, or cell in the matrix. Cramer's-V values range from 0, meaning that the two variables are completely randomly associated, to 1.0, meaning that they are perfectly associated with each other.

3. The percentage figures under the "EU" column of both tables vary slightly due to different sample sizes. Both tables include only those cases in which both variables have been coded. If data from *either* of the juxtaposed variables was missing, the entire case was dropped from the analysis.

4. It should be noted that the question prompt refers to the bringing together of European countries, which, if literally interpreted by respondents, arguably implies only the very utilitarian notion of cooperation toward some goal. On the other hand, only some of the offered responses lend themselves to this strict interpretation. Looked at together, the full collection of response choices suggests a wider interpretation of the question prompt that includes both utility items as well as shared attitudes and attributes.

5. This seeming statistical anomaly is explained by the fact that respondents could select *up to* three options in response to the question prompt. This means they could also select fewer, and in fact they did so in a manner reflective of their response to the identity-strength question. Thus the 5,676 respondents who never thought of themselves as European could have given three times that many responses to the identity-definition question. In fact, however, they gave only 9,569 responses, or 56.2 percent of the 17,028 maximum possible. Among the 1,602 respondents who often thought of themselves as European, on the other hand, 3,855 responses were given to the definition question, equal to 80.2 percent of the 4,806 maximum possible. This disproportionate response rate to the identity-definition question across the three identification-level categories

permits a situation in which strong identifiers can more frequently pick *every* characteristic as descriptive of European identity than do weak and nonidentifiers.

6. These three groups are not necessarily exclusive of one another in terms of
membership.

7. Again, these are mostly European sympathizers and identifiers, though there
were also some ardent Euroskeptics in the interview pool, as well as individuals with
views in-between these poles.

6

How "European" Are the Europeans? The Depth of European Identification

Who will die for Europe?
—Anthony Smith (1995: 139)

THE EMPIRICAL CHAPTERS OF this study have so far examined several key dimensions of European identity, including its popular extent and temporal dynamics, the factors associated with its variance in level across individuals, and the nature of its content. The task of this chapter is to explore the depth dimension of the phenomenon. What do we mean by *depth of identity*? As employed here, the term invokes a concept not dissimilar to degree of identity, which is accounted for by some of the dependent-variable measures examined in Chapter 3. Yet its meaning refers to something else, a concept that is principally operationalized in terms of willingness to sacrifice, but that also concerns a shared sense of community.

Thus it is possible—to make this distinction more clear—that a person could describe himself or herself as very attached to Europe, but nevertheless possess a European identity of rather shallow depth, as measured by willingness to sacrifice for Europe. Such a scenario might be all the more plausible to the extent that the content of the identity were highly instrumentally determined. To make the point more concretely, one might imagine a person who is quite attached to Europe because his friends are scattered across the continent, and because integration provides high mobility and access to people and things that enrich and enhance his life. In this sense, he may feel very European (especially in contrast to the nationalism of his grandparents), but when asked to sacrifice either for Europe or for other Europeans, he may immediately balk.

The point of the foregoing discussion is not so much to split conceptual hairs as it is to define the contours of this chapter's thematic focus. As in the previous chapters, the analyses in this chapter are based on multiple sources, with the intent of triangulating on the topic and yielding a more accurate assessment of its character. Quite a number of existing survey datasets contain

131

questions that address the issue of identity depth and willingness to make sacrifices. This chapter examines data from the European Community Studies of
1970, 1971, and 1973, and from Eurobarometers 3 (1975), 5 (1976), 8 (1977),
10 (1978), 13 (1980), 15 (1981), 18 (1982), 24 (1985), 30 (1988), and 34-0
(1990). The analyses also draw on the Survey of European Identifiers (SEI)
dataset, and on responses to interview questions. As in the previous chapter,
responses to survey questions concerning identity depth have been arrayed
against indicators of nationality and, where available, levels of European identification. The analysis proceeds in the direction of increasing specificity, beginning with discussion of the overall importance of the European integration
project, and then moving to willingness to make shared national and then personal sacrifices of various types for Europe and for fellow Europeans.

Eurobarometers 30 and 34-0 both posed a question to respondents that
asked them to select those political and cultural institutions and movements of
the day that they deemed worthy of the greatest concern. The text of the question read:

> In your opinion, in this list [show list] which are the great causes which
> nowadays are worth the trouble of taking risks and making sacrifices for?
> [Several answers possible.]

Included in the list of possible responses were such items as human rights,
world peace, freedom of the individual, the struggle against racism, and others. Table 6.1 presents frequency distributions from both surveys (one row of
figures each), by nationality, for three of the prompted responses: defense of
country, religious faith, and the unification of Europe. The data in the table indicate that, of the three causes, Europeans still hold national defense as most
worthy of their risks and sacrifices (though, interestingly, less than 30 percent
of respondents are of this opinion even for this most popular cause). Approximately 15 percent of respondents believe European unification to be worthy
of risks and sacrifices, a figure that, incidentally, is equivalent in size to the co-
hort labeled "core identifiers" in Chapter 3. While 15 percent is not a lot relative to the whole of the sample, it may be considered a rather remarkable
amount for a cause that is simultaneously young, controversial, threatening to
the established political order, and generally rather vaguely specified.

Relative to the popularity of the other causes, moreover, the figure becomes even more impressive. In 1990, more of those sampled believed Europe
worthy of risk and sacrifice than did those holding that view of their religion,
and only 6 percent more of respondents held that opinion with respect to their
country than with regard to Europe. Considering the centuries and even mil-
lennia of tradition (and traditions of sacrifice, at that) associated with faith and
country, these are remarkable comparisons indeed. Given the rather dimin-
ished figures for all three measures, however, the headline emerging from

Table 6.1 Causes Worth Risks and Sacrifices, by Nationality (Eurobarometers 30, 1988; and 34-0, 1990)

Percentage Choosing: Eurobarometer 30, 1988 (first row) / Eurobarometer 34-0, 1990 (second row)

	France	Belgium	Netherlands	Germany	Italy	Luxembourg	Denmark	Ireland	UK	Greece	Spain	Portugal	EU	Cramer's V
Defense of my country	31.0	26.6	7.6	26.8	24.4	28.4	21.4	13.3	40.8	36.4	26.9	49.5	29.5	.18***
	26.3	16.2	5.3	16.6	17.3	21.2	11.0	16.0	27.7	28.2	22.1	42.8	21.2	.17***
My religious faith	13.4	13.4	16.2	17.5	22.3	19.0	10.7	35.3	18.4	34.5	19.6	31.7	18.8	.13***
	12.9	8.5	16.1	9.3	16.5	13.9	5.4	23.0	12.4	20.2	16.7	23.6	13.5	.11***
The unification of Europe	24.7	26.6	9.9	19.1	22.2	39.4	8.8	8.3	8.8	20.0	13.0	28.4	17.9	.17***
	17.8	17.1	14.6	19.6	13.9	20.5	13.1	8.8	7.7	16.4	12.1	16.7	14.9	.12***
Number of respondents														11,794
														12,588

Note: *** p ≤ .001

Table 6.1 may have less to do with the relative depth of European identity than the degree to which contemporary Europeans resist all such calls on their health, wealth, and longevity. With respect to the effects of nationality on European identification tendencies, the table shows both more variance (Cramer's V = .17) and more predictable variance for Eurobarometer 30 data than for Eurobarometer 34-0 data (V = .12), though the latter also loosely fit the general pattern of national attitudes toward Europe observed in Chapter 4 and elsewhere.

Table 6.2 arrays the same data from the risk/sacrifice questions against the European identification–level question, which asks respondents how frequently they think of themselves as European. Not surprisingly, the degree of identification with Europe has little effect on the extent to which respondents think risks or sacrifices are worthwhile for their country (V = .04) or their religious faith (V = .02), but has enormous implications for their opinion with respect to European unification (V = .22). Indeed, more than three times as many of those who frequently think of themselves as European support risk or sacrifice for European unification (33.2 percent)[1] compared to those who never think of themselves as European (10.0 percent), just as might be expected. And, just as might also be expected, 55.3 percent of the generally Europhile sample of SEI respondents also described European unification as worthy of risk and sacrifice.

The identity-depth survey questions discussed so far are (purposely?) silent with respect to who or what would be taking or making the posited risks and sacrifices for each cause—they simply ask whether the cause is worthy of risk and sacrifice as a general proposition. A more specific scenario places the respondent's country in the role of active agent, and also specifies a particular need to be addressed. The following question was posed in Eurobarometers 8, 10, 15, and 24:

Table 6.2 Causes Worth Risks and Sacrifices, by European Identity Level (Eurobarometer 30, 1988)

| | Percentage Choosing | | | | |
| | Thinks of Self as European | | | | |
	Never	Sometimes	Often	EU	Cramer's V
Defense of my country	29.8	30.8	25.8	29.5	.04***
My religious faith	17.8	19.5	19.7	18.8	.02*
The unification of Europe	10.0	21.2	33.2	18.1	.22***
Number of respondents					11,379

Notes: * p ≤ .05
*** p ≤ .001

> If one of the countries of the European Community other than our own finds itself in major economic difficulties, do you feel that the other countries including [your country], should help it or not?

Responses to this question, by nationality, are presented in Table 6.3. These results display a remarkable willingness to sacrifice on behalf of other Europeans—that is, a depth of European identity[2]—to the extent that more than 80 percent in every survey answered this question affirmatively and, astonishingly, nearly 90 percent did so in two out of the four surveys. Respondents from all countries agreed that EC countries should assist one another in times of trouble, but there was substantial variance around the survey means, as the V values ranging from .18 to .24 indicate. Yet the figures do not necessarily follow the typical national patterns of public opinion on European questions. The Netherlands, for example, which generally runs toward the low end of European identity, is consistently above the mean on this question, as is Italy, which is consistently high on European identity scores. France, generally high in European identity, hovers near the mean in each survey on the assistance question. And Ireland and Britain, both of which tend to possess the lowest proportion of European identifiers, go separate ways on this question, with Ireland always above the mean, and Britain always below. Perhaps much of what drives this pattern of variance is each country's status as a net-contributor or a net-recipient of European funds, but in any case, these national variations should not obscure the more remarkable finding that support for the notion of assisting other countries is quite profound, with national samples in no case ever falling below two-thirds of the sample, and on average approaching 90 percent. This consistent mean at so high a level is rare among opinion-polling questions, but is perhaps even more astonishing for a question involving sacrifices.

A third level of specificity on the question of identity depth brings the issue directly to the respondent, testing his or her willingness to personally sacrifice for Europe or Europeans. Three question prompts were employed across Eurobarometers 5, 10, 13, 15, 18, and 24 to generate the data in Table 6.4. All prompts concern willingness to pay a European tax, and all required yes/no responses. The first prompt, used in Eurobarometer 5, asked respondents:

> In a European Parliament the members of Parliament for [country] would not have the majority, even if they were all in agreement. Would you, or would you not, accept that the European Parliament passes laws in the fields that I am going to list, which would be applicable to all countries of the European Community, including [country] . . . As far as taxation matters are concerned (e.g., create a European tax)?

For Eurobarometers 10, 15, 18, and 24, the prompt was:

Table 6.3 Should EC Countries Assist Another in Trouble? (by nationality)

	Percentage Agreeing														Number of
	France	Belgium	Netherlands	Germany	Italy	Luxembourg	Denmark	Ireland	UK	Greece	Spain	Portugal	EU	Cramer's V	Respondents
Eurobarometer 8, 1977	86.3	87.2	93.0	87.6	97.1	89.7	82.3	89.5	81.2	—	—	—	88.2	.18***	8,027
Eurobarometer 10, 1978	88.9	89.5	93.3	84.4	97.6	81.4	78.9	92.3	77.9	—	—	—	87.7	.22***	7,587
Eurobarometer 15, 1981	85.0	69.3	88.1	79.8	95.5	92.2	75.1	84.0	71.4	93.9	—	—	83.2	.24***	18,623
Eurobarometer 24, 1985	87.0	73.5	91.5	80.8	95.6	92.0	66.5	86.4	77.6	87.1	85.7	94.3	85.3	.20***	10,596

Note: *** p ≤ .001

> Are you, personally, prepared or not to make some personal sacrifice, for example paying a little more taxes, to help another country in the European Community experiencing economic difficulties?

And for Eurobarometer 13, a paired set of questions allowed an interesting comparison between the extent of respondent largess for fellow countrymen and countrywomen and for fellow Europeans. Those questions asked:

> Do you agree or not that a part of the taxes you are paying (e.g. income tax, VAT [value-added tax], etc.) . . . be used for the development of the most needy regions in [country]? [or] be used for the development of the neediest regions of the European Community even if they are not in our country?

As Table 6.4 demonstrates, the phrasing of the prompt can substantially affect the response from those surveyed. Presumably, this is why the rather more vaguely stated burden posited in Eurobarometer 5 generates much higher agreement than the specific and personal tax burden of the question asked in Eurobarometers 10, 15, 18, and 24. Nearly 80 percent agree with the first question, though there is very wide variation across national frontiers (V = .28), ranging from 55.7 percent in Denmark to 92.3 in Luxembourg (or 88.9 in the larger country of Italy). When the second prompt is employed, on the other hand, the agreement rate falls to a fairly consistent 46–48 percent (Eurobarometer 18 is the one exception). Remarkably, this rate of agreement for the entire sample is mostly consistent despite enormous variance across countries (V ranges from .23 to .33), as well as within countries across the four surveys.

Finally, the pairing of aid questions from Eurobarometer 13 provides an interesting comparative measure of the depth of European identity relative to national identities. Close to 90 percent of respondents would be willing to pay taxes to aid needy regions of their own countries, and this figure is quite consistent across the countries sampled (V = .07). When asked to make the same sacrifice for needy regions of the EC, though, less than half as many (38.5 percent) would agree to do so, though the variance between countries is extensive (V = .31), ranging from 19.0 percent agreement in Britain to 60.2 percent in Germany, more than three times the British commitment. In any case, the depth of European identification is clearly less than the national, according to these figures, by a vast degree.

Table 6.5 presents a similar set of questions from four surveys, though in this case respondents could choose from four ordinal responses, rather than simply agreeing or disagreeing with the prompt. In the European Community Studies of 1970 and 1971, the question asked was:

Table 6.4 Various Questions Regarding Personal Sacrifice, by Nationality

								Percentage Agreeing								
	France	Belgium	Netherlands	Germany	Italy	Luxembourg	Denmark	Ireland	UK	Greece	Spain	Portugal	EU	Cramer's V	Number of Respondents
Accept a European tax voted by the European Parliament?															
Eurobarometer 5, 1976	84.8	87.4	84.6	76.5	88.9	92.3	55.7	80.3	57.5	—	—	—	77.0	.28***	7,011
Sacrifice (e.g., taxes) for another EU country?															
Eurobarometer 10, 1978	41.8	34.8	68.3	36.1	72.4	41.9	51.2	45.4	39.0	—	—	—	48.3	.30***	7,305
Eurobarometer 15, 1981	32.4	24.5	57.0	36.9	73.6	56.6	47.8	46.3	38.8	60.4	—	—	46.5	.33***	18,040
Eurobarometer 18, 1982	34.6	24.4	46.9	38.7	56.2	39.0	32.5	26.7	24.1	45.2	—	—	38.1	.23***	8,374
Eurobarometer 24, 1985	44.5	26.3	57.1	40.3	69.6	54.4	34.9	34.7	41.5	52.6	48.4	47.5	48.1	.23***	10,290
Okay for use of taxes to aid neediest regions of own country?															
Eurobarometer 13, 1980	89.2	84.0	89.1	85.0	90.3	95.2	90.0	93.5	86.4	—	—	—	87.8	.07***	179,478
Okay for use of taxes to aid neediest regions of EC?															
Eurobarometer 13, 1980	30.6	30.6	54.3	60.2	44.8	44.1	24.6	27.5	19.0	—	—	—	38.5	.31***	173,041

Note: *** p ≤ .001

Would you be willing to make certain personal sacrifices, for example, on the financial level, to accomplish European unification? Would you be completely willing, fairly willing, slightly willing, or not at all willing?[3]

In the European Community Study of 1973 and Eurobarometer 3, the prompt was:

Would you or would you not be willing to make some personal sacrifice, for example, pay a little more taxes, to help bring about the unification of Europe? Would you be very willing, fairly willing, not very willing, or not at all willing?

Table 6.5 indicates a relatively broad distribution of responses. Approximately 40 percent of all respondents across all four surveys rule out personal sacrifices altogether. Yet about 40 percent of all respondents in the first three surveys (and nearly 30 percent in the last) are either completely/definitely/very willing or fairly/somewhat willing to reach into their pockets and pay extra for the development of Europe. This is all the more remarkable for several reasons. First, "European unification" is an enormously broad and vague aspiration against which to request quite specific, financial sacrifice. In particular, as phrased in the prompt, it promises no specified benefit, such as lower prices or freedom of movement, in exchange for the respondent's mark, franc, or pound sterling. Second, the questions were asked at a point in time before the integration of Europe had substantially begun to deliver any such benefits to its citizens. And, finally, the integration process itself was at perhaps its all-time nadir during and especially directly preceding the period in which these surveys were taken. For all these reasons, it seems striking that such a substantial proportion of respondents would be willing (and for almost 10 percent, almost anxious) to make a personal sacrifice for Europe.

There are, of course, differences between national samples on these questions; these differences appear to generally follow the standard pattern of attitudes toward Europe within the member-states. Finally, Table 6.6 presents the same personal sacrifice data as the previous table, but this time cross-tabulated with the European identity–level variable (where available—two of the four surveys do not contain such measures). As should clearly be expected, there is a relationship between the two variables ($V = .17$ and $.14$), such that the proportion of those definitely or very willing to pay for European unification is about three times as high among those who named Europe as their first identity as the proportion among those who didn't name Europe first or second. Likewise, roughly twice as many in the latter group are not at all willing to sacrifice for Europe as that proportion of the former group.

A final and quite interesting collection of survey data is summarized in Table 6.7. This table presents the results of various tests of willingness to make

Table 6.5 Willingness to Sacrifice for European Unification, by Nationality

	France	Belgium	Netherlands	Germany	Italy	Luxembourg	Denmark	Ireland	UK	Greece	Spain	Portugal	EU	Cramer's V	Number of Respondents
European Communities Study, 1970														.12***	7,827
Completely willing	5.4	5.4	9.4	14.1	7.6	—	—	—	—	—	—	—	8.6		
Fairly willing	24.3	20.4	35.3	30.7	32.1	—	—	—	—	—	—	—	28.8		
Slightly willing	24.5	21.1	20.0	26.1	22.9	—	—	—	—	—	—	—	23.3		
Not at all willing	45.8	53.0	35.3	29.1	37.5	—	—	—	—	—	—	—	39.3		
European Communities Study, 1971														.17***	7,422
Definitely willing	6.9	5.8	10.7	14.0	15.7	—	—	—	—	—	—	—	10.9		
Somewhat willing	24.7	18.7	39.4	27.7	31.1	—	—	—	—	—	—	—	28.0		
A little willing	19.6	19.5	31.4	29.1	21.4	—	—	—	—	—	—	—	24.1		
Not at all willing	48.8	56.1	18.4	29.2	31.8	—	—	—	—	—	—	—	37.1		
European Communities Study, 1973														.17***	11,684
Very willing	7.0	8.6	12.6	5.6	10.8	15.8	7.0	8.7	4.0	—	—	—	7.9		
Fairly willing	26.0	20.3	30.7	49.0	43.4	31.3	31.6	34.2	25.8	—	—	—	33.0		
Not very willing	20.9	23.7	25.1	30.5	22.3	21.5	29.7	24.2	22.5	—	—	—	24.5		
Not at all willing	46.1	47.5	31.6	14.9	23.5	31.3	31.7	32.8	47.8	—	—	—	34.6		
Eurobarometer 3, 1975														.10***	8,903
Very willing	5.9	5.1	7.0	6.6	6.4	12.4	2.7	2.9	4.4	—	—	—	5.8		
Fairly willing	23.0	14.2	24.1	19.2	25.5	22.3	17.5	22.0	23.2	—	—	—	22.2		
Not very willing	19.7	19.5	30.2	35.5	23.9	22.7	33.7	17.4	21.3	—	—	—	25.5		
Not at all willing	51.5	61.2	38.8	38.7	44.2	42.6	46.1	57.6	51.0	—	—	—	46.5		

Percentage Agreeing

Note: *** p ≤ .001

Table 6.6　Willingness to Sacrifice for European Unification, by European Identity Level

| | Percentage Choosing | | | | | |
| | European Identity As | | | | | |
	Not Chosen	Second Choice	First Choice	EU	Cramer's V	Number of Respondents
European Communities Study, 1971					.17***	7,016
Definitely willing	8.2	16.6	27.4	11.1		
Somewhat willing	25.7	36.6	38.4	28.3		
A little willing	25.8	22.0	15.1	24.3		
Not at all willing	40.3	24.8	19.2	36.3		
European Communities Study, 1973					.14***	11,163
Very willing	6.2	13.6	16.3	7.8		
Fairly willing	30.6	45.4	46.4	33.5		
Not very willing	26.0	19.4	17.4	24.6		
Not at all willing	37.2	21.7	19.9	34.1		

Note: *** p ≤ .001

sacrifices on behalf of various polities. The data thus provide an excellent opportunity to examine identity depth in a context that is comparative in two dimensions: across types of sacrifice, and across beneficiaries of such sacrifice. The downside of the data is that they are derived from the SEI instrument, and thus reflect the sentiments of mostly strong Europhiles. While responses to these questions from a representative sample of Europeans (especially one that could be further cut along a European identity–level dimension) would certainly be preferable, these data may at least provide a sense of willingness to sacrifice for Europe at its current plausible limits. The data in Table 6.7 were gathered by asking SEI respondents a set of four questions, repeated three times, once each with respect to Europe, the respondent's country, and locality/region. For each of the twelve resulting questions, respondents could check one of three boxes, marked "Not very willing," "Possibly willing," or "Very willing." The questions posed were:

What sort of sacrifices would you be willing to make for the sake of . . .

. . . your country;
. . . your region or province (e.g., Scotland, Bavaria);
. . . Europe or the EU?

Accept a modestly lower standard of living to help raise the standard of living in poorer parts of . . .

Table 6.7 Willingness to Sacrifice for Regional, National, and European Polities, by Type of Sacrifice (Survey of European Identifiers, 1998; percentages of respondents)

Polity	Lower Standard of Living			Pay Additional Taxes			Serve in a Volunteer Corps			Fight in a War During Crisis		
	Not Very Willing	Possibly Willing	Very Willing	Not Very Willing	Possibly Willing	Very Willing	Not Very Willing	Possibly Willing	Very Willing	Not Very Willing	Possibly Willing	Very Willing
Region	26.7	47.6	25.7	28.2	47.2	24.6	41.6	38.9	19.5	65.6	25.4	8.5
Country	15.2	51.0	33.8	14.4	53.6	32.1	34.8	38.8	26.4	54.4	30.1	15.5
Europe	19.6	50.3	30.2	18.6	50.5	30.4	31.3	39.5	29.2	52.3	33.2	14.6

Note: Number of respondents = 189–209 (depending on question).

. . . your country?;
. . . your province?;
. . . Europe?

Pay additional taxes to ease a crisis in another . . .

. . . province?;
. . . community/town?;
. . . European country?

Serve in a volunteer corps for a year?

Fight in a war in a time of crisis, or approve of a family member doing so?"

Comparing first the four tests of willingness to sacrifice to one another, it is largely the case that they descend in order of popularity, regardless of which polity is in question, just as might be expected a priori, based on the ascending level of sacrifice these tests would be expected to entail for most individuals. Of course, a more interesting question concerns what respondents would be willing to sacrifice on behalf of one polity relative to what they'd give for another. Based on the figures in Table 6.7, the answer to this question can be interpreted in at least three ways, all providing valid and interesting commentary on the relative depth of competing identities.

In the first instance, it might be noted that the depth of national identity still trumps its regional and continental rivals. But this is true in only three of the four tests when looking at the "very willing" category, and in only two of the four tests when looking at the combined "very willing" and "possibly" categories. Thus, second, one might just as well note the relative depth of European identity evident in these figures, especially considering again that the European polity is weak, young, and controversial. That nearly 15 percent of respondents would be very willing to fight a war on behalf of Europe in a crisis is quite noteworthy, though it must be remembered again that this is a highly biased sample. Finally, perhaps the most interesting conclusion to be drawn from the table is the relative equality of the three polities when it comes to respondents' willingness to make sacrifices. In particular, members of the SEI sample are just about equally inclined to sacrifice on behalf of Europe as for their countries, while the depth of identity with respect to their regions is lower, but not vastly so.

As a final data source, interviewed informants (again, largely but not exclusively Europhiles) were also queried on the depth of their identification with Europe. The prompt verbally put to them read:

People are often asked to make certain sacrifices for the benefit of their country, such as paying taxes to aid a less developed region, serving in a volun-

teer corps, or even fighting in a war during a time of crisis. How would you
feel about being called upon to make similar sacrifices at the European level?

The initial response of many informants to this question ran along the
lines of "we are already doing so," either in the form of value-added or other
taxes, or perhaps preparation sacrifices during the run-up to monetary union.
Whether or not informants made that comment, however, they almost always
agreed in principle with the idea of making sacrifices on behalf of Europe.
There were certainly some who did not wish to do so, including the Dane who
said, "I would probably prefer to make sacrifices in Denmark. I'm still not European enough." Or the ardent British Euroskeptic (and nationalist) who
blurted out emphatically, "I would rather go to jail!" and seemed to quite mean
it. On the other hand, there were those who were equally enthusiastic about the
prospect of paying dues to Europe. A Portuguese informant said, "I would do
it without any problem. I hope to have the chance to do this." And a British
businessman pronounced his preference for making sacrifices at the European
level over the national, including fighting in a European army, or paying taxes
to Brussels (while noting that he felt sure his sentiments were unusual among
the European public generally, let alone the British).

These represent the two extremes of responses to this question. Yet there
was little real variation—most interviewees expressed a general willingness to
make sacrifices on behalf of the European polity, as did the Spanish informant
who said he had no problem with European taxes and the like, noting, "I could
make the same sacrifices for Brussels as for Madrid." The typical responses did
not give the impression that informants were necessarily motivated by affection
for Europe, however (though that sentiment may have been preventing a knee-
jerk rejection of the prospect of sacrifices for Europe). Rather, informants projected a sense of fair play that caused them to recognize that benefits must be
paid for, regardless of the polity providing them. Said one Italian informant, for
example, "I am a citizen and am receiving benefits, so I would have no problem contributing." The only caveats to this general willingness to make sacrifices in return for the benefits provided were the somewhat frequently expressed concerns about the execution of said sacrifices and the programs they
supported. Informants wanted a Europe that would make demands of them to
be efficient, democratic, and fair. A Swede, for example, said, "I would have no
problem if all others made the same sacrifices, because I believe in the European idea." While an Irish informant noted, "It would depend on what Europe
is doing in return." If Europe were providing quality services, that is, she would
have no problem making the necessary sacrifices to support them.

Some rejected military service in principle, regardless of the polity in
question, while others had pragmatic concerns about the notion of a European
military (e.g., language incompatibility, nondemocratic political institutions
making deployment decisions, relations with national services). There were,

again, the extremes of those who rejected the idea completely, such as the British informant who simply found the idea too foreign from his notion of military service, and those who actively embraced it, such as the Belgian who said, "I would be glad to serve Europe," or the French student who was already trying to fulfill his national military/civil commitment in European institutions. Generally, however, the idea of European military service was approached with the same pragmatic detachment that characterized most responses to questions of sacrifice for Europe. It seemed fair and necessary in principle, and therefore informants understood the need to contribute, just as they did within their national communities. Their only stipulation was that such sacrifices met their standards for good governance, which were also applied universally to all polities—that is, government institutions that are efficient, fair, and democratic.

Conclusion

This chapter has sought to add another dimension—depth, generally operationalized as willingness to sacrifice—to the other European identity dimensions developed in the preceding empirical chapters: width, or the popular and temporal dynamic of the affect (Chapter 3), determinants of its variance across individuals (Chapter 4), and the meaning of the identity (Chapter 5). As before, evidence from both quantitative and qualitative sources has been marshaled toward a better understanding of how deep European identities run.

Willingness to take risks and make sacrifices toward the goal of European unification is exhibited in substantial amounts, especially when the relatively young age of the European polity is considered, as well as its vague ultimate aspirations, its threat to the existing political order, and its controversial nature. It would appear, for example, that about the same number of Europeans are willing to risk and sacrifice for the unification of Europe as there are those who would do the same for their religious faiths. Nor does the higher proportion of those willing to risk and sacrifice for their countries dwarf those who would do so for Europe. Some survey data also demonstrate a remarkable willingness of Europeans to have their countries make sacrifices in order to aid other Europeans—often at a level approaching 90 percent of those polled. When it comes to personal sacrifices in the form of increased taxes, levels of support do drop, depending on the phrasing of the question, but still roughly 40–50 percent maintain a willingness to pay more taxes in order to aid other Europeans. By comparison, however, the number of respondents in one survey who supported higher taxes to aid needy regions of their country was close to 90 percent. Among surveyed Europhiles, meanwhile, willingness to sacrifice for Europe is slightly higher than for the local/regional polity, and about the same as for the nation-state. Interviewed Europhiles saw little distinction between Europe or any other polity when it came to the question of making sacrifices. Their very pragmatic approach to the question recognized the need for services and benefits to be paid for, wherever they are provided. They only asked in return that such services and processes meet contemporary standards of quality in execution—that is, they should be fair, efficient, and democratic.

Notes

1. This figure also provides empirical support for the argument, discussed at the beginning of this chapter, that level and depth of identification represent separate ideas. Since only 33.2 percent of those who often think of themselves as European also think that European unification is worthy of risks and sacrifices, the two concepts would appear to be manifestly separate.

2. It could be argued that willingness to assist is not related to identity at all, but simply represents humanitarianism on the part of respondents. For this to be the case, however, such willingness would need to extend equally to all peoples of the world. Data are not available from these surveys to determine whether or not this is true, but it seems unlikely that such largess would extend equally to, say, African or Latin American countries. Still, it might be argued that even if this supposition of an asymmetrical willingness to assist other countries is true, it could possibly be accounted for by the perception that developing countries would represent a constant drain on donor resources rather than an ad hoc emergency requiring assistance. Perhaps a simpler explanation, however, is that Europeans regard one another as part of a common community, and would thus be more willing to begin their charity "at home." Such an explanation strongly implies the existence of a European identity operating in responses to this question.

3. The response choices presented here are those that were offered in the 1970 European Communities Study. In the 1971 European Communities Study, the wording of the question varied slightly, offering choices of "definitely willing," "somewhat willing," "a little willing," and "not at all willing."

7

Conclusion: European Identity and Its Context

Germany is my fatherland, Europe is my future.
—Helmut Kohl (quoted in Howe 1995: 32)

THIS STUDY HAS SOUGHT to examine the phenomenon of European identity from the perspective of several important dimensions. For this final chapter, three tasks remain. In the first part of the chapter, the results of the empirical investigations from Chapters 3–6 are briefly recapitulated. Next, an attempt is made to interpret the meaning of these findings, to locate them in the wider context of political identities more generally, and to assess their possible trajectories under conditions of postmodern society. Finally, the implications of these findings are considered for the process of European integration and for a number of issues now facing the European polity.

Summary of Findings

Four chapters in this study have presented empirical analyses of the several dimensions of European identity. Chapter 3 began the investigation by asking to what extent European identifiers could be found in Europe. Answering that question is complicated in part by variation in the form of prompt put to survey respondents, and by the interpretive judgment required of analysts as to which responses should be considered indicative of the affect. Yet, regardless of these intricacies, two conclusions are plain across the many variations of question form and response analysis. One is that a European identity clearly exists, while the other is that it is just as clearly a minority sentiment. Chapter 3 went on to show that there is considerable variance in levels of European identification across EU member-state borders. Moreover, the data allow for a cross-continental comparison as well, demonstrating that Europe is not the only place in the world where such regional identities may be found, though it is there that they are most pronounced.

Chapter 3 also looked at how European identity levels have changed over time. Based on the survey data available for examining this question, it appears that there has been little movement over the three decades from about 1970 to 2000. Qualitative evidence, on the other hand, suggests a sea change in attitudes among today's youth in Europe, but whether or not this is accurate, it does not necessarily imply an identity shift. Rather, there are good reasons to believe that young people have more experience of Europe than do their elders, that they hold less enmity toward other European countries, and that they are more comfortable living and moving about in a Europe-wide social and political space, having even come to take this behavior for granted over the course of a single generation. Still, such attitudes do not necessarily equate to an attachment to Europe in the form of an identity.

Chapter 4 provided a core analysis of the study. In it, a wide range of hypotheses were tested against an equally wide range of quantitative and qualitative data, in order to determine which factors and characteristics predict variances in levels of European identification. The chapter's findings showed that European identification may rather confidently be predicted by certain measures of elite status and cosmopolitanism, and that it is likewise associated with postmaterialist attitudes, leftist and centrist ideologies, male gender, perceived instrumental benefits accruing from EU membership, and possession of a normative belief in the idea of European integration. In terms of political culture, those from richer, more Catholic, and southern member-states have a greater tendency to identify with Europe.

There also appears to be a link between European identification and those who are high in political efficacy, those who are members of a religious and/or regional minority, and those who are from a country that has relatively recently joined the EU, though these relationships are not as clearly marked as the ones enumerated above. Finally, a number of factors hypothesized to affect levels of European identification turn out to manifest little relationship to it. These include age, nontraditionalist attitudes, country size, and national legacy from World War II. Similarly, there is little to suggest that European identification is driven by socialization processes or leadership effects, though due to a lack of data the latter hypothesis remains more unproven either way than necessarily disproved.

Chapter 5 turned to the question of meaning, exploring how the identity is conceived by those who possess it. A sense of what it means to be European emerged from the analyses, though it was neither precise nor consistent across data sources examined. Nevertheless, certain themes were clearly manifest, at least in rough form. The first of these is that the very idea of a unified, singular European identity is much contested. Only a bit less than half of those surveyed generally agreed to its existence.

As to the thematic content of the identity, the idea of peace was referred to most frequently and with greatest salience among those surveyed and interviewed. Europeans sometimes also see a shared sense of culture as a feature of the identity, along with fundamental sociopolitical ideas like democracy, human rights, and economic solidarity. Additionally, for some, the meaning of European identity is wrapped up in perceived instrumental benefits that are seen to improve their standard of living. This instrumentalist association appears to be found especially among those who least-identify as European.

Two other themes seemed to be at the core of what many ascribe Europeanness to mean. One—which is especially attractive to European identifiers—revolves around notions of shared history and a common heritage. The other certainly constitutes one of the more ironic aspects of this identity, as it invokes the very notions that have previously been most antithetical to other political identities such as nationalism or provincial identity. Thus we find the concepts of diversity, multiculturalism, and tolerance as the chief defining aspect of Europeanness for many, and again, especially among those who possess the identity.

A final and important distinction about European identity concerns its constitutional nature and flavor. Where national identities have traditionally struck (and, for some respondents and informants, still strike) emotional chords within them, and where local and regional identities tend to invoke notions of home, comfort, and familiarity, European identity takes on a rather different cast. Its character suggests a relationship based far more on the logic of cognitive calculation in the minds (but not really the hearts) of Europeans. Identification with Europe is thus largely the product of a rational assessment that suggests the necessity of certain political structures and the utility of locating administrative competences at certain geopolitical levels in order to most efficiently improve the living conditions (peace, prosperity, mobility, etc.) of the citizenry. Europeans, in short, love their nations (at least those who still do, nowadays), and rather unconditionally so. Europe, on the other hand, they tend more to *appreciate,* and even this only on the condition that it provides to them certain functional returns.

Finally, Chapter 6 added the discussion of another dimension to those already examined. This is the question of the depth of European identity, a concept that is generally operationalized in terms of willingness to make sacrifices. That willingness does in fact substantially appear, a finding that is all the more remarkable when one considers how historically recent the phenomenon of European integration and its latest product, the EU, are; how vague and yet also how controversial that process and that entity are; and how both represent a palpable threat to the existing political order. Nevertheless, if depth of European identity is measured in terms of willingness to make sacrifices, then this identity surely has some depth to it. Indeed, Europeans are about equally inclined to risk and sacrifice for Europe as they are for their religious faiths. And even though the past century's decline in religiosity in Europe might make that seem faint praise indeed, the somewhat higher number of those willing to risk and sacrifice for their countries does not dwarf those who would do so for Europe.

More remarkably, Europeans are quite willing for their countries to make sacrifices in order to aid fellow Europeans, often in astonishingly high percentages. This willingness to assist does in fact drop to significantly lower levels when personal sacrifice is substituted for the national in the question prompt, but agreement still remains at surprisingly robust levels of 40–50 percent. For Europhiles, of course, the proportions are even higher, such that their willingness to sacrifice for other Europeans essentially matches their willingness to do the same for others within their respective country and province.

And these same Europhiles tend to see little difference between Europe or other polities when it comes to the question of sacrifice and financial support. In their very pragmatic and rationalistic approach to such matters, they acknowledge the requirement of fiscal support for public services, and the realization that such support can only be generated through taxation. They tend to be as willing to pay taxes for services provided by Europe as they are for services offered by national or provincial governments. They only ask of Europe—as they do equally of the other polities—maximal quality and efficiency in the implementation of such programs and the expenditure of their resources.

Interpreting European Identity

What do these findings mean? How should the phenomenon of European identity, with its characteristics summarized above, best be interpreted? And what are its wider implications, if any? Three broad interpretations of the European identification trends uncovered in this study seem most plausible.

It may be the case, first, that European identity is simply unlike any other political identity. The political identities we've grown used to—nationalisms, essentially—are highly emotive affairs, generally built on distinctions of ethnos. They are typically quite jealous of their claim to the total devotion of subscribers' hearts and minds, and are usually willing to share popular loyalties only with religions (and sometimes not even that—or, more often, massively integrating religious identities in support of their nationalist projects). Now comes an identity built on cognitive calculations dispassionately assessing that which best serves the welfare of Europeans, based on the universalism of their shared interests. It tells no tale of the European nation emerging from the mists of history, nor of its destiny for redemption on the world stage. It does not even require that the identifier hold before it no other identity. It is quite happy to share, in both the external sense—that is, to coexist with other identities—and the internal sense—that is, unlike most prior identities, to celebrate diversity rather than its opposite, some sort of ethnic homogeneity.

And, what is more, it is an identity quite apparently in stasis, not growing as might be expected were it exhibiting a pattern similar to that of others at a similar point in their historical trajectory. There is limited evidence for this conclusion, but certainly the apparent lack of substantial change in levels of European identification from 1971 to 2001 suggests that the identity has not spread in popularity. The evidence from survey data that young Europeans are actually slightly *less* likely to adopt this identity further argues against the spread of Europeaness that might be anticipated given the institutional development of the polity over the past five decades. Of course, several mitigating caveats should be considered before too rapidly concluding that the identity is not growing, not least including the comments to the contrary repeatedly manifest in the qualitative data. All that said, however, there remains in sum a certain amount of evidence for this sui generis interpretation of European identity, which sees the phenomenon as substantially unique among identities and likely to remain so. But there are also ample reasons to resist leaping precipitously to that conclusion.

If the first approach to understanding the empirical observations of this study calls for rejecting comparisons to other identities, the second does the opposite, drawing special attention to the nation-state analogy. Understanding European identity in this context requires apprehending that nation-states are always works in progress, not the unchanged communities of destiny their rhetoric would often have us believe. This observation, in turn, forces the realization that a view of European identity as locked in stasis may be historically myopic in the extreme. We have taken a snapshot of a moment in time, that is, and inappropriately projected that image into the past and future without limitation or modification of any sort. Without the nation-state model to guide us, we might be excused for coming to this conclusion, since, after all, we have only one photograph, one image, one data point, with which to work.[1] But in fact we *do* have the nation-state model to draw from, and it reminds us that polities develop and change over time. Scholars may hope to extract generalized patterns from these transitions, but whether or not they are successful in this enterprise, the more important point to note is the dynamism of polities.

Applied to the subject of this study, the lesson suggests that Europe is on a trajectory of some sort, not fixed forever in its present characteristics. In particular, past patterns have suggested that states give birth to nations at least as often as, if not more than, the reversed and more mythologized construal;[2] that, moreover, the process of nation-building does not necessarily occur rapidly; and that there are often certain prompts or forces that bring nations into being. If one considers the European case according to these experiences, the analogy suggests that it is far too premature to write off European identity after only five decades of any sort of polity existing on the continent. It also suggests that the articulation of such an identity could well follow the creation of the legal and political space—the polity—in question, just as nations often followed the creation of states. And, finally, the model would argue that such an identity may require certain developments in order to be forged, such as an external crisis or challenge of some sort, or perhaps large leaps in the quantity and qualities of internal communications of all types.

Anthony Marx's treatment (2003) of nationalism's origins in Western Europe provides one such analogical blueprint. To begin with, Marx dissents from the general chronology of nationalism's development that is broadly held by other scholars, dating the advent of the phenomenon to early, not late, modernity. If he is correct, discounting the possibility of a European identity developing would be even more premature than it already seemed, since the analogous national identities of Europe took five hundred years—not two hundred—to develop. Marx also highlights the degree to which state-building and nation-building in Europe were concurrent developments, with the latter being necessary to the evolution of the former, since forced mass compliance is too expensive, if not impossible, thus rendering voluntary cooperation induced through affective attachment to the state—that is, nationalism—a sustainable, far more efficient, and therefore more attractive substitute. Were Marx's story of nationalism applied to Europe in the form of an analogy, one could certainly argue that the European Union's nation-building efforts have kept rough pace with its state-building program of the past (mere) half century.

In any case, where Linda Colley (1992) and others see an external "Other" as key to the development of nationalism, the core mechanism in Marx's theory involves the selective exclusion of internal out-groups (generally marked by religious differentiation) in order to enhance the identity-building of the remaining majority. Thus, "to augment core cohesion, often a scapegoat is selected precisely because it is present, visible, and powerless to resist and therefore useful for displacing aggression from some faction of the in-group too powerful to exclude. Purportedly minor differences are often thus magnified by elites and/or commoners eager to build cohesion" (Marx 2003: 24).

Europe today lacks any sufficient core around which to cohere, even if the normative implications of Marx's theory wouldn't prove entirely noxious as prescription (a fact the author himself acknowledges, and struggles with at some length). But, purely for purposes of theoretical discussion alone, one might imagine Poles, for example, with their conservatism and attachment to the United States, playing the role of scapegoated pariah, or more likely Greeks or certainly Turks, should they join the club, because of religious differences. Perhaps most likely of all—rather than an entire member-state—would be the use of Muslim minority populations found within a variety of the predominantly Christian EU countries to star in this role. While we can hope that no such scapegoating or attendant violence will occur in Europe's future, we should also be conscious that—to the (debatable) degree that Marx's pattern is a requirement of identity-building generally—Europe may again experience both or, alternatively, may in the absence of both be unable to forge a common identity.

In any case, however intriguing the mechanics of Marx's specific ideas and analogies, what is more to the point is the general argument that, according to this second interpretation of the empirical findings presented here, writing off the possibility of enhanced European identification would be a foolish exercise in historical myopia. According to relevant time scales, the European polity is very young, and therefore the potential for turning French political identities into European identities, given the right circumstances and sufficient time, should be seen as no more improbable than was turning Norman or Burgundian identities into French.

That said, there is also a third possible interpretation of the empirical data assayed in this study. Humans today live in what is arguably the most exciting period since the birth of modernity, where "a bonfire of the certainties" (Horsman and Marshall 1994: 267)[3] generates a world "about to be remade" (Ruggie 1993: 139). Where, "in sum, the world enters a period of exceptional fluidity—of the sort which historically has usually come about through the dislocation of a major war. Nation and state, as we have known them, are interrogated by history and alternative visions of the future" (Young 1993: 29–30).

It would seem unlikely, given these conditions, that political identities will emerge from this period possessing quite the same characteristics with which they entered it. With careful attention to the historical trajectory of political identities and the current set of forces acting upon them, it may be possible to predict their shape in the world approaching. It may also be the case that the identity constellation and characteristics possessed by Europeans today in fact already reflect the impact of those changes and, what is more, preview the future of postmodern political identities everywhere, or at least everywhere in the developed world. Consideration of this possibility requires a discussion of these tectonic changes and their implications for political identities.

To begin with, there is the question of the state, a form of political organization that today manifests the strains of being challenged by multiple forces buffeting it from multiple directions. And, since states historically often created nations, and since it is states that in any case often provide a crucial focal point for mass affect, we may safely assume that the assault on the state has considerable implications for the nation and for national identity. Today there are myriad factors placing pressure on the state. Some of these may be described as structural in character, such as globalization of all sorts (economic, cultural, environmental, ideational, etc.)—each form of which, by definition, impinges on the capacity of the state to control its own destiny, diminishing its sovereignty and its relevance, and therefore also its capacity to promote and engender national identification. Additionally, the contemporary proliferation of international organizations and the increasing scope of their functional capacity also pose a major structural threat to states. Nowhere is this more true than in Europe, where the European Union has assumed increasingly broad chunks of its member-states' portfolios, a trend that may accelerate significantly in the form of long-term spillover from monetary union.

In addition to these external difficulties, states also face additional structural challenges from within, taking the form of regional autonomy and secessionary movements, as well as their own devolutionary schemes offered in response, in order to defuse such campaigns. (Such programs may indeed prove efficacious in blocking further centrifugal tendencies, but nevertheless by definition entail a loss of sovereignty for the capital.) On another front, state capacity has been drained not only upward and downward, but also sideways, toward the private sector, as increasingly wide swathes of once-core state services have been privatized.

A second set of challenges facing the state might be described as political in character, including, for example, neoliberalism's assault on the welfare-state—one of the modern state's two primary functions—which in turn "inevitably undermines the universalistic core of any republican polity" (Habermas 1998: 413). Other political assaults on the state include what might be labeled as a Thatcherist antistatist ideology (Young 1993: 17), which tends to view all (nonmilitary) things public as evil, and which seriously threatens the state's capacity to mobilize a disaffected body politic. To this should also be added a late-twentieth-century general cynicism about politics and politicians that leaves the state less relevant to the public than was previously the case.

Martin van Creveld synthesizes many of these structural and political forces arrayed against the state in his anthropological and historical essay *The Rise and Decline of the State* (1999). He notes that both of the state's chief functions, warfare and welfare—combined, the essential raison d'être for the entity itself—have been significantly limited in recent decades, sometimes voluntarily so, other times not. To this prescription for irrelevance and destruction, he adds the ironic effects of technology (which, having helped to create the state, now assists in its undoing), and the inability or unwillingness of states to provide for the personal and property security of their citizens. All told, van Creveld finds, the state is losing its historic grip on power and people's imaginations, both in an absolute sense, and also relative to its newly empowered competitors.

Third and finally, there are normative factors that further diminish the power and autonomy of states. Both domestically and at the international level, for example, there is growing recognition of certain norms or regimes (e.g., on human rights, aggression) that impinge on the ability of states to act with completely autonomy. One thing seems clear about the world we inhabit today: this is not, so to speak, our grandfathers' Westphalian system, in which the internal sovereignty of states was normatively absolute, and in which the only limit on the external application of their power was the counterbalancing tendencies of other states in an identical pursuit of territory, plunder, and power of their own.

In sum, recent years have not been kind to the nation-state as a form of polity, though in that form it still retains supremacy of power in factual and probably ideal terms as well. Nevertheless, the relative diminishment of the state is real, and these effects should be assumed to have, and indeed have had, serious implications for the way in which people identify, since states often provide the focal points for national identities. Thus, if we seek to plot the future trajectory of political identity by means of inventorying the present, the assault on the state is one of several trends we must highlight.

Another of these is the degree to which formerly homogeneous societies are now struggling with the implications of pluralization. One estimate, now more than a dozen years old, is that over 200 million people are living in countries other than the one in which they were born,[4] whether because of war, political oppression, economic opportunity, or other reasons. This development presents different challenges of different magnitude to each society in which it appears. For all, however, the phenomenon forces a reconsideration of the nation-state itself—rarely true to form in application anyhow—as an ideal type. As Arjun Appadurai notes, "the formula of hyphenation (as in Italian-Americans, Asian-Americans, and African-Americans) is reaching the point of saturation, and the right-hand side of the hyphen can barely contain the unruliness of the left-hand side" (1996: 172). This development is perhaps even more pronounced in Europe, and is bound to put pressure on the idea of the monolithic nation, further distancing that ideal from practice.

Moreover, the exposure that pluralization provides to alternative cultures is part of a third general trend of interest, characterized by rising levels of cosmopolitanism (though such exposure is of course hardly always conflict-free). The globe is surely shrinking, and the horizon of people's sense of community is surely widening, not least because of the astonishing effect of electronic media and the increasing access to long-distance transportation. Levels of travel, study, and work abroad have risen higher by an order of magnitude compared to past practice, with attitudes following close behind (Habermas 1988: 8). Nowhere is this process more evident than in Europe (to no small degree because the Common Market and EU-sponsored educational exchange programs like ERASMUS and SOCRATES have been constructed in part for this very purpose), where changes in attitudes across just three generations mark out these effects. It would not be uncommon to find there, that is, a member of the World War II generation who still loathed and distrusted nationals from former enemy states, whose children instead viewed those countries as economic partners and perhaps holiday destinations, and whose grandchildren have traveled, studied, lived, dated, married, and worked in those same countries. The effect of such exposure on individuals' psychospatial sense of community should not be underestimated. As Jürgen Habermas avers: "Mass communication and mass tourism exert their influence less dramatically, almost beneath the surface. Both work to change a group morality tailored to what is nearby. They accustom our eyes to the heterogeneity of forms of life and to the reality of the differentials between living conditions here and elsewhere" (1988: 8).

The dramatic rise over the past century in the general standard of living provides a fourth current of which we must take notice. Notwithstanding either the fact that the blessings of this development are mostly limited to industrial-

ized countries, or that even many of the people within such countries are partially excluded from such benefits, the effect is still remarkable. Today, vast
numbers of people live substantially longer, healthier, and more prosperous
lives than they would have had they been born only a hundred years earlier, let
alone at any other point during the one or two million years humans have
walked the earth. There are several repercussions of this development that are
significant with respect to the question of identity.

First, evolving beyond a short life span that is necessarily devoted primarily
to survival provides people with the time, latitude, and disposition to ponder ex-
tramaterial questions, such as the nature of identity. Orrin Klapp notes that "perhaps it is only as material problems are solved that we get time to sit around and
ask questions about ourselves" (1969: 4). Second, prosperity may well steer individuals toward thinking about identity differently when they do think about it.
As Habermas (1998: 409) argues, the development of the welfare state, and the
expansion and reform of educational, criminal justice, and social institutions,
improved people's standard of living dramatically in the space of a single generation, and thus reoriented the content of national identities toward notions of
citizenship rights, and away from ethnic definitions.

Both these effects of prosperity on the character of identity are subtle yet
significant, and those qualities are even more true of a third effect. However ig-
norant of history many people are today, most are nevertheless at least vaguely
aware of the uniqueness of our time. Many alive today have even experienced
this transition over the course of their own lifetimes.[5] And if asked, not many,
it would seem, would ascribe these massive changes to some sort of divine
blessing bestowed upon the last three generations of humans, but withheld for
some reason from the entirety of our ancestors. In short, whatever people's religious commitments (which in Europe are far less intense than they once
were), and however much they may idealize the simpler life of this or that historical period, modernity's core message has triumphed. People recognize that
humans control growing portions of their own destiny, and that the fruits of past
achievements—world wars, nuclear terror, and environmental depredations
notwithstanding—have dramatically improved living conditions, while dou-
bling or even tripling the years in a lifetime available to enjoy such enviable
conditions. This recognition, this rationalist orientation, however subcon-
sciously held, has important implications for the future of political identity.

To sum, the context for the determination of identities provided by the just-
cataloged conditions of postmodernity is thus substantially different from that
of modernity. Given this predicate, the third model for interpreting the empirical findings of this study would see Europe today neither as an anomaly among
identities nor as an example of typical identity development in its early evolu-
tionary stages. Rather, the characteristics of European identifiers uncovered in
this study may be seen as a harbinger for postmodern identities more generally,
driven by the contemporary metacultural factors just cataloged. That is, rather

than the European model moving ultimately toward other identity forms, other identity forms are likely to emulate that which is found in Europe today, that which has been precipitated by the conditions described above.

A number of characteristics define these "postmodern" identities, with five seeming especially prominent. To begin with, there is the proliferation of polities and dispersion of power delineated above, and their effects on attitudes. To the extent that identities are instrumentally driven, as they often appear to be, such new or revived polities as the EU or devolved regional governments should become the foci of new or revived political identities. As the European Union does more, and does it more successfully—if this in fact transpires—a European identity already possessed by some should also be expected to become more widespread, and likely deeper as well. The monetary union project, with its considerable potential for further integrative spillover, seems especially likely to provide a fillip in this direction. The general point, however, is that identities will more than ever be multiple and diverse, perhaps taking the form of the concentric circles pattern some scholars have suggested (Beer 1975).[6]

Hedley Bull wrote of this concept—which he dubbed a "neo-mediaeval-ism"—several decades ago. Noting that a return to a theocratic system might seem fanciful to imagine, he nonetheless anticipated "that there might develop a modern and secular counterpart of it that embodies its central characteristic: a system of overlapping authority and multiple loyalty" (1977: 254). Given the findings of the present study, Bull could well be described as prescient in having posited this concept, but for two important caveats. The first is that this scenario was only one of several possibilities he surveyed as potential alternatives to his existing "anarchical society," better known as the Westphalian system. The other is that he went on to reject the likelihood that any of these others would actually come into existence, favoring instead a continuation of the existing order. Nevertheless, Bull's discussion of this possibility nicely summarizes both the structural and identity implications of a diversifying system:

> We might imagine, for example, that the government of the United Kingdom had to share its authority on the one hand with authorities in Scotland, Wales, Wessex and elsewhere, and on the other hand with a European authority in Brussels and world authorities in New York and Geneva, to such an extent that the notion of supremacy over the territory and people of the United Kingdom had no force. We might imagine that the authorities in Scotland and Wales, as well as those in Brussels, New York and Geneva enjoyed standing as actors in world politics, recognised as having rights and duties in world law, conducting negotiations and perhaps able to command armed forces. We might imagine that the political loyalties of the inhabitants of, say, Glasgow, were so uncertain as between the authorities in Edinburgh, London, Brussels and New York that the government of the United Kingdom could not be assumed to enjoy any kind of primacy over the others, such as it possesses now. If such a state of affairs prevailed all over the globe, this is what we may call, for want of a better term, a neo-mediaeval order. (1977: 255)

Such a state of affairs does *not* prevail all over the globe, but—as the history of institutional integration in Europe has demonstrated over the past half century, and as the findings of this book make clear with respect to identity questions—Bull's neomediaeval model is not so far off the mark in contemporary Europe. Political authority *is* shared by the state with polities both below and above it, and the loyalties—or identities—of Europeans *are* very much mixed, multiple, and simultaneous, and likely to become more so. Gary Marks observed this tendency in his comparison of state-building experiences to European integration: "In some respects, the structuration of authority in this polity has more in common with feudalism than with the state system. Both the feudal and European political orders are characterized by multiple spheres of legitimate authority and by a corresponding propensity for individuals to have nested, rather than exclusive, political identities" (1997: 38).

To this new proliferation of identities under postmodern conditions should be added a second characteristic, the greater likelihood that identities will be contextually driven, as they often already are. Widening cosmopolitanism and communication networks will insert individuals into an increasing number of group memberships, forcing them to juggle multiple identities. Moreover, shifts in context may be contingent on either geographical location or events on the ground. The comments of informants regarding such contextuality that were mentioned in Chapter 1 are worth reiterating here. One noted how he felt German when in London, European when in the United States, and Western when visiting Latin America, while a second informant inverted the effect, saying, "At home [in Ireland], I feel proud to be European, while away from home, I feel proud to be Irish." And, illustrating the contingent effect that events (as opposed to location) may have on identities, another said that he too felt very European in the United States, but also felt German when the French were fighting for the presidency of the European Central Bank.

Third, it is increasingly likely that postmodern political identities will need to be built and maintained on a set of normative civic values, rather than on essentializing or "primordial" characteristics, or as contradistinctions against an "Other" of some sort. This change will be forced by the growing pluralization of domestic societies, the normative discrediting of ethnic nationalism, and the difficulty in a shrinking world of disaggregating "others" from the in-group. This new limitation may seem to put bigger and newer associations such as Europe at a competitive disadvantage relative to the proven emotional appeal of national or regional identities, yet such a formulation has in fact worked rather successfully in the United States,[7] albeit under less daunting circumstances than those that conditions in Europe now present, with the continent's linguistic diversity, its long-established sovereign states, and the bloody history of conflict between them.

Fourth, prominent among these civic values—which may include commitments to democracy, liberty, and tolerance, and to the social solidarity model of political economy—is found perhaps the most ironic element on which any common identity might be built: the respect for, and even celebration of, diversity. Jude Bloomfield renders mellifluously this new and historically unexpected embrace of cultural pluralism as a desirable quality, describing it as a cross-fertilizing polyphony, "the kind of cultural convergence embodied in jazz" (1993: 266–267). Again, this change will be the product of the shifts in the conditions facing communities discussed above, but also may be seen as part of a wider change of values in developed countries. In any case, the evidence presented in Chapter 5 shows that diversity is perhaps the single most defining element of European identity, and thus perhaps a model for other identities in the future.

Fifth and finally, identities are increasingly likely to be the product of instrumental quid pro quo relationships (Bauman 1991: 249), as opposed to socialized emotional responses to specified tribes and tropes. Hence, they will take on more of an intellectualized and abstract quality than have previously ascendant political identities such as nationalism. This is a quality that arguably is already diluting national identities, and may increasingly apply to all but the most local of affective ties. In any case, it would seem particularly true of geographically disperse and historically shallow-rooted identities—like Europe's—that popular associations in the future will be based more on cognitive calculations than on the emotive fabric that has tied together people and polities to date.

Taken together, the above characteristics describe the European identifiers observed within these pages, with their multiple, contingent, and instrumental identities, their rationalistic approach to these affinities, and their insistence on construing their European identity in normative terms wholly contradictory to those more traditionally employed to define national and other affiliations. Perhaps Europe is an anomaly, and what is observed there will neither spread internally nor replicate externally. Alternatively, however, given the roots of these manifestations in the tectonic shifts buffeting all of the postmodern world, perhaps these characteristics represent the future of political identification not only in Europe, but elsewhere as well.

Implications

Whether Europe's new, postmodern identity structures are harbingers of what to expect elsewhere in the world, or are sui generis on one continent, they certainly suggest the potential to reverberate with powerful implications across a plethora of issues on the European Union's agenda. Attempting to predict how identity factors might impact these issues and vice versa, let alone how the issues will play out more generally, is of course a highly speculative exercise. However, between the theoretical ideas in the identity literature and the empirical findings of this book, we can at least hope that the speculation we are engaged in is of an informed kind.

A key contingency for Europe's future concerns its relations with the United States. This is likely to be both cause and effect with respect to the construction of a European identity. As noted above, much of the literature on nationalism suggests that the existence and significance of an "Other" is a primary factor in identity-building. For reasons already explained, the closer such an "Other" is to those integrating their identities, the better it serves the purpose of making that distinction. For Europe, the obvious choice is the United States, and recent events have certainly facilitated that process. Commentators such as Robert Kagan (2002, 2003) are correct to note presently strained transatlantic relations, but wrong in attributing their cause. Relations have been strong throughout the postwar period, and as recently as the late 1990s. On September 11, 2001, European sympathy—in the sense of both affinity and compassion—for the United States was powerfully felt. However, amid the Kyoto Protocol, the Anti–Ballistic Missile Treaty, the International Criminal Court, the Iraq War, "Old Europe," the Middle East, extraordinary renditions, secret Central Intelligence Agency prisons on European soil, and more, the George W. Bush administration has managed to alienate Europeans no less successfully than it has much of the rest of the world. Whether those attitudes are maintained may depend on the duration of neoconservative politics in the United States, and thus on the willingness and plausibility of Europeans hoping to excuse the present moment as an aberration. And whether such politics in the United States—however long they last—translate into a stimulus for identity formation in Europe as against an American "Other" is equally unknown, but will certainly be very interesting to observe in coming years.

Europe, of course, has been deeply divided on the Iraq question—though, importantly, this is only true at the governmental level, not with respect to popular sentiments, which are remarkably uniform. But as the war's promised benefits and its rationales atrophy over time, we might expect within the EU either changes of governmental policy (e.g., Italy's announced withdrawal of its deployed troops ahead of a coming election), or changes in those governments themselves (e.g., the 2004 victory of the Socialist Party in Spain). Thus, the Atlantic breach, if continued, could conceivably drive Europeans into one another's arms, even at the governmental level, and into a heightened sense of separate Europeaness, eclipsing currently powerful Western identities. That new identity, along with associated ideological and policy differences with the United States, could then in turn reamplify the breach, creating a cycle either vicious or virtuous, depending perhaps on the reader's own politics. In any case, current international policy disputes, the absence of a unifying adversary as in the Cold War years, and the contextual quality of postmodern identities argue for greater levels of European identification and greater differentiation across the Atlantic, at least if existing conditions continue unabated. Additional terrorist attacks by Islamic radicals, on the other hand, would have the potential to drive Europeans back into the arms of the Americans, or, alternatively, to generate even greater transatlantic antipathy should the United States be seen by Europeans as responsible for recklessly precipitating such attacks.

Whatever external factors come into play, however, there remains the internal dimension with which to grapple. At present, two items are highest on that agenda: the assimilation of twelve new members of the Union, and the prospect of one now just outside but clamoring to come in—Turkey.[8] The former situation is the more innocuous of the two, with Europe's latest enlargement so far proceeding with a hiccup or two over foreign policy issues, but with little of the economic and social disruptions some had feared. In identity terms, however, adding so many people and so many new member-states— both groups at least moderately different from those of "The Fifteen" of Western Europe—represents a definite if temporary victory for widening over deepening. That is, it is reasonable to conclude that the greater the sheer number of bodies to integrate, let alone the greater the gap among them in terms of economic fortunes or cultural differences, the harder such identity integration will prove to be, almost by definition.

Certainly the prospect of Turkish accession underscores that point, with European Caucasian Christendom manifesting substantial unease as it contemplates the addition of a very large, very Muslim, very Asian neighbor to the south. One scenario, leaving out the Turks, would posit European identities reinforced and cohering against this traditional "Other." It is also possible (but does not now seem probable for the foreseeable future) that Turkey could actually be invited to join the EU, the likely effect of which would be to diminish identity coherence, at least in the (rather long) short term. But, given the new qualities of diversity, contextuality, and a values-centered defining core ascribed to postmodern identities in Europe, the longer-term integration of Turkey within Europe—not only in terms of membership and adoption of the *acquis communautaire,* but also with respect to identity—is not inconceivable, however distant it now appears. If that seems an improbable outcome today, it's useful to recall that there was a time when the same could have been said about Scotland and England, Brittany and other parts of France, and—just a moment ago in grand historical terms—France and Germany, as well. Indeed, it could still be said today with respect to Northern Ireland, Corsica, and the Basque Lands.

It would be hard to imagine, though, that Turkey would take on quite such frightening dimensions were it not for the half century of failed (when even attempted) integration of large Muslim minorities in countries like France, Germany, Britain, and the Netherlands, each of which having experienced very recent and very unpleasant manifestations of these failures on their respective streets. In this sense, then, while the Turkish accession question is quite real, it also becomes a stalking horse of sorts for existing domestic social maladies, and even racism. This is the black eye on Europe's vision of itself as the land of tolerance and even political maturity, and it is not at all clear that conditions are improving or even remaining in stasis. (Nor is it clear that non-Muslim Europeans view this deterioration of communal relations as a necessarily bad thing, or that they would blame themselves if they did. To the extent that such views are held within Europe, the term "black eye" and its connotations may therefore be inappropriate from their perspective, with all the connotations this would imply for the future of ethnic relations.) In any case, from the perspective of a purely theoretical interest in how such developments affect identity questions, a Europe united around mutual antipathy toward an internal religious minority-group pariah could not come more directly out of Anthony Marx's playbook (2003) for how to build a common identity. The normative implications of doing so in this fashion are an entirely different matter, of course.

Nor does the existence of large and restless Muslim minorities represent Europe's only internal issue that implicates identity causes and consequences, though it is likely to be the most consequential. Already, "integrated" Europe continues to struggle, with no end in sight, with the dissension born of differing visions for the Union itself. Should Europe integrate faster, more slowly, no further at all, or should it reverse some or all of the past half century's development? If it does move forward, should it focus on deepening or widening? What is the wisdom, and what are the implications, for the use of "flexibility" to produce "two-speed" integration, in which a "core Europe" integrates at a faster pace than fellow member-states, as seen most prominently in the monetary union project? Does it matter whether Europe can agree on a constitution, or instead continues to be governed by a series of treaties?

Most of these issues probably have some long-term consequences for the question of identity-building, to the extent that identities require some institutional focal point around which to aggregate—like a seed at the core of a cloud—just as nations and states historically reciprocated and perhaps required one another for mutual development. That is, any serious development of European identity may depend (and may have depended so far) on further development of the European Union. Flags, borders, anthems, capitols, and presidents do matter, and they matter beyond their tangible purposes—they are also symbols around which affective sentiments can align, and in the long run the degree to which the questions of the prior paragraph are resolved in favor of more institutional integration might well provide European identity some additional purchase for its own growth as well. As Franz Mayer and Jan Palmowski (2004) note, there are also more tangible, nonsymbolic effects by which the institutional integration of Europe may be seen to already have strengthened the continent's integrated identity, including by fostering common values, moderating nationalist sentiments, and guaranteeing certain citizenship rights to all Europeans.

But, as in the case of the nation-state, these are reciprocal effects, and they therefore work in the other direction as well. Indeed, it would seem fair to say that the effect (or absence of effect) of identities on institutions is the more powerful and least speculative of the two causal directions in this relationship. Why is Europe divided on everything from foreign policy to currency to social and economic legislation to constitutional language to, ultimately, whether the Union should exist at all and, if so, in what form and with what dimensions? In part—though only in part—this is a reflection of the very absence of identity across the continent. That the European state is now caught in a transitory netherworld located somewhere in the unhappy and unstable conceptual region dividing confederalism from federalism is no doubt in part a consequence of the fact the Europeans only partially see themselves as Europeans, while also retaining multiple and powerful simultaneous identities, not all of which are even territorial in nature. If Europeans felt themselves more strongly to be just that, the EU might today have a single integrative speed (fast), a constitution, a real Common Foreign and Security Policy, and a universal currency. That it has none of these things is in part a reflection of the fact that it also has a rather weak and diffuse common identity, to the degree it has one at all.

To some extent, according to the vision of our third, or "postmodern," interpretation of the empirical findings in this book, European identity will ever be thus. This form of identity—cerebral rather than emotive, instrumental rather than devoted—is unlikely ever to inspire the sort of passions associated with nationalism. For good reason, it is nearly impossible now to imagine today's Europeans cohering together, invading Russia, and digging in for a half decade's worth of bloody trench warfare, all to glorify and honor the European fatherland. Their grandparents did something analogous to that, as had nearly every generation prior, but it is as unlikely that the present generation's grandchildren will as that they themselves would today. For equally good reason, it is hard to imagine another Scramble for Africa–type extravaganza of European colonialism, widely popular and driven by a heady mixture of identity and religious fervor, neither of which exist in today's Europe, and neither of which seem likely to exist anytime soon. Whatever sentiments arise in Europe in coming decades, this will not be our grandfathers' identity.

In a normative sense, it would be difficult to see this as other than a good thing. Indeed, to a large extent such stripped-down and emotionally vacated identities are the product of conscious choices made by Europeans to reject the mistakes of the past, and they therefore represent an undeniable example of learning in international politics, and as such also a refutation to those, such as "realist" scholars of international relations, who posit as immutable (and thereby ultimately tragic) the at least partially predatory character of human nature. Talk to Europeans today, and many of them will tell you that the kind of expressions of national pride, let alone superiority, that were common less than a century ago, are now considered a cultural faux pas, too embarrassing for most people ever to engage.

If there is a "downside" to this development from the perspective of fans of European integration (and it must be remembered that this is only one perspective—the vision of a "United States of Europe" being the worst nightmare for not a few Europeans), it is that a passionless identity cannot serve the same function for the EU that nationalism did for state-builders. Thus, internal struggles over the constitution, currency and foreign policy integration, and other related areas will not be assisted by the presence of a continent-wide identity, voice, or will. Of course, even integrated polities are quite capable of massive internal disruptions, the historical likes of which have dwarfed anything seen in the ECSC or its successor institutions. Moreover, Europeans seem quite comfortable with the condition of integration on the continent at the moment. It is hard to find anywhere a serious mass (or even elite) movement of significant proportions that champions the idea of substantial further integration. If anything, it is considerably easier to find passionate Euroskeptic associations in a number of member-states, though the bulk of the general public is situated somewhere in-between, forming the broad bulge of a bell curve.

European identity is unlikely to ever approximate the power of its best historical analogue, nationalism, which can be argued to have been the single most consequential political force of the past two centuries. That is probably bad news for the Monnets and Spinellis of this world, but it could be the best thing that has happened to the rest of us. For, whatever good can be said to have been brought forth by nationalism, it would certainly have a very hard time competing with the horrors of the war, colonialism, genocide, brutality, hatred, and ethnosuperiority that the identity also spawned. An emotionally dessicated form of political identity (with religious sentiment following a similar arc across European history) would not be available as an animating force for integration on the continent. But if its absence saves Europe from a repeat of the scourge of world war, imperialism, and mass murder, that seems a small price to pay, even for those there who share the vision of Jean Monnet.

Notes

1. Of course, as noted in Chapter 3, there are in fact at least twenty survey measurements of European identity, covering about a thirty-year period since the early 1970s. But in the longer historical view most relevant to this discussion, thirty years looks more like a single period—or even a piece of a single period—than it does a series of data points.

2. Compare Habermas 1988: 6; Schwartz 1993: 218.

3. The authors credit George Robertson with first use of the phrase "a bonfire of the certainties."

4. Provided to Crawford Young (1993: 16) by Kumar Rupesinghe of the International Peace Research Institute, Oslo, Norway.

5. "And the old remembered," wrote Eugen Weber (1976: 492) of French peasants, for whom modernization erased prior deprivations.

6. See also Appadurai 1996: 176; Gibbins 1989: 23; Horsman and Marshall 1994: 264, 266. Furio Cerutti (1992: 157) describes a new, "modular" identity structure.

7. Paul Howe (1995: 32) mentions both the United States and Canada as examples of a successful non-ethnos-based model, though the latter case arguably provides more evidence against the model's viability than for it.

8. There are others, as well. But Turkey is economically, geographically, politically, and especially culturally, sui generis.

Appendix 1

Summary of Elite Informants Interviewed

Informant	Title	Organization
European Union		
Thomas Jansen	Adviser to the Commission president	Forward Studies Unit, European Commission
Neil Kinnock	Member of the Commission, Transport	European Commission
Anna Michalski	Project coordinator	Forward Studies Unit, European Commission
Risto Raivio		Directorate for Consultative Work, Committee of the Regions
Various MEPs and staff		European Parliament
Scotland		
Elaine Ballantyne	European and International Unit	City of Edinburgh Council
Colin Bartie	Political assistant	David Martin, MEP and vice president of the European Parliament
Malcolm Chisholm	MEP, Leith	British House of Commons
Chris Eynon	Managing director	System Three Marketing and Social Research
Iain Gray	Deputy head of Campaigns	Oxfam
Craig Milroy	Research assistant	Scottish National Party
Kenneth Munro	Head of Representation	European Commission Representation in Scotland
Iain Stewart	Head of Research	Scottish Conservative and Unionist Party
Ian Swanson	Scottish political editor	Edinburgh Evening News
David Wallace		European Affairs Unit, Scottish Office
Northern England		
Nigel Ashford	Principal lecturer in politics	Staffordshire University
John Begg	Former MEP candidate	Liberal Democrat Party
Andy Fear	Professor	University of Keele
Peter Johnson	Chairman	REA Metal Windows Limited
Terry Martin		Resource Procurement Group, Chief Executive's Office, City of Manchester
Laura McAllister	Professor	University of Liverpool

continues

Informant	Title	Organization
London		
Richard Balfe	MEP	European Parliament
Tony Barber	European news editor	Financial Times
Mark Cottle	Constituency media manager	Pauline Green, MEP and leader of the Socialist Group in the European Parliament
Joe Griffin		European Union Department, Foreign and Commonwealth Office, UK
Mark Leonard	Senior researcher	Demos
Julian Satterthwaite	Senior researcher	Liberal Democrat Party
Anthony Staddon	Staff	Sir Edward Heath, British House of Commons
John Stevens	MEP	European Parliament
James Stewart		EMU Team, Her Majesty's Treasury, UK
Lorna Windmill		EMU Team, Her Majesty's Treasury, UK
Wales		
Wayne David	MEP and leader of the European Parliamentary Labour Party	European Parliament
Russell Deacon	Lecturer in government and politics	University of Wales Institute, Cardiff
Siôn Ffrancon	Communication officer	Plaid Cymru Party
Terry Gwilym	Media coordinator	European Affairs Division, Welsh Office
Elizabeth Haywood	Director	Wales Confederation of British Industry
Wyn Mears	Secretary	British Broadcasting Corporation
Jonathan Morgan	Welsh Assembly candidate	Conservative Party
Rhodri Morgan	MP, Cardiff West	British House of Commons
John Osmond	Director	Institute of Welsh Affairs
Geoff Roberts	Media coordinator	European Affairs Division, Welsh Office
Nick Speed	Reporter	Western Mail
Dublin		
Alan Dukes	Teachtaí dála (member of parliament), and former leader of Fine Gael Party	Dáil Éireann (House of Representatives), Republic of Ireland
Barbara Fitzgerald	Director	Irish Association
Garret FitzGerald	Former taoiseach (prime minister)	Republic of Ireland
Paul Gillespie	Foreign editor	Irish Times
Deidre Healy	Information and development officer	European Movement, Ireland
Colm Larkin	Director	European Commission representation in Ireland
Patricia Lawler	Chief executive	European Movement, Ireland
Ian McShane	Managing director	Market Research Bureau of Ireland (MRBI)
Jim O'Brien	Director	European Parliament representation in Ireland
Patricia O'Donovan	Deputy general secretary	Irish Congress of Trade Unions
Seán O'Regan	Press officer	Department of Foreign Affairs, Republic of Ireland
Terry Stewart	Director	Institute of European Affairs

continues

Informant	Title	Organization
Galway		
Liam Connolly	Agricultural economist	Teagasc Agriculture and Food Development Authority
John Cunningham	Editor	Connaught Tribune
Pat Diskin	Journalist	Freelance
Seamus Keating	Former county manager	County Galway
Michael Marren	Area manager	AIB Bank
Tom O'Connor	Managing director	O'Connors of Galway
Jim Reidy	Rural development specialist	Teagasc Agriculture and Food Development Authority

Appendix 2

Summary of Targeted European Identifiers (and Some Nonidentifiers) Interviewed

Nationality of Respondent	Number of Respondents Interviewed at the College of Europe, Bruges	Number of Respondents Interviewed at the Congress of Europe, The Hague	Number of Respondents Interviewed at the People's Europe Conference, London	Number of Respondents Interviewed at Field Locations in the UK and Ireland	Total
EU countries					
Austria	4				4
Belgium	3				3
Denmark	2	1			3
Finland	1				1
France	6	2			8
Germany	5	2			7
Greece	1				1
Ireland	3			3	6
Italy	1				1
Luxembourg	1				1
Netherlands	3	4			7
Portugal	1				1
Spain	4				4
Sweden	4				4
United Kingdom	3	1	5	11	20
Non-EU countries					
Hungary	2				2
Norway	1	2			3
Switzerland	1				1
Total	46	12	5	14	77

Appendix 3

Summary of Respondents to the Survey of European Identifiers (SEI)

Nationality of Respondent	Number of Survey Responses from the Congress of Europe, The Hague	Number of Survey Responses from the People's Europe Conference, London	Number of Young European Movement Survey Responses Returned via E-mail	Total
EU countries				
Austria	6			6
Belgium	30	3		33
Denmark				0
Finland	11			11
France	19			19
Germany	18	2		20
Greece	4			4
Ireland	3	1		4
Italy	19	2		21
Luxembourg	3			3
Netherlands	9			9
Portugal	6	1		7
Spain	4			4
Sweden	8			8
United Kingdom	14	51	12	77
Non-EU countries				
Croatia	2			2
Czech Republic	6	1		7
Hungary		2		2
Latvia	2			2
Lithuania	2	1		3
Macedonia	5			5
Malta	5			5
Norway	1			1
Poland	3			3
Romania	1	1		2
Russia		2		2
Slovakia	1			1

continues

Nationality of Respondent	Number of Survey Responses from the Congress of Europe, The Hague	Number of Survey Responses from the People's Europe Conference, London	Number of Young European Movement Survey Responses Returned via E-mail	Total
Switzerland	4			4
Turkey	1			1
Ukraine		1		1
Yugoslavia	3			3
Unspecified		1		1
Total	190	69	12	271

Appendix 4

Summary of Survey Datasets Analyzed

European Communities Study, 1970
European Communities Study, 1971
European Communities Study, 1973

Eurobarometer 3, May 1975
Eurobarometer 5, May 1976
Eurobarometer 6, October/November 1976
Eurobarometer 8, October/November 1977
Eurobarometer 10, October/November 1978
Eurobarometer 10A, October/November 1978
Eurobarometer 12, October/November 1979
Eurobarometer 13, April 1980
Eurobarometer 15, April 1981
Eurobarometer 18, October 1982
Eurobarometer 24, October 1985
Eurobarometer 27, March/May 1987
Eurobarometer 30, October/November 1988
Eurobarometer 31, March/April 1989
Eurobarometer 33-0, Spring 1990
Eurobarometer 34-0, October/November 1990
Eurobarometer 36-0, Fall 1991
Eurobarometer 37-0, March/April 1992
Eurobarometer 38-0, September/October 1992
Eurobarometer 41-1, June/July 1994
Eurobarometer 50-0, October/November 1998
Eurobarometer 51-0, March/May 1999
Eurobarometer 52-0, October/November 1999
Eurobarometer 54-1, November/December 2000
Eurobarometer 56-3, January/February 2002
Eurobarometer 58-1, October/November 2002

International Social Survey Program (ISSP), Survey of National Identity, 1995

World Values Survey I, 1980–1984
World Values Survey II, 1990–1993
World and European Values Survey, 1999–2001

Appendix 5

Basic Script for Interviews of Elite Informants

1. I'd like to start with a very broad question about life and politics in this region. Arguably, this period represents a momentous historical juncture, politically, economically, culturally and otherwise, for [Scotland/Britain/Wales/Ireland]. Do you have any thoughts on where the country has been, and where you see it heading?
2. How visible has the EU been in this region? Does it affect people's lives much?
3. Have these effects, if any, been positive or negative? How so?
4. How would you characterize the perception of "Europe" and the EU here? Do people know much about the EU and/or think much about being European?
5. Do you think these perceptions have changed much over time? How so, and why?
6. Do different groups in the region hold substantially different perceptions? Which groups, and why?
7. If European integration were to speed-up substantially, how would the people here react?
8. Which do you think people have the strongest emotional sentiments toward here, the region, the country, or Europe? What accounts for these feelings?
9. Why do you think that some people tend to identify with Europe and others do not? What factors would you imagine are associated with European identification?
10. What do you think Europeans have in common? Are there any characteristics which you associate with Europe?
11. If Europe wanted to draw people closer to it—to win their hearts and minds—what would it need to do? Would it even be possible? What would be the best way to do it?

Appendix 6

Basic Script for Interviews of Targeted European Identifiers (and Some Nonidentifiers)

1. In general, are you for or against efforts being made to unify Europe? Why?
2. What would you like to see Europe and the EU look like in 50 years?
3. Taking everything into consideration, would you say that your country has on balance benefitted or not from being a member of the European Union? In what ways? In what ways not?
4. Would you say that you, personally, have benefitted from the EU and European integration? In what ways? In what ways not?
5. How attached do you personally feel toward Europe?
6. How would you compare that feeling to your feelings toward your country and province?
7. How would you say your feelings toward Europe compare toward those of . . .
   a. your co-workers?
   b. your parents when you were growing up?
   c. the people you know in your community when growing up?
   d. your friends in secondary school or college?
   e. political leaders you've admired?
8. What factors do you think have most shaped your sentiments toward Europe, especially your degree of "Europeaness" or your attachment to Europe?
9. What does being European mean to you? What words, ideas or feelings come to mind when you think of being European?
10. What does being part of your nation mean to you? What words, ideas or feelings come to mind when you think of being _____?
11. What does being part of your regional or provincial community mean to you? What words, ideas or feelings come to mind when you think of being _____?
12. What do you think Europeans have in common? Are there any characteristics which you associate with Europe?
13. Countries often call on their citizens to make certain sacrifices for the sake of the national welfare, such as paying taxes to help out less fortunate individuals or regions, military conscription, serving in a volunteer corps, etc. How willing would you be to make these sort of sacrifices at the European level?

14. Why do you think that some people tend to identify with Europe and others do not? What factors would you imagine are associated with European identification?
15. If Europe wanted to draw people closer to it—to win their hearts and minds—what would it need to do? Would it even be possible? What would be the best way to do it?

Appendix 7

Survey of European Identifier (SEI) Instruments (English and French Versions)

Dear Congress of Europe Participant: The questions on this form are being asked as part of a University of Wisconsin—Madison research project concerning attitudes toward European integration. Your assistance in responding to them accurately and completely will be very much appreciated. Please note that all responses are completely confidential — it is not necessary to write your name on this survey. Thank you very much for your assistance and participation in this research. **Please place the completed form in the box marked "WISCONSIN SURVEY"**. (*Version française disponible, a votre demande.*)

1. In which country do you reside? _____ Province/region? _____
2. In general, are you for or against efforts being made to unify Europe?
   ❏ For—very much ❏ For—to some extent ❏ Against—to some extent ❏ Against—very much
3. What reasons best explain your answer to the previous question? Why are you for or against European unification? _____

4. One can imagine different developments happening in the European Union in the course of the next ten or fifteen years. Among the following ones, which development appears, to you personally, to be the most desirable? (please select one response only):
   ❏ The European Union is scrapped ❏ The European Union continues as now ❏ The European Union becomes a place within which economic, scientific and cultural exchanges between Europeans are more intense ❏ The countries of the European Union, while still governing themselves, form a European federation with a federal government with responsibility in certain important areas ❏ The frontiers between the countries of the European Union completely disappear and the community becomes one single large country

	National Government	European Union
Environmental protection?	❏	❏
Education?	❏	❏
Economic policy?	❏	❏
Trade policy?	❏	❏
Criminal justice?	❏	❏
Foreign policy?	❏	❏
Security/defense?	❏	❏

5. Which of the following government functions would you prefer to see performed by your national government, and which by the European Union?

6. Taking everything into consideration, would you say that your country has on balance benefitted or not from being a member of the European Union?
   ❏ Benefitted extensively ❏ Benefitted to some extent ❏ Not Benefitted
7. In what ways, if any, has your country benefitted from membership in the European Union? _____

8. In what ways, if any, has your country NOT benefitted from membership in the European Union? _____

9. To what extent have you personally benefitted from the EU and European integration? ❏ Extensively ❏ Somewhat ❏ Not at all
10. In what ways, if any, have you personally benefitted from the EU and European integration? _____

11. In what ways, if any, have you NOT personally benefitted from the EU and European integration? _____

12. Do you ever think of yourself not only in terms of your nationality (German, Irish, etc.) but also European?
    ❏ Often ❏ Sometimes ❏ Never
13. To which of these geographical groups would you say you belong first of all (please mark "1")? And the next (please mark "2")?
    _____ The locality or town where you live _____ The region or province where you live _____ Your country as a whole
    _____ Europe _____ The world as a whole

14. People may feel different degrees of attachment to their town or village, to their region, to their country, to the European Community or to Europe as a whole. Please indicate how attached you feel to each of these:

	Not At All Attached	Not Very Attached	Fairly Attached	Very Attached
Town/Village	❏	❏	❏	❏
Region	❏	❏	❏	❏
Country	❏	❏	❏	❏
The EU	❏	❏	❏	❏
Europe As a Whole	❏	❏	❏	❏

15. Thinking about how attached you feel toward Europe, how would you compare your feelings to those of... ...your coworkers

	I Am Much Less Attached	I Am Somewhat Less Attached	Probably About the Same	I Am Somewhat More Attached	I Am Much More Attached
...your coworkers	❏	❏	❏	❏	❏
...your parents when you were growing up	❏	❏	❏	❏	❏
...the people you knew in your community when you were growing up	❏	❏	❏	❏	❏
...your friends when you were in secondary school or college	❏	❏	❏	❏	❏
...political leaders you've admired	❏	❏	❏	❏	❏

16. What does being European mean to you? What words, ideas or feelings come to mind when you think of being European? _____

17. What does being part of your nation mean to you? What words, ideas or feelings come to mind when you think of being French, Italian, etc.? _____

18. What does being part of your regional or provincial community mean to you? What words, ideas or feelings come to mind when you think of being Scottish, Bavarian, etc.? _____

19. What factors do you think have most shaped your sentiments toward Europe, especially your degree of 'Europeaness' or your attachment to Europe? _____

	Not very Important	Somewhat Important	Very Important

20. There is a certain way of life, a standard of behavior and values,   "Culture": ☐ ☐ ☐
that may be considered more specifically European than others.   "Peace": ☐ ☐ ☐
Please indicate the degree to which you think each of the   "Democracy": ☐ ☐ ☐
following are important aspects of being European: "Way of Life": ☐ ☐ ☐
    "Standard of Living": ☐ ☐ ☐
    "Quality of Life": ☐ ☐ ☐
    Other (please specify) _____: ☐ ☐ ☐
    Other (please specify) _____: ☐ ☐ ☐
    ☐ I don't think specifically European values exist.

21. What sort of sacrifices would you be willing to make for the sake of your country?

	Not Very Willing	Possibly Willing	Very Willing
Accept a modestly lower standard of living to help raise the standard of living in poorer parts of your country?	☐	☐	☐
Pay additional taxes to ease a crisis in another province?	☐	☐	☐
Serve in a volunteer corps for a year?	☐	☐	☐
Fight in a war in time of crisis, or approve of a family member doing so?	☐	☐	☐

22. What sort of sacrifices would you be willing to make for the sake of your region or province (e.g., Scotland, Bavaria)?

	Not Very Willing	Possibly Willing	Very Willing
Accept a modestly lower standard of living to help raise the standard of living in poorer parts of your province?	☐	☐	☐
Pay additional taxes to ease a crisis in another community/town?	☐	☐	☐
Serve in a volunteer corps for a year?	☐	☐	☐
Fight in a war in time of crisis, or approve of a family member doing so?	☐	☐	☐

23. What sort of sacrifices would you be willing to make for the sake of Europe or the EU?

	Not Very Willing	Possibly Willing	Very Willing
Accept a modestly lower standard of living to help raise the standard of living in poorer parts of Europe?	☐	☐	☐
Pay additional taxes to ease a crisis in another European country?	☐	☐	☐
Serve in a volunteer corps for a year?	☐	☐	☐
Fight in a war in time of crisis, or approve of a family member doing so?	☐	☐	☐

24. When you yourself hold a strong opinion, do you ever find yourself persuading your friends, relatives or fellow workers to share your views? How often does this happen?   ☐ Often   ☐ From time to time   ☐ Rarely   ☐ Never

25. Some people say they sometimes feel that what they think doesn't count very much. Do you yourself ever happen to think that?
    ☐ Yes   ☐ No

26. Can you name one or several political leaders whom you've very much admired in your lifetime? _____

27. In your opinion, which of the items on this list are the great causes nowadays for which it is worth the trouble of taking risks and making sacrifices?
(Please check all that apply):   ☐ Sexual equality   ☐ Protection of wildlife   ☐ The fight against poverty
☐ World peace   ☐ Human rights   ☐ The revolution   ☐ Your religious faith   ☐ The unification of Europe
☐ Defense of your country   ☐ Freedom of the individual   ☐ The struggle against racism   ☐ None of these

28. Below are three basic attitudes vis-a-vis the society we live in. Please choose the one which best describes your own opinion.
☐ The entire way our society is organized must be radically changed by revolutionary action
☐ Our society must be gradually improved by reforms   ☐ Our present society must be defended against all subversive forces

29. There is a lot of talk these days about what each country's goals should be for the next ten or fifteen years. Below are listed some of the goals that different people say should be given top priority. Would you please indicate which one of them you yourself consider to be most important for your country in the long run (please mark "1")? And what would be your second choice for your country's most important goal (please mark "2")?
_____Maintaining order in the country   _____Fighting rising prices
_____Giving the people more say in important government decisions   _____Protecting freedom of speech

30. Would you say you live in a...?   ☐ Rural area or village;   ☐ Small/middle size town;   ☐ Large town

31. What is your age? _____   32. How many languages do you read or speak at least moderately well? _____

33. What is your religion? (circle):   Roman Catholic;   Protestant;   Orthodox;   Jewish;   Muslim;   Buddhist;   Hindu;   Other;   None

34. In political matters people talk of "the left" and "the right". How would you place your views on this scale from 1 to 10?
(Left)   1   2   3   4   5   6   7   8   9   10   (Right)

35. How old were you when you finished your full-time education?   ≤14   15   16   17   18   19   20   21   ≥22   Still Studying

36. What is your occupation?   ☐ Farmer   ☐ Fisherman   ☐ Professional   ☐ Employed Professional   ☐ Shopowner/Craftsmen/Proprietor ☐ General Management   ☐ Middle Management   ☐ Supervisor   ☐ Other Office Employee   ☐ Non-office Employee
☐ Skilled Manual Worker   ☐ Non-manual Worker (Shop Assistant, etc)   ☐ Other Manual Worker   ☐ Military Service
☐ Housewife/Not Otherwise Employed   ☐ Student   ☐ Retired   ☐ Temporarily Unemployed

37. On average, how often do you travel outside your country?   ☐ About once every 10 years, or less often   ☐ About once every 5-10 years   ☐ About once every 1-5 years   ☐ About once a year   ☐ Several times per year, or more often

38. Do you consider yourself to be a member of an ethnic or religious minority group in your country?   ☐ Yes   ☐ No

Please place the completed form in the box marked "WISCONSIN SURVEY". Thank you very much for your participation!

Cher membre du Congrès Européen: Le questionnaire suivant s'inscrit dans le cadre d'un projet de recherche portant sur les attitudes envers l'intégration européenne. Nous apprécierons grandement si vous pouviez répondre le plus justement possible aux questions suivantes. Veuillez noter que toutes les réponses seront confidentielles; vous n'avez pas à inscrire votre nom sur ce questionnaire. Merci de collaborer à ce projet de recherche. **Une fois complété, veuillez déposer ce questionnaire dans la boîte "WISCONSIN SURVEY".** (*English version available — please request.*)

1. Quel est votre nationalité _____ Quelle province/région habitez-vous? _____
2. De manière générale, êtes-vous pour ou contre les efforts mis dans l'unification de l'Europe.
   ❏ Pour — fortement ❏ Pour — moyennement ❏ Contre — moyennement ❏ Contre — fortement
3. Quelles sont les raisons. qui expliquent le mieux votre réponse à la question précédente? Pourquoi êtes-vous pour ou contre l'unification européenne?
   _____
   _____

4. On peut imaginer plusieurs développements différents au sein de l'Union Européenne au cours des dix ou quinze prochaines années. Parmi les propositions suivantes, laquelle vous semble la plus désirable? (veuillez sélectionner une seule réponse)
   ❏ l'Union Européenne tombe en désuétude ❏ l'Union Européenne se maintient telle qu'elle est aujourd'hui
   ❏ l'Union Européenne devient tel au sein duquel les échanges économiques, scientifiques, et culturels entre Européens s'intensifient
   ❏ Les pays de l'Union Européenne, bien que se gouvernant eux-mêmes, forment une fédération européenne, laquelle possède des responsabilités dans d'importants secteurs.
   ❏ Les frontières entre pays de l'Union Européenne disparaissent complètement et la communauté devient un seul et même pays

	Gouvernement national	Union Européenne
Protection de l'environnement?	❏	❏
5. Quelles fonctions gouvernementales suivantes préféreriez-vous voir administrées par votre gouvernement national, et lesquelles par l'Union Européenne? — Éducation?	❏	❏
Politiques économiques?	❏	❏
Politique commerciale?	❏	❏
Justice criminelle?	❏	❏
Politique étrangère?	❏	❏
Sécurité/Défense?	❏	❏

6. De manière générale, diriez-vous que votre pays a bénéficié de son adhésion à l'Union Européenne?
   ❏ fortement bénéficié ❏ plus ou moins bénéficié ❏ pas bénéficié
7. De quelle manière, si tel est le cas, votre pays a-t-il bénéficié de son adhésion à l'Union Européenne? _____
8. De quelle manière, si tel est le cas, votre pays n'a PAS bénéficié de son adhésion à l'Union Européenne? _____
9. Dans quelle mesure avez-vous personnellement bénéficié de l'Union Européenne et de l'intégration européenne?
   ❏ fortement bénéficié ❏ plus ou moins bénéficié ❏ pas bénéficié
10. De quelle manière, si tel est le cas, avez-vous personnellement bénéficié de l'Union Européenne et de l'intégration européenne? _____
11. De quelle manière, si tel est le cas, n'avez-vous PAS personnellement bénéficié de l'Union Européenne et de l'intégration européenne? _____
12. Vous arrive-t-il de vous définir non seulement en terme de votre nationalité (Allemand, Irlandais), mais aussi en tant qu'Européen?
    ❏ Souvent ❏ Quelques fois ❏ Jamais
13. Auquel de ces groupes géographiques diriez-vous que vous appartenez en premier lieu (indiquez "1")? En second lieu (indiquez "2")?
    _____ à la localité ou ville où vous habitez _____ à la région ou province où vous habitez _____ à votre pays dans sa totalité
    _____ à l'Europe _____ au monde dans sa totalité

		pas du tout attaché	peu attaché	plutôt attaché	vraiment attaché
14. Les gens peuvent éprouver différents degrés d'attachement à leur ville ou village, à leur région, à leur pays, à la Communauté Européenne, ou à l'Europe en générale. Veuillez indiquer dans quelle mesure vous vous sentez attaché à chacune des catégories suivantes:	ville/village	❏	❏	❏	❏
	region	❏	❏	❏	❏
	pays	❏	❏	❏	❏
	Union Europénne	❏	❏	❏	❏
	Europe en général	❏	❏	❏	❏

	Je suis beaucoup moins attaché	Je suis plutôt moins attaché	Le même attachement	Je suis plutôt plus attaché	Je suis beaucoup plus attaché
15. Considérant le degré d'attachement que vous éprouvez envers l'Europe, comment compariez-vous votre attachement à celui de...					
...vos collègues de travail	❏	❏	❏	❏	❏
...vos parents durant votre jeunesse	❏	❏	❏	❏	❏
...les gens de votre communauté durant votre jeunesse	❏	❏	❏	❏	❏
...vos amis lorsque vous étiez à l'école secondaire ou à l'université	❏	❏	❏	❏	❏
...les hommes ou femmes politiques que vous admiriez	❏	❏	❏	❏	❏

16. Que signifie "être Européen" pour vous? Quels sont les mots, idées, ou sentiments qui vous viennent à l'esprit lorsque vous pensez à ce qu'est être "Européen" signifie?
    _____
17. Qu'est-ce que l'appartenance à votre nation signifie pour vous? Quels sont les mots, idées, ou sentiments qui vous viennent à l'esprit lorsque vous pensez à ce qu'est être "Français", "Italien", etc.?
    _____
18. Qu'est-ce que l'appartenance à votre région ou province signifie pour vous? Quels sont les mots, idées, ou sentiments qui vous viennent à l'esprit lorsque vous pensez à ce qu'est être "Écossais", "Bavarois", etc.?
    _____

19. D'après vous, quels sont les facteurs qui ont le plus influencé vos sentiment envers l'Europe, et plus précisemment, votre degré d'attachement à l'identité européenne?

_____
_____

	Peu important	Assez important	Très important
20. Il y aurait une certaine manière de vivre, certains codes de conduites, et certaines valeurs qui peuvent être considérés comme plus 'européens' que d'autres. Veuillez indiquer dans quelle mesure vous pensez que chacun des éléments suivants sont des aspects importants de ce qu'est "être européen": "Culture":	☐	☐	☐
"Paix":	☐	☐	☐
"Démocratie":	☐	☐	☐
"Manière de vivre":	☐	☐	☐
"Niveau de vie":	☐	☐	☐
"Qualité de vie":	☐	☐	☐
Autre (précisez) _____:	☐	☐	☐
Autre (précisez) _____:	☐	☐	☐

☐ Je ne crois pas qu'il existe des valeurs proprement européennes.

	Peu prêt à consentir	Plutôt prêt à consentir	Très prêt à consentir
21. Quelle sorte de sacrifice seriez-vous prêts à consentir pour votre pays?			
Accepter une diminution modeste de votre niveau de vie afin d'améliorer le niveau de vie d'endroits plus pauvres de votre pays?	☐	☐	☐
Payer des impôts supplémentaires afin d'aider une autre région en crise dans votre pays?	☐	☐	☐
Servir dans un "corps volontaire" durant un an?	☐	☐	☐
Prendre part à un conflit armé en temps de crise, ou bien approuver qu'un membre de votre famille y participe	☐	☐	☐

	Peu prêt à consentir	Plutôt prêt à consentir	Très prêt à consentir
22. Quelle sorte de sacrifice seriez-vous prêts à consentir pour votre région ou province (ex. Écosse, Bavière, etc.)?			
Accepter une diminution modeste de votre niveau de vie afin d'améliorer le niveau de vie d'endroits plus pauvres de votre région?	☐	☐	☐
Payer des impôts supplémentaires afin d'aider une autre communauté/ville en crise dans votre région?	☐	☐	☐
Servir dans un "corps volontaire" durant un an?	☐	☐	☐
Prendre part à un conflit armé en temps de crise, ou bien approuver qu'un membre de votre famille y participe	☐	☐	☐

	Peu prêt à consentir	Plutôt prêt à consentir	Très prêt à consentir
23. Quelle sorte de sacrifice seriez-vous prêts à consentir pour l'Europe ou l'Union Européenne?			
Accepter une diminution modeste de votre niveau de vie afin d'améliorer le niveau de vie de régions plus pauvres d'Europe?	☐	☐	☐
Payer des impôts supplémentaires afin d'aider un autre pays européen en crise?	☐	☐	☐
Servir dans un "corps volontaire" durant un an?	☐	☐	☐
Prendre part à un conflit armé en temps de crise, ou bien approuver qu'un membre de votre famille y participe	☐	☐	☐

24. Lorsque vous possédez une opinion tranchée, vous arrive-t-il d'essayer de persuader vos amis, vos collègues de travail, ou votre famille, de partager vos opinion? À quelle fréquence?   ☐ Souvent   ☐ De temps en temps   ☐ Rarement   ☐ Jamais

25. Certaines personnes disent que parfois ce qu'elles pensent ne compte pas véritablement. Croyez-vous que cela soit votre cas?
☐ oui   ☐ non

26. Pouvez-vous nommer une ou plusieurs personalités politiques que vous avez admiré dans votre vie?
_____

27. D'après vous, pour quels éléments de la liste suivante faudrait-il prendre des risques et faire des sacrifices? (indiquez tous les cas qui s'appliquent):
☐ égalité des sexes   ☐ protection de la nature   ☐ lutte contre la pauvreté   ☐ la paix mondiale
☐ les droits de la personne   ☐ défendre votre pays   ☐ votre foi religieuse   ☐ l'unification de l'Europe
☐ liberté individuelle   ☐ la révolution   ☐ lutte contre le racisme   ☐ aucun de ces éléments

28. Sont énumérés ci-dessous trois attitudes portant sur la société dans laquelle nous vivons. Veuillez choisir celle qui décrit le mieux votre opinion.
☐ La manière dont notre société est organisée doit changer radicalement par des actions révolutionnaires   ☐ Notre société doit être réformée graduellement par des réformes   ☐ Notre société actuelle doit être défendue contre toutes forces subversives

29. Dernièrement on a beaucoup parlé des objectifs que chaque pays se donne pour les dix à quinze prochaines années. Vous trouverez ci-dessous quelques objectifs que certaines personnes considèrent comme primordiaux. Pourriez-vous indiquer lequel de ces objectifs vous considérez comme étant le plus important pour l'avenir de votre pays. (indiquez "1"). Quel serait le deuxième objectif le plus important pour votre pays? (indiquez "2"). _____ maintenir l'ordre dans le pays _____ combattre la hausse des prix _____ donner aux gens plus de poids dans la prise de décisions gouvernementales importantes _____ protéger la liberté d'expression

30. Diriez-vous que vous habitez dans une....?   ☐ région rurale ou village   ☐ Petite ou moyenne ville   ☐ Grande ville

31. Quel est votre âge? _____   32. Combien de langues parlez-vous ou lisez-vous de manière satisfaisante? _____

33. De quelle religion êtes-vous? (encerclez):   Catholique Protestante Orthodoxe Juive Musulmane Bouddhiste Hindu Autres Aucune

34. En politique, on parle généralement de la "droite" et de la "gauche". Où vous situeriez-vous sur une échelle de 1 à 10?
(gauche)   1   2   3   4   5   6   7   8   9   10   (droite)

35. Quel âge aviez-vous quand vous avez terminé votre scolarisation?   ≤14   15   16   17   18   19   20   21   ≥22   Encore étudiant

36. Quelle est votre occupation?   ☐ Agriculteur   ☐ Pêcheur   ☐ Professionnel   ☐ Professionnel employé   ☐ Cadre supérieur
☐ Cadre intermédiaire   ☐ Superviseur   ☐ Propriétaire de boutique/propriétaire/artisan   ☐ Employé de bureau
☐ Employé (autre que de bureau)   ☐ Travailleur manuel qualifié   ☐ Travailleur non-manuel   ☐ Travailleur manuel (autre)
☐ Service militaire   ☐ Femme au foyer/non-employé(e)   ☐ Etudiant   ☐ Retraité   ☐ Chômeur temporaire

37. En moyenne, combien de fois voyagez-vous à l'extérieur de votre pays?   ☐ Environ tous les 10 ans; ou moins souvent
☐ Environ tous les 5-10 ans   ☐ Environ tous les 1-5 ans   ☐ Environ une fois par année   ☐ Plusieurs fois par année

38. Vous considérez-vous comme membre d'une minorité ethnique ou religieuse dans votre pays?   ☐ oui   ☐ non

Appendix 8

Summary of Ancillary Events Attended During 1998 Fieldwork

Fiftieth-anniversary Congress of Europe, May 8–10, The Hague

Scottish Labour Party fund-raiser, May 29, Edinburgh

"The New Scotland: Politics, Society, Culture, and the Future of Scotland," May 29–31, Glasgow

People's Europe Conference, June 5–7, London

Bruges Group meeting, June 8, London

European Union summit (public events), June 14–16, Cardiff

References

Anderson, Benedict. 1991. *Imagined Communities: Reflections on the Origin and Spread of Nationalism.* London: Verso.

Appadurai, Arjun. 1996. *Modernity at Large: Cultural Dimensions of Globalization.* Minneapolis: University of Minnesota Press.

Aron, Raymond. 1954. *The Century of Total War.* Garden City, N.Y.: Doubleday.

Atkins, Ralph, and Lionel Barber. 1996. "Kohl Tries to Allay Fears About Germany." *Financial Times,* December 13: 2.

Bauman, Zygmunt. 1991. *Modernity and Ambivalence.* Ithaca: Cornell University Press.

Beer, Francis A. 1975. "The Structure of World Consciousness." In *Planning Alternative World Futures: Values, Methods, and Models,* edited by Louis Rene Beres and Harry R. Targ, pp. 276–291. New York: Praeger.

Berger, Peter L., and Thomas Luckmann. 1995. *Modernity, Pluralism, and the Crisis of Meaning: The Orientation of Modern Man.* Gutersloh, Germany: Bertelsmann Foundation.

Birch, Anthony H. 1989. *Nationalism and National Integration.* London: Unwin Hyman.

Bloom, William. 1990. *Personal Identity, National Identity, and International Relations.* Cambridge: Cambridge University Press.

Bloomfield, Jude. 1993. "The New Europe: A New Agenda for Research?" In *National Histories and European History,* edited by Mary Fulbrook, pp. 255–284. Boulder: Westview.

Bosch, Agusti, and Kenneth Newton. 1995. "Economic Calculus or Familiarity Breeds Content?" In *Public Opinion and Internationalized Governance,* edited by Oskar Niedermayer and Richard Sinnott, pp. 73–105. Oxford: Oxford University Press.

Brewer, John, and Albert Hunter. 1989. *Multimethod Research: A Synthesis of Styles.* Newbury Park, Calif.: Sage.

Bueno de Mesquita, Bruce. 1981. *The War Trap.* New Haven: Yale University Press.

Bugliarello, George. 1997. "Telecommunities: The Next Civilization." *The Futurist* 31 (September–October): 23–26.

Bull, Hedley. 1977. *The Anarchical Society.* New York: Columbia University Press.

Caporaso, James A. 1996. "The European Union and Forms of State: Westphalian, Regulatory, or Post-Modern?" *Journal of Common Market Studies* 34 (1): 29–52.

Cerutti, Furio. 1992. "Can There Be a Supranational Identity?" *Philosophy and Social Criticism* 18 (2): 147–162.

Chebel d'Appollonia, Ariane. 1998. "National and European Identities: Between Myths and Realities." In *Political Symbols, Symbolic Politics: European Identities in Transformation,* edited by Ulf Hedetoft, pp. 65–79. Aldershot: Ashgate.

Claude, Inis. 1971. *Swords Into Plowshares.* New York: Random House.

Colley, Linda. 1992. *Britons: Forging the Nation, 1707–1837.* New Haven: Yale University Press.

Commission of the European Communities. 1985. "A People's Europe." *Bulletin of the European Communities,* supp. 7/85.

Deflem, Mathieu, and Fred C. Pampel. 1996. "The Myth of Postnational Identity: Popular Support for European Unification." *Social Forces* 75 (1): 119–143.

Delanty, Gerard. 1998. "Redefining Political Culture in Europe Today: From Ideology to the Politics of Identity and Beyond." In *Political Symbols, Symbolic Politics: European Identities in Transformation,* edited by Ulf Hedetoft, pp. 23–43. Aldershot: Ashgate.

———. 1995. "The Limits and Possibilities of a European Identity: A Critique of Cultural Essentialism." *Philosophy and Social Criticism* 21 (4): 15–36.

Deutsch, Karl. 1953. *Nationalism and Social Communication: An Inquiry into the Foundations of Nationalism.* Cambridge: Massachusetts Institute of Technology Press.

Deutsch, Karl, et al. 1957. *Political Community and the North Atlantic Area: International Organization in the Light of Historical Experience.* Princeton: Princeton University Press.

Dinan, Desmond. 1998. *Encyclopedia of the European Union.* Boulder: Lynne Rienner.

———. 1994. *Ever Closer Union?* Boulder: Lynne Rienner.

Dogan, Mattei. 1994. "The Erosion of Nationalism in the West European Community." In *Toward a European Nation? Political Trends in Europe—East and West, Center and Periphery,* edited by Max Haller and Rudolph Richter, pp. 31–54. Armonk, N.Y.: Sharpe.

Dougherty, James, and Robert Pfaltzgraff. 1990. *Contending Theories of International Relations.* New York: HarperCollins.

Duchesne, Sophie, and André-Paul Frognier. 1995. "Is There a European Identity?" In *Public Opinion and Internationalized Governance,* edited by Oskar Niedermayer and Richard Sinnott, pp. 193–226. Oxford: Oxford University Press.

Easton, David. 1965. *A Systems Analysis of Political Life.* New York: Wiley.

Easton, David, and Jack Dennis. 1969. *Children in the Political System: Origins of Political Legitimacy.* New York: McGraw-Hill.

The Economist. 1995a. "France Prepares for EMU." (337): 11–12.

———. 1995b. "More-or-Less European Union." (336): 46.

Eichenberg, Richard C., and Russell J. Dalton. 1993. "European and the European Community: The Dynamics of Public Support for European Integration." *International Organization* 47 (4): 507–534.

Etzioni, Amitai. 1965. *Political Unification, a Comparative Study of Leaders and Forces.* New York: Holt, Rinehart, and Winston.

Featherstone, Kevin. 1994. "Jean Monnet and the 'Democratic Deficit' in the European Union." *Journal of Common Market Studies* 32 (2): 149–170.

Feldstein, Martin S. 1997. "EMU and International Conflict." *Foreign Affairs* 76 (6): 60–73.

Flickinger, Richard S., Staci L. Rhine, Linda L. M. Bennett, and Stephen E. Bennett. 1997. "In Search of European Citizens: A Policy Preference Based Approach." Paper presented to the European Community Studies Association Conference, Seattle, pp. 1–24.

Fukuyama, Francis. 1992. *The End of History and the Last Man.* New York: Free Press.

Fulbrook, Mary. 1993. "Introduction: States, Nations, and the Development of Europe." In *National Histories and European History,* edited by Mary Fulbrook, pp. 1–17. Boulder: Westview.

Gabel, Matthew. 1998. *Interests and Integration: Market Liberalization, Public Opinion, and European Union.* Ann Arbor: University of Michigan Press.

Gabel, Matthew, and Harvey D. Palmer. 1995. "Understanding Variation in Public Support for European Integration." *European Journal of Political Research* (27): 3–19.

Gabel, Matthew, and Guy D. Whitten. 1997. "Economic Conditions, Economic Perceptions, and Public Support for European Integration." *Political Behavior* 19 (1): 81–93.

Gamble, Andrew, and Anthony Payne. 1996. "Conclusion: The New Regionalism." In *Regionalism and World Order,* edited by Andrew Gamble and Anthony Payne, pp. 247–264. New York: St. Martin's.

García, Soledad. 1993. "Europe's Fragmented Identities and the Frontiers of Citizenship." In *European Identity and the Search for Legitimacy,* edited by Soledad García, pp. 1–29. London: Pinter.

Gärtner, Manfred. 1997. "Who Wants the Euro—And Why? Economic Explanations of Public Attitudes Towards a Single European Currency." *Public Choice* (93): 487–510.

Geertz, Clifford. 1973. *The Interpretation of Cultures.* New York: Basic.

Gibbins, John R. 1989. "Contemporary Political Culture: An Introduction." In *Contemporary Political Culture: Politics in a Postmodern Age,* edited by John R. Gibbins, pp. 1–30. London: Sage.

Gibbins, John, and Bo Reimer. 1995. "Postmodernism." In *The Impact of Values,* edited by Jan W. van Deth and Elinor Scarbrough, pp. 301–331. Oxford: Oxford University Press.

Giner, Salvador. 1994. "The Advent of a European Society." In *Toward a European Nation? Political Trends in Europe—East and West, Center and Periphery,* edited by Max Haller and Rudolph Richter, pp. 15–30. Armonk, N.Y.: Sharpe.

Glen, Carol. 1995. "Growing Together or Coming Apart? The Causes and Consequences of National and Regional Disparities in the European Union." PhD diss., Tallahassee, Florida State University.

Gowland, David, Basil O'Neill, and Alex Reid. 1995. "Epilogue: A European Identity?" In *The European Mosaic: Contemporary Politics, Economics, and Culture,* edited by David Gowland, Basil O'Neill, and Alex Reid, pp. 287–290. London: Longman.

Greenfeld, Liah. 1992. *Nationalism: Five Roads to Modernity.* Cambridge: Harvard University Press.

Haas, Ernst. 1975. *The Obsolescence of Regional Integration Theory.* Research Series, no. 25. Berkeley: Institute of International Studies, University of California.

———. 1971. "The Study of Regional Integration: Reflections on the Joy and Anguish of Pretheorizing." In *Regional Integration: Theory and Research,* edited by Leon Lindberg and Stuart Scheingold, pp. 3–42. Cambridge: Harvard University Press.

———. 1964. *Beyond the Nation-State.* Stanford: Stanford University Press.

———. 1958. *The Uniting of Europe: Political, Social, and Economic Forces, 1950–1957.* Stanford: Stanford University Press.

Habermas, Jürgen. 1998. "The European Nation-State: On the Past and Future of Sovereignty and Citizenship" *Public Culture* 10 (2): 397–416. [Reprinted from *The Inclusion of the Other: Studies in Political Theory,* 1998.]

————. 1995. "Citizenship and National Identity: Some Reflections on the Future of Europe." In *The Nationalism Reader,* edited by Omar Dahbour and Micheline R. Ishay, pp. 333–343. Atlantic Highlands, N.J.: Humanities Press.

————. 1988. "Historical Consciousness and Post-Traditional Identity: Remarks on the Federal Republic's Orientation to the West." *Acta Sociologica* 31 (1): 3–13.

————. 1979. *Communication and the Evolution of Society.* Boston: Beacon.

————. 1975. *Legitimation Crisis.* Boston: Beacon.

————. 1974. "On Social Identity." *Telos* 19 (Spring): 90–103.

Halecki, Oskar. 1963. *The Millennium of Europe.* Notre Dame, Ind.: University of Notre Dame Press.

Haller, Max. 1994. "Epilogue: Europe as a New Nation or a Community of Nations?" In *Toward a European Nation? Political Trends in Europe—East and West, Center and Periphery,* edited by Max Haller and Rudolf Richter, pp. 226–263. Armonk, N.Y.: Sharpe.

Havel, Václav. 1996. "The Hope for Europe." *New York Review of Books,* June 29: 40–41.

Hayward, Fred. 1971. "Continuities and Discontinuities Between Studies of National and International Political Integration: Some Implications for Future Research Efforts." In *Regional Integration: Theory and Research,* edited by Leon Lindberg and Stuart Scheingold, pp. 313–337. Cambridge: Harvard University Press.

Heller, Agnes, and Ferenc Feher. 1988. *The Postmodern Political Condition.* New York: Columbia University Press.

Hewstone, Miles. 1986. *Understanding Attitudes to the European Community: A Social-Psychological Study in Four Member States.* Cambridge: Cambridge University Press.

Hobsbawm, E. J. 1997. "An Afterword: European Union at the End of the Century." In *European Integration in Social and Historical Perspective: 1850 to the Present,* edited by Jytte Klausen and Louise A. Tilly, pp. 267–275. Lanham: Rowman and Littlefield.

————. 1995. "Nationalism in the Late Twentieth Century." In *The Nationalism Reader,* edited by Omar Dahbour and Micheline R. Ishay, pp. 362–371. Atlantic Highlands, N.J.: Humanities Press.

————. 1992. *Nations and Nationalism Since 1780: Programme, Myth, Reality.* Cambridge: Cambridge University Press.

Hodges, Michael. 1978. "Integration Theory." In *Approaches and Theory in International Relations,* edited by Trevor Taylor, pp. 237–256. London: Longman.

Hodgson, Godfrey. 1993. "Grand Illusion: The Failure of European Consciousness." *World Policy Journal* 10 (2): 13–18.

Hogg, Michael A., and Dominic Abrams. 1988. *Social Identifications: A Social Psychology of Intergroup Relations and Group Processes.* London: Routledge.

Hoover, Kenneth. 1975. *A Politics of Identity: Liberation and the Natural Community.* Urbana: University of Illinois Press.

Horowitz, Donald. 1985. *Ethnic Groups in Conflict.* Berkeley: University of California Press.

Horsman, Mathew, and Andrew Marshall. 1994. *After the Nation-State: Citizens, Tribalism and the New World Disorder.* London: HarperCollins.

Howe, Paul. 1995. "A Community of Europeans." *Journal of Common Market Studies* 33 (1): 27–46.

Huntington, Samuel P. 1996. *The Clash of Civilizations and the Remaking of World Order.* New York: Simon and Schuster.

Inglehart, Ronald. 1986. Foreword to *Understanding Attitudes to the European Union,* by Miles Hewstone. Cambridge: Cambridge University Press.

———. 1977. *The Silent Revolution: Changing Values and Political Styles Among Western Publics.* Princeton: Princeton University Press.

Jacobson, Harold. 1984. *Networks of Interdependence.* New York: Knopf.

Judt, Tony. 1996. *A Grand Illusion? An Essay on Europe.* New York: Hill and Wang.

Kaase, Max, and Kenneth Newton. 1995. *Beliefs in Government.* Oxford: Oxford University Press.

Kagan, Robert. 2003. *Of Paradise and Power: America and Europe in the New World Order.* New York: Knopf.

———. 2002. "Power and Weakness." *Policy Review* (113) (Summer). http://www.policyreview.org/jun02/kagan_print.html.

Kazancigil, Ali. 1993. "A Prospective View on the European Nation State and Unification." In *The Future of the Nation State in Europe,* edited by Jyrki Iivonen, pp. 117–129. Aldershot: Elgar.

Keane, John. 1992. "Questions for Europe." In *The Idea of Europe: Problems of National and Transnational Identity,* edited by Brian Nelson, David Roberts, and Walter Veit, pp. 55–60. New York: Berg.

Keohane, Robert, and Stanley Hoffmann. 1994. "Institutional Change in Europe in the 1980's." In *The European Union: Readings on the Theory and Practice of European Integration,* edited by Brent F. Nelsen and Alexander C-G. Stubb. Boulder: Lynne Rienner.

Klapp, Orrin E. 1969. *Collective Search for Identity.* New York: Holt, Rinehart, and Winston.

Koenigsberg, Richard A. 1977. *The Psychoanalysis of Racism, Revolution, and Nationalism.* New York: Library of Social Science.

Kroes, Rob. 1995. "Supranationalism and Its Discontents." In *European Identities: Cultural Diversity and Integration in Europe Since 1700,* edited by Nils Arne Sørensen, pp. 75–84. Odense, Denmark: Odense University Press.

Laffan, Brigid. 1996. "The Politics of Identity and Political Order in Europe." *Journal of Common Market Studies* 34 (1): 81–102.

Leonard, Mark. 1997. *Britain.* London: Demos.

Lewis, David. 1993. *The Road to Europe.* New York: Peter Lang.

Lindberg, Leon, and Stuart Scheingold. 1970. *Europe's Would-Be Polity: Patterns of Change in the European Community.* Cambridge: Harvard University Press.

Livingston, Robert Gerald. 1997. "Life After Kohl? We'll Always Have Germany." *Foreign Affairs* 76 (November–December): 2–7.

Llobera, Josep R. 1993. "The Role of the State and the Nation in Europe." In *European Identity and the Search for Legitimacy,* edited by Soledad García, pp. 64–80. London: Pinter.

Lodge, Juliet (ed.). 1993. *European Community and the Challenge of the Future.* 2nd ed. New York: Palgrave Macmillan.

Mann, Michael. 1993. "Nation-States in Europe and Other Continents: Diversifying, Developing, Not Dying." *Daedalus* 122 (3): 115–140.

Marks, Gary. 1997. "A Third Lens: Comparing European Integration and State Building." In *European Integration in Social and Historical Perspective: 1850 to the Present,* edited by Jytte Klausen and Louise A. Tilly, pp. 23–43. Lanham: Rowman and Littlefield.

Marx, Anthony. 2003. *Faith In Nation.* Oxford: Oxford University Press.

Mayer, Franz, and Jan Palmowski. 2004. "European Identities and the EU: The Ties That Bind the Peoples of Europe." *Journal of Common Market Studies* 42 (3): 573–599.

Merritt, Richard. 1966. *Symbols of American Community, 1735–1775.* New Haven: Yale University Press.

Middlemas, Keith. 1995. *Orchestrating Europe: The Informal Politics of the European Union, 1973–95.* London: Fontana.

Mikkeli, Heikki. 1998. *Europe as an Idea and an Identity.* London: Macmillan.

Moïsi, Dominique. 1996. "Gloom of the Sick Man: The Deep Sense of Malaise in France Is Endangering Monetary Union." *Financial Times:* 20.

Monnet, Jean. 1978. *Memoirs.* New York: Doubleday.

Nelsen, Brent F., and James L. Guth. 2003. "Roman Catholicism and the Founding of Europe: How Catholics Shaped the European Communities." Paper presented at the annual meeting of the American Political Science Association, Philadelphia, August 28–31.

———. 2000. "Exploring the Gender Gap: Women, Men, and Public Attitudes Toward European Integration." *European Union Politics* 1 (3): 267–291.

Nicoll, William, and Trevor C. Salmon. 1990. *Understanding the European Communities.* Savage, Md.: Barnes and Noble.

Niedermayer, Oskar. 1995. "Trends and Contrasts." In *Public Opinion and Internationalized Governance,* edited by Oskar Niedermayer and Richard Sinnott, pp. 53–73. Oxford: Oxford University Press.

Niedermayer, Oskar, and Richard Sinnott. 1995. Introduction to *Public Opinion and Internationalized Governance,* edited by Oskar Niedermayer and Richard Sinnott, pp. 1–9. Oxford: Oxford University Press.

Nørgaard, Asbjørn Sonne. 1994. "Institutions and Post-Modernity in IR: The New EC." *Cooperation and Conflict* 29 (3): 245–287.

Papcke, Sven. 1992. "Who Needs European Identity and What Could It Be?" In *The Idea of Europe: Problems of National and Transnational Identity,* edited by Brian Nelson, David Roberts, and Walter Veit, pp. 61–74. New York: Berg.

Payne, Anthony, and Andrew Gamble. 1996. "Introduction: The Political Economy of Regionalism and World Order." In *Regionalism and World Order,* edited by Andrew Gamble and Anthony Payne, pp. 1–20. New York: St. Martin's.

Protzman, Ferdinand. 1994. "Intellectual Oz Embracing an Ideal Grounded in Reality." *New York Times:* 12.

Reif, Karlheinz. 1993. "Cultural Convergence and Cultural Diversity as Factors in European Identity." In *European Identity and the Search for Legitimacy,* edited by Soledad García, pp. 131–153. London: Pinter.

Ruggie, John Gerard. 1993. "Territoriality and Beyond: Problematizing Modernity in International Relations." *International Organization* 47: 139–174.

Russett, Bruce. 1993. *Grasping the Democratic Peace.* Princeton: Princeton University Press.

Said, Edward. 1979. *Orientalism.* New York: Vintage.

Schlesinger, Philip. 1994. "Europeanness: A New Cultural Battlefield? In *Nationalism,* edited by John Hutchinson and Anthony D. Smith, pp. 316–325. Oxford: Oxford University Press.

———. 1993. "Wishful Thinking: Cultural Politics, Media, and Collective Identities in Europe." *Journal of Communications* 43 (Spring): 6–17.

Schmidtke, Oliver. 1998. "Obstacles and Prospects for a European Collective Identity and Citizenship." In *Political Symbols, Symbolic Politics: European Identities in Transformation,* edited by Ulf Hedetoft, pp. 44–64. Aldershot: Ashgate.

Schmitter, Philippe. 1970. "A Revised Theory of Regional Integration." *International Organization* 24 (Autumn): 836–868.

Schmitter, Philippe, and Wolfgang Streeck. 1994. "Organized Interests and the Europe of 1992." In *The European Union: Readings on the Theory and Practice of European Integration,* edited by Brent F. Nelsen and Alexander C-G. Stubb. Boulder: Lynne Rienner.

Schuman, Robert. 1994. "The Schuman Declaration." In *The European Union: Readings on the Theory and Practice of European Integration,* edited by Brent F. Nelsen and Alexander C-G. Stubb. Boulder: Lynne Rienner.

Schwartz, Benjamin I. 1993. "Culture, Modernity, and Nationalism: Further Reflections." *Daedalus* 122 (3): 207–226.

Shively, W. Phillips. 1974. *The Craft of Political Research: A Primer.* Englewood Cliffs, N.J.: Prentice-Hall.

Sinnott, Richard. 1995. "Bringing Public Opinion Back In." In *Public Opinion and Internationalized Governance,* edited by Oskar Niedermayer and Richard Sinnott, pp. 11–33. Oxford: Oxford University Press.

Slater, Martin. 1982. "Political Elites, Popular Indifference, and Community Building." *Journal of Common Market Studies* 21 (1): 69–87.

Smith, Anthony D. 1995. *Nations and Nationalism in a Global Era.* Cambridge: Polity.

———. 1992. "National Identity and the Idea of European Unity." *International Affairs* 68 (1) (January): 55–76.

———. 1990. "Towards a Global Culture?" *Theory, Culture & Society* 7 (2–3): 171–191.

Smith, Dale L., and Jurgen Wanke. 1993. "Completing the Single European Market: An Analysis of the Impact on the Member States." *American Journal of Political Science* 37 (2) (May): 529–554.

Squires, Josephine. 1994. "National, Sub-National, and Supra-National Identities: The Case of UK Political and Business Leaders in the Context of the European Community." PhD thesis, Boulder, University of Colorado.

Stanley, Alessandra. 1998. "For Ambitious Entrepreneurs, All Europe Is Just One Nation." *New York Times,* December 24: A1, A10.

Strange, Susan. 1996. *The Retreat of the State: The Diffusion of Power in the World Economy.* New York: Cambridge University Press.

Tajfel, Henri. 1982. "Social Psychology of Intergroup Relations." *Annual Review of Psychology* 33: 1–39.

Tilly, Charles. 1998. "International Communities, Secure or Otherwise" (draft version). In *Security Communities,* edited by Emanuel Adler and Michael Barnett. Cambridge: Cambridge University Press.

Tranholm-Mikkelsen, Jeppe. 1991. "Neo-Functionalism: Obstinate or Obsolete? A Reappraisal in the Light of the New Dynamism of the EC." *Millennium: Journal of International Studies* 20 (1): 1–22.

Trillin, Calvin. 1997. "European Unification: The Short Version." *The Nation* 265 (1): 6.

United Nations Research Institute for Social Development. 1995. *States of Disarray: The Social Effects of Globalization.* Geneva.

van Creveld, Martin. 1999. *The Rise and Decline of the State.* Cambridge: Cambridge University Press.

van Tartwijk-Novey, Louise. 1995. *The European House of Cards: Towards a United States of Europe?* New York: St. Martin's.

Wallace, William. 1990. *The Transformation of Western Europe.* New York: Council on Foreign Relations Press.

Weber, Eugen. 1976. *Peasants Into Frenchmen: The Modernization of Rural France, 1870–1914.* Stanford: Stanford University Press.

Weilenmann, Hermann. 1963. "The Interlocking of Nation and Personality Structure." In *Nation-Building,* edited by Karl Deutsch and William Foltz, pp. 33–55. New York: Atherton.

Weiler, Joseph H. H. 2001. "Federalism Without Constitutionalism: Europe's *Sonderweg.*" In *The Federal Vision: Legitimacy and Levels of Governance in the United States and the European Union,* edited by Kalypso Nicolaidis and Robert Howse, pp. 54–72. Oxford: Oxford University Press.

Wessels, Bernard. 1995a. "Development of Support: Diffusion or Demographic Replacement?" In *Public Opinion and Internationalized Governance,* edited by Oskar Niedermayer and Richard Sinnott, pp. 105–137. Oxford: Oxford University Press.

———. 1995b. "Evaluations of the EC: Elite or Mass-Driven?" In *Public Opinion and Internationalized Governance,* edited by Oskar Niedermayer and Richard Sinnott, pp. 137–162. Oxford: Oxford University Press.

Wilterdink, Nico. 1993. "The European Ideal: An Examination of European and National Identity." *Archives Européennes de Sociologie* 34 (1): 119–136.

———. 1990. "Where Nations Meet: National Identities in an International Organization." *EUI Working Papers in Political and Social Sciences* 90 (3): 1–106.

Wintle, Michael. 1996. "Cultural Identity in Europe: Shared Experience." In *Culture and Identity in Europe: Perceptions of Divergence and Unity in Past and Present,* edited by Michael Wintle, pp. 9–32. Aldershot: Avebury.

World Values Study Group. 1994. *World Values Survey, 1981–1984 and 1990–1993.* Computer file, ICPSR version. Ann Arbor: produced by the Institute for Social Research, distributed by the Interuniversity Consortium for Political and Social Research.

Young, Crawford. 1993. "The Dialectics of Cultural Pluralism: Concept and Reality." In *The Rising Tide of Cultural Pluralism: The Nation-State At Bay?* edited by Crawford Young, pp. 3–35. Madison: University of Wisconsin Press.

Index

Adonnino Committee, 45
Age. *See under* European
   identification level predictive
   factors
Attitudes toward other countries. *See*
   European identification level
   predictive factors
Attitudinal factors of European
   identity, 29, 75–76(tab), 80(tab),
   82(tab), 84(tab), 89–92. *See also*
   European identification level
   predictive factors
Attributional factors of European
   identity, 28, 72–89, 74–75(tab),
   79(tab), 82(tab), 84(tab). *See also*
   European identification level
   predictive factors

Change in European identity over time.
   See European identity over time
Characteristics of European identifiers.
   See European identifier
   characteristics
Character of European identity. *See*
   Meaning of European identity
Class. *See under* European
   identification level predictive
   factors

Cohesion policy, 47
College of Europe, 20
Common European
   heritage/history/lifestyle, 114, 115,
   116, 119, 125, 127, 128. *See also*
   Elements of European identity
Community size. *See under* European
   identification level predictive
   factors
Congress of Europe, 19
Constitution. *See* European Union
   constitution
Constructivism, 25–26, 40–41
Content of European identity. *See*
   Meaning of European identity
Cosmopolitanism, 40. *See also under*
   European identification level
   predictive factors
Country size. *See under* European
   identification level predictive
   factors: size of member-state
Creation of European identity. *See*
   Efforts to foster European identity
Cross-national relationships. *See under*
   European identification level
   predictive factors
Culture and European identity. *See*
   Meaning of European identity

Data sources, 19–24, 52–54, 55, 62, 66, 72, 109–110, 131–132, 167–187; elite interviews, 20–21; European identifiers interviews, 19–20; extant surveys, 22–23; original survey, 21–22. *See also* Survey of European Identifiers

Democracy and European identity, 119, 121, 122, 126, 127

Dependent-variable question formats, 23, 27–28, 52, 66, 70(nn2,4,5)

Depth of European identity, 29, 131–146, 149–150; comparative tests of, 139–143; definition, 131; depth of other identities versus, 137, 139–143; European identification level and, 134, 139, 141(tab); nationality and, 133(tab), 134, 135, 136(tab), 137, 138(tab), 139, 140(tab)

Diffuse support, 7

Diversity/tolerance and European identity, 125, 126, 127, 128, 158–159. *See also* Elements of European identity; Meaning of European identity; Postmodern identity

Education. *See under* European identification level predictive factors

Education abroad/exchange programs, 47–48, 86, 87, 155. *See also under* European identification level predictive factors

Efficacy. *See* European identification level predictive factors, political efficacy

Efforts to foster European identity, 44–49

Elements of European identity, 43–44. *See also* Meaning of European identity

Elites. *See* European identification level predictive factors: socioeconomic status

ERASMUS. *See* Education abroad/exchange programs

Eurobarometer, 22, 175–176

European identification level predictive factors: age, 68–69, 75(tab), 79(tab), 82(tab), 84(tab), 87–88, 148; attitudes toward other countries, 86; class, 73, 74(tab), 79(tab), 82(tab), 84(tab); community size, 74(tab), 79(tab), 82(tab), 83–86; cosmopolitanism, 74(tab), 83–87; cross-national relationships, 87; education, 73–83, 84(tab); education abroad/exchange programs, 86, 97; EU/integration support, 62–66, 68, 76(tab), 80(tab), 82(tab), 84(tab), 91–92; EU membership, 83(tab), 85(tab), 100–102; feelings toward other people, 74(tab), 79(tab), 82(tab), 86; frequency of travel, 74(tab), 79(tab), 86; frontier proximity, 74(tab), 79(tab), 86; gender, 75(tab), 79(tab), 82(tab), 84(tab), 89; ideology, 75(tab), 80(tab), 82(tab), 84(tab), 90–91; income, 73, 74(tab), 79(tab), 82(tab), 84(tab); instrumentalism, 76(tab), 80(tab), 82(tab), 85(tab), 94–95; interest in other countries, 74(tab), 79(tab), 86; languages spoken, 74(tab), 79(tab), 86; leadership, 77(tab), 81(tab), 82(tab), 85(tab), 98–99; marital status, 75(tab), 80(tab), 82(tab), 91; media, 97; minority culture/status, 77(tab), 80(tab), 82(tab), 85(tab), 95–96; mixed-nationality parents, 86–87; moral issues, 75–76(tab), 80(tab), 82(tab), 91; nontraditionalism, 75(tab), 80(tab), 82(tab), 84(tab), 91; normative values, 76(tab), 80(tab), 84(tab), 92; occupation,

73, 74(tab), 79(tab), 82(tab),
84(tab); "Other," the, 41–42, 43,
77(tab), 81(tab), 82(tab), 96, 127,
152, 158, 160–162; political
efficacy, 76(tab), 80(tab), 82(tab),
84(tab), 93–94; postmaterialism,
75(tab), 80(tab), 82(tab), 84(tab),
89–90; race, 77(tab), 80(tab),
95–96; regionalism, 62, 83(tab),
85(tab), 96, 104; religion, 62,
75(tab), 80(tab), 82(tab), 83(tab),
84(tab), 85(tab), 91, 95, 103;
size of member-state, 83(tab),
85(tab), 102–103; socialization,
including parents, peers, 77(tab),
81(tab), 82(tab), 85(tab), 96–98;
societal change, 75(tab), 80(tab),
91; societal wealth, 83(tab),
85(tab), 103; socioeconomic status,
72–83; trust in other Europeans,
74(tab), 79(tab), 82(tab), 84(tab),
86; World War II, 83(tab), 85(tab),
103–104. *See also* Attitudinal
factors of European identity;
Attributional factors of European
identity; Political-cultural factors of
European identity; Postmodern
identity; Social-psychological
factors of European identity
European identifier characteristics,
71–107, 148. *See also* European
identification level predictive
factors
European identity as a unique form,
150–151
European identity compared to other
continents, 62–66, 147
European identity compared to other
identities, 55–57, 62
European identity over time, 28,
66–69, 148, 151–152
European institutions and the
significance of European identity,
5–6, 6–9, 162–163
European Parliament, 46

European Union constitution, 48
European Union/integration
support. *See under* European
identification level predictive
factors
European Union membership. *See
under* European identification level
predictive factors
Examples (fictional composite
archetypes) of European identifiers,
71, 105–106
Existence of European identity,
110–112, 122, 125, 127. *See also*
Extent of European identity
Extent of European identity, 28,
52–55, 147

Factors associated with European
identity. *See* Attitudinal factors of
European identity; Attributional
factors of European identity;
European identification level
predictive factors; Political-cultural
factors of European identity;
Social-psychological factors of
European identity
Factors favorable to creating European
identity, 39–40
Feelings toward other people. *See
under* European identification level
predictive factors
Frequency of travel. *See under*
European identification level
predictive factors
Frontier proximity. *See under*
European identification level
predictive factors

GDP. *See* European identification level
predictive factors, societal wealth
Gender. *See under* European
identification level predictive factors
Generational effect. *See* European
identification level predictive
factors, age

History of European identity. *See* Idea of European identity

Hypotheses of European identity factors, 28–29, 72. *See also* Attributional factors of European identity; Attitudinal factors of European identity; European identification level predictive factors; Social-psychological factors of European identity; Political-cultural factors of European identity

Idea of European identity, 28, 33–36

Identity: contextuality and, 158; multiplicity and, 157–158; nature of, 24–26. *See also* Political identity, general; Postmodern identity

Ideology. *See under* European identification level predictive factors

Implications of European identity, 29, 159–164

Income. *See under* European identification level predictive factors

Informants, 19–21, 167–169, 171, 177, 179–180. *See also* Data sources

Instrumentalist interpretation of European identity, 114–116, 118, 119, 121, 123, 128, 159. *See also* European identification level predictive factors; Postmodern identity

Integration: definition of, 13, 30(n6); significance of European identity to, 6, 12–16, 162. *See also* European identification level predictive factors, instrumentalism, European Union/integration support

Interest in other countries. *See under* European identification level predictive factors

Interpretation of European identity findings, 150–159

Languages spoken. *See under* European identification level predictive factors

Leadership. *See under* European identification level predictive factors

Length of European Union membership. *See* European identification level predictive factors, EU membership

Lifestyle and European identity. *See* Meaning of European identity

Maastricht Treaty, 46

Marital status. *See under* European identification level predictive factors

Meaning of European identity, 29, 68, 109–130, 148–149; European identification level and, 114–116, 118, 121; nationality and, 112, 113(tab), 114, 116, 117(tab), 119, 120(tab)

Measures of European identity. *See* Dependent-variable question formats

Media. *See under* European identification level predictive factors

Methodology, 17–19

Minority culture/status. *See under* European identification level predictive factors

Mixed-nationality parent. *See under* European identification level predictive factors

Monnet, Jean, 36

Moral issues. *See under* European identification level predictive factors

Muslims, and European identity, 161–162

National levels of European identity, 57–62, 147

National identities, 124(tab), 125–126, 129

Nationalism, as a European identity analogue, 1–2, 17, 37, 39, 151–153, 164

Nationalism, negative aspects, 40, 164

Nationality and European identity, 77(tab), 81(tab), 83(tab), 85(tab), 99–100. *See also* Meaning of European identity; National levels of European identity

Nature of European identity. *See* Meaning of European identity

Nontraditionalism. *See under* European identification level predictive factors

Normative implications of European identity, 163–164

Normative values, 114, 158. *See under* European identification level predictive factors

Obstacles to study of European identity, 17–18, 24–28, 109

Occupation. *See under* European identification level predictive factors

"Other," the. *See under* European identification level predictive factors

Parents. *See under* European identification level predictive factors, socialization

Peace, European identity and, 114–115, 116, 119, 121, 122, 125, 126, 127, 128. *See also* European identification level predictive factors, normative values; War

Peers. *See* European identification level predictive factors, socialization

People's Europe Conference, 20

People's Europe initiative, 45

Political activism. *See* European identification level predictive factors, political efficacy

Political-cultural factors of European identity, 29, 77(tab), 81(tab), 83(tab), 85(tab), 99–104, 101(tab), 102(tab). *See also* European identification level predictive factors

Political efficacy. *See under* European identification level predictive factors

Political identity, general, 1–3

Political integration. *See* Integration

Population. *See* European identification level predictive factors, size of member-state

Possibility of European identity, 37–43

Postmaterialism. *See* European identification level predictive factors

Postmodern identity, 2–3, 153–159; characteristics of, 157–159; cultural pluralism as a contributing factor, 155; definition, 29–30(n1); European identity interpreted as, 153–159; significance of European identity and, 6, 16–17; standard of living as a contributing factor, 155–156; states, pressures on, as contributing factor, 153–155

Primordialism, 25–26, 40–41, 100

Problems of creating a European identity, 37–39

Race. *See under* European identification level predictive factors

Rational/cognitive/cerebral quality of European identity, 126–127, 128, 129, 146, 149, 150, 159, 163–164. *See also* Meaning of European identity; Postmodern identity

Regional identities, 124(tab), 126, 129

Regionalism. *See under* European identification level predictive factors

Religion. *See under* European identification level predictive factors

Sacrifice/risk: causes worth personal sacrifice/risk, 132–134; 138(tab); Europe/Europeans, for, 135–145; national sacrifices for other European countries, 134–135. *See also* Depth of European identity

Scholarly attention to European identity questions, 3–4

SEI. *See* Survey of European Identifiers

Sex. *See* European identification level predictive factors, gender

Shared European Cultural Identity, 111(tab). *See also* Meaning of European identity

Significance of European identity, 3, 4–17, 159–164

Size of member-state. *See under* European identification level predictive factors

Socialization. *See under* European identification level predictive factors

Social-psychological factors of European identity, 29, 76–77(tab), 80–81(tab), 82(tab), 84–85(tab), 92–99. *See also* European identification level predictive factors

Societal change. *See under* European identification level predictive factors

Societal wealth. *See under* European identification level predictive factors

Socioeconomic status. *See under* European identification level predictive factors

SOCRATES. *See* Education abroad/ exchange programs

Sources. *See* Data sources

Standard of living, 119, 121, 122

Structure of the book, 28–29

Summaries of findings, 4, 69, 104–105, 128–129, 145–146, 147–150

Survey data, 21–24, 173–174, 175–176, 181–185. *See also* Data sources

Survey of European Identifiers (SEI), 21–22, 173–174, 181–185 *See also* Data sources

Time and European identity. *See* European identity over time

Town size. *See under* European identification level predictive factors, community size

Travel. *See* European identification level predictive factors, frequency of travel

Trust in other Europeans. *See under* European identification level predictive factors

Turkey, implications of EU membership, 161

United States, relations with, 42, 160–161. *See also* European identification level predictive factors, "Other," the

Variance in degree of European identification. *See* European identifier characteristics

War: factors preventing in Europe, 10; significance of European identity and, 6, 9–12

World War II. *See under* European identification level predictive factors

About the Book

TO WHAT EXTENT AND for what reasons do citizens of the European Union think of themselves not as being French, German, Hungarian, or the like, but as being European? How have the answers to these questions changed over time? What explains variations among individuals? Addressing these and related questions, David Green draws on a vast quantity of empirical data to thoroughly investigate the phenomenon of European identity.

Green finds that there is indeed a sense of European identity among a substantial segment of the EU population—but that it has a very different character compared to traditional political identities. His demonstration of the "postmodern," instrumental nature of European identity has serious implications not only for the development of the EU, but also for international politics more broadly.

David Michael Green is associate professor of political science at Hofstra University, New York.